The Demb Family Journey

from Mlynov to Baltimore

Author: Howard I. Schwartz, PhD

JewishGen
מרכז עולמי לגנאלוגיה יהודית
The Global Home for Jewish Genealogy

A Publication of JewishGen, Inc.
Edmond J. Safra Plaza, 36 Battery Place, New York, NY 10280
646.494.5972 | info@JewishGen.org | www.jewishgen.org

An affiliate of New York's Museum of Jewish Heritage – A Living Memorial to the Holocaust

MUSEUM OF
JEWISH HERITAGE
A LIVING MEMORIAL
TO THE HOLOCAUST

The Demb Family Journey from Mlynov to Baltimore 1840 - 1940

Author: Howard I. Schwartz, PhD

Cover Design: Rachel Kolokoff Hopper
Indexing: Jonathan Wind

Library of Congress Control Number (LCCN): 2023941656

ISBN: 978-1-954176-78-2 (hard cover: 254 pages, alk. paper)

About JewishGen.org

JewishGen, an affiliate of the Museum of Jewish Heritage - A Living Memorial to the Holocaust, serves as the global home for Jewish genealogy.

Featuring unparalleled access to 30+ million records, it offers unique search tools, along with opportunities for researchers to connect with others who share similar interests. Award winning resources such as the Family Finder, Discussion Groups, and ViewMate, are relied upon by thousands each day.

In addition, JewishGen's extensive informational, educational and historical offerings, such as the Jewish Communities Database, Yizkor Book translations, InfoFiles, Family Tree of the Jewish People, and KehilaLinks, provide critical insights, first-hand accounts, and context about Jewish communal and familial life throughout the world.

Offered as a free resource, JewishGen.org has facilitated thousands of family connections and success stories, and is currently engaged in an intensive expansion effort that will bring many more records, tools, and resources to its collections.

Please visit https://www.jewishgen.org/ to learn more.

Executive Director: Avraham Groll

About JewishGen Press

JewishGen Press (formerly the Yizkor Books-in-Print Project) is the publishing division of JewishGen.org, and provides a venue for the publication of non-fiction books pertaining to Jewish genealogy, history, culture, and heritage.

In addition to the Yizkor Book category, publications in the Other Non-Fiction category include Shoah memoirs and research, genealogical research, collections of genealogical and historical materials, biographies, diaries and letters, studies of Jewish experience and cultural life in the past, academic theses, and other books of interest to the Jewish community.

Please visit https://www.jewishgen.org/Yizkor/ybip.html to learn more.

Director of JewishGen Press: Joel Alpert
Managing Editor - Jessica Feinstein
Publications Manager - Susan Rosin

The Demb Family Journey

from Mlynov to Baltimore

1840–1940

By

Howard I. Schwartz, PhD

For Rivka (Gruber) and Israel Jacob Demb,

Progenitors of Our Demb Family

A note about the researcher/author:
Howard I. Schwartz, PhD, is descended from
the Demb and Gruber families in Mlynov.

Howard Schwartz's
Paternal Ancestry

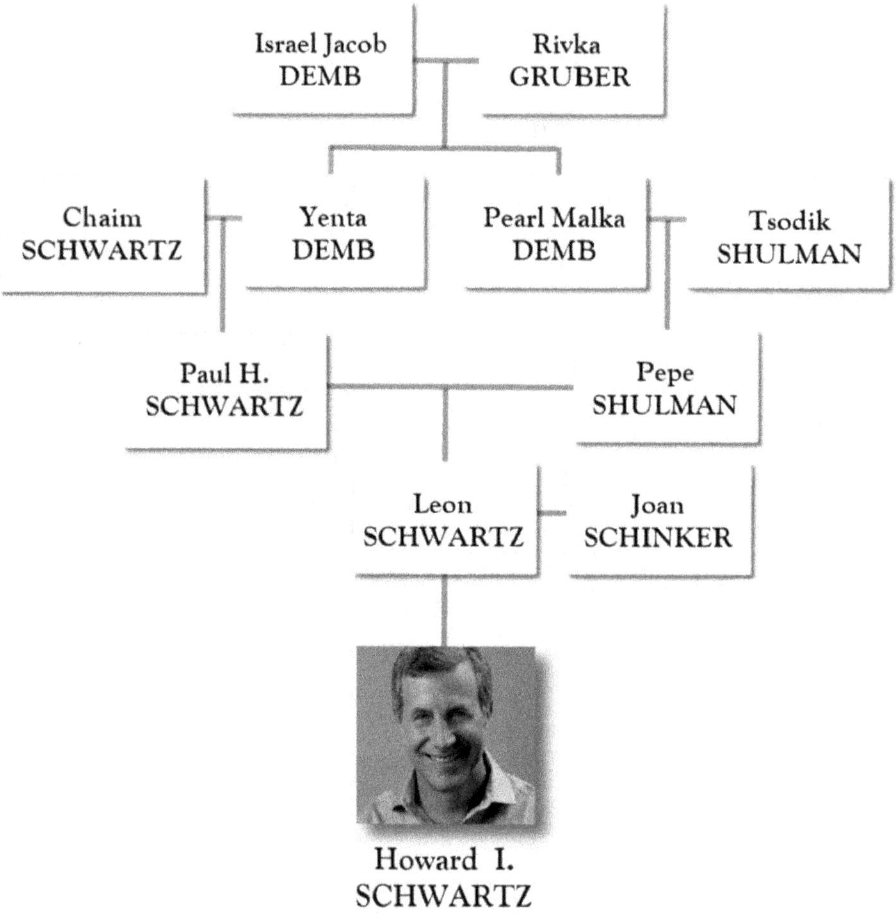

Israel Jacob
DEMB

Rivka
GRUBER

Chaim
SCHWARTZ

Yenta
DEMB

Pearl Malka
DEMB

Tsodik
SHULMAN

Paul H.
SCHWARTZ

Pepe
SHULMAN

Leon
SCHWARTZ

Joan
SCHINKER

Howard I.
SCHWARTZ

*Figure 1 A gathering in 2019 of descendants
on grounds of Star-Spangled Banner Flag House where first Demb immigrants lived*

The Demb Family from Mlynov

Rivka Gruber (1842–after 1913) m Israel Jacob Demb (1838?–after 1929) Wed in 1863. They had nine children.*

Pesse Demb m David Rivetz/ Hurwitz
- Gulza Hurwitz Mazer
- Minnie Hurwitz Fox
- Isaac Hurwitz
- Rose Hurwitz Finkelstein m1 Margalit m2
- Clara Hurwitz Fram

Pearl Malka Demb m Tsodik Shulman
- Nehuma Shulman Meiler
- Liza Shulman Koszhushner
- Simon Shulman
- Harry Shulman
- Sarah Shulman Shulman
- Clara Shulman Fishman
- Pepe Shulman Schwartz

Simha Gruber Chava m1
- Mollie Gruber Herman
- Nathan Gruber
- Samuel Gruber

Yenta Demb m Chaim Schwartz
- Benjamin Schwartz
- Norton Schwartz
- Paul H. Schwartz

Motel Demb/ Demming m Freida Kozusnia
- Sylvia Demb Penn
- Julius Deming
- Marion Demb Laken

Mollya Demb m Samuel Roskes
- David S. Roskes
- Herman Roskes

Aaron Demb m Baila Woladski
- Louis Demb
- Hyman Demb

Marriage of First Cousins
Pepe Shulman & Paul Schwartz

/ Name Change
() Birth Surname Unknown
m Married
m1 First Marriage
m2 Second Marriage
~ Circa

Tree designed by Audrey Goldseker Polt

*Rivka and Israel Jacob had two more children, Edle Demb and Hanna Demb (), born after Mollya and before Aaron. Tragically, Edle drowned. Nothing is known about Hanna and her child Edith.

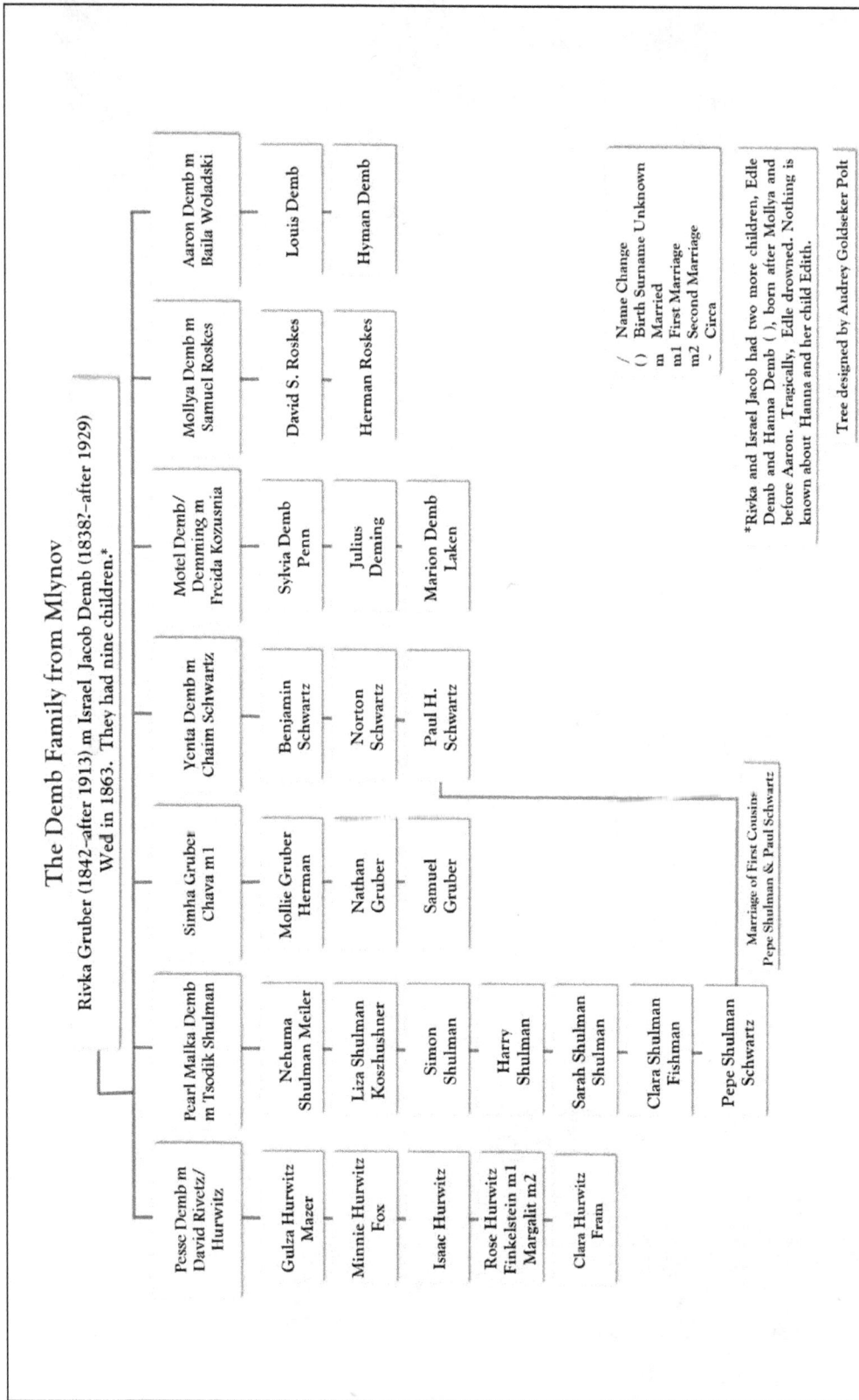

Figure 2 The Demb Family Tree

Contents

TABLE OF FIGURES

***

PREFACE

I wrote a version of this Demb Family story several years ago, but in the process, I became interested in so many intriguing tangents about people in Baltimore that it evolved into a sprawling saga about much more than the Demb family. Every little clue pulled me into the fascinating story of someone else whose life intersected with our family. As one thread led to another, I realized that my understanding of the Demb family could be enriched – indeed could not be fully understood – without also getting my arms around the stories of other Mlynov immigrants who landed in Baltimore.

That effort expanded into my growing interest into the history of the shtetl and people of Mlynov and the sister town of Mervits. In the process, I developed the Mlynov web site, connected with and created a virtual community of more than two hundred Mlynov family descendants, documented the story of dozens of other Mlynov families, and helped translate and publish a complete and fully annotated version of Mlynov-Mervits Memorial Book.

With the publication of that new translation in 2023, I felt it was time to go back and revisit the Demb family story so that Demb descendants could have a consolidated version of our story. This is the consolidated story. I hope other descendants find the story of the Demb family to be as interesting and illuminating as I have.

My daughter, Penina, between tombstones of her two Mlynov great-great grandfathers.
Shomrei Mishmeres Hakodesh Cemetery. Rosedale, Maryland.

* * *

ADDITIONAL RESOURCES

- The Mlynov Mervits website:
  https://kehilalinks.jewishgen.org/Mlyniv/index.html

- Families from Mlynov
  https://kehilalinks.jewishgen.org/Mlyniv/families.html

- Translation of the Mlynov-Mervits Memorial Book in Print
  https://www.jewishgen.org/yizkor/ybip/YBIP_Mlyniv.html

- Translation of the Mlynov-Merivts Memorial Book Online
  https://www.jewishgen.org/yizkor/Mlyniv/Mlyniv.html

FROM MLYNOV TO BALTIMORE

***

CHAPTER 1

THE DEMB FAMILY STORY

Sometime not long before 1868 in a small shtetl called Mlynov, located in what was then the Western part of Russia and is now Western Ukraine, a young woman named Rivka Gruber married a man named Israel Jacob Demb. The marriage had no particular historical significance, though it may have been noteworthy in that small shtetl for reasons discussed below. Still, the marriage was a productive one. Rivka became the matriarch of the Demb family, the mother of nine children, twenty-seven grandchildren, 67 great-grandchildren whom we know about, the majority of whom would end up living in Baltimore, the thriving port in Maryland.

We don't know much about this original couple. Only two photos are extant showing what they looked like. And a precious brief memoir by a granddaughter, written when she was 80, recalls a bit about them when she was still a young girl living in Mlynov.

The story of this Demb family, and its migration to Baltimore, is reconstructed in what follows from oral traditions, a memoir, a family tree scroll that circulated in the family and supplemented where possible by historical records.

My name is Howard I. Schwartz, and I am one of Rivka and Israel Jacob's great-great-grandsons. Both of my father's parents were born in Mlynov and were first cousins. Their mothers were sisters and both were daughters of Rivka and Israel Jacob Demb. I am thus descended along two different paths to Rivka and Israel Jacob Demb, making this story particularly interesting to me.

Growing up, I never heard the names of Rivka and Israel Jacob Demb. Indeed, I can't remember my father ever mentioning the name Mlynov, the birthplace of his parents. Like so many other American families, the first generation in America was happy to have left shtetl life behind.

My interest in the family and its migration story began when I was taking down the ancestral photos off the wall of my parents' home after they had passed away. As I looked at those photos, I realized how little I knew about the origin of my father's family. Thus began my interest in my family history which blossomed into my larger interest in Mlynov.[1]

Thankfully, I didn't have to start research on the Demb family story from scratch. A memoir written by Mlynov-born Clara Fram (~1902–1994) was circulating in the family by the early 1990s and a paper scroll of a family tree written down originally by Rivka and Israel Jacob's granddaughter

---

[1] Most of my research on Mlynov is documented at the Mlynov website hosted by the nonprofit JewishGen at https://kehilalinks.jewishgen.org/Mlyniv/

Clara Shulman (~1903–1990) living in Baltimore and documented by Julius Edlavitch (1954–), was also circulating in the family.

Figure 3 Mlyniv in Western Ukraine on today's maps.

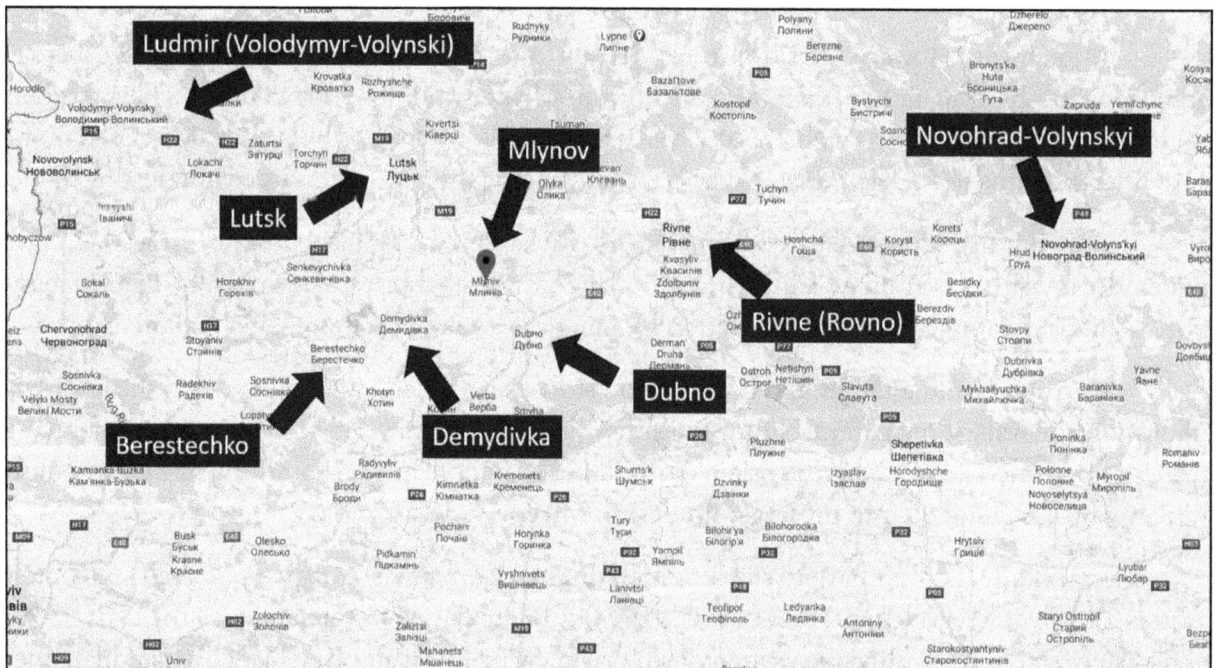

Figure 4 Mlynov in relationship to other close towns

The following narrative of the Demb family draws on these earlier efforts supplemented by interviews of various Demb family descendants, US immigration, naturalization and census records, and the few original Russian records that have been located and translated.

***

A Funny Story: On the Origins of the Demb Family Tree

As I began looking for information on the Demb family history, I discovered that Demb descendant, Ted Fishman (1927–2020), then in his eighties, was a great source of information, stories and photos. Growing up in Baltimore, Ted was my father's best friend and first cousin (their mothers were sisters). Both of his parents were born in Mlynov and he was a great-grandson of Rivka and Israel Jacob Demb.[2]

I used to call Ted regularly on Sundays before he passed away in 2020. He was a great raconteur and knew quite a bit about the Demb family history, especially after it arrived in Baltimore. On several occasions Ted told me the funny story of how the Demb family tree originally came into being.

The story begins when Ted fell in love with and then married a woman named Anabel who was from New York. After they were married Ted's mother would often point to someone they saw and tell Anabel, "That's a cousin, and there's another cousin."

At one point, when Ted and Anabel were buying their first home, they were visiting an area where the developer was a cousin (Joseph Herman). Some other cousins (Mitchell Penn and Etta) also were buying in the development and they "used to meet there on weekends to see how our homes were being built." In Ted's words:

"One Sunday when my mother was with us, she saw the Penns and took Anabel over to meet a cousin. This set Anabel off as it seemed to her my mother was introducing her to everyone in Baltimore as a cousin." By this point, Anabel was skeptical.

"You can't be related to all these people," she insisted. "Prove it to me." So Ted's mother, Clara, sat down and drew the first Demb family tree on a piece of paper. As new members of the family were born, they would add to the tree.

---

[2] Ted's mother was born Clara (Chaika) Shulman (1904–1990) in Mlynov, one of the granddaughters of Rivka and Israel Jacob Demb. She arrived in Baltimore with the Shulman family in 1921. In Baltimore, Clara married Benjamin Fishman (1902–1993) who was also from Mlynov. Ben, a son of Moishe Fishman, came to Baltimore a year earlier in 1920 as a teenager with a group of three Mlynov wives and their children in a story told in more detail later. In Baltimore, Ben married his Mlynov sweetheart, Clara Shulman.

Nothing much happened with the family tree until one time in 1979 Ted was traveling west for business and had a stopover in Minneapolis. He gave his cousin Julius Edlavitch[3] a call. Julius informed Ted that his new son Michael had just been born.

"I know," said Ted, "Michael is already in the family tree." At that moment, Ted laughingly tells me, "Julius jumped down my throat."

"What family tree?" Julius pressed.

When Ted told him about the family tree his mother had written down on paper, Julius asked for a copy. From that point forward, Julius became obsessed, a feeling I can relate to. He would hound family members for information. He would call Ted at all hours of the night and ask for more information.

*Figure 5 Wedding of Ted Fishman and Anabel
Courtesy of Karen Passero*

Julius began reaching out to many Demb relatives. Lynne (Herman) Sandler recalls that she corresponded regularly with Julius during those years and helped him organize the first Demb reunion in 1992 at the party room of her mother's apartment building.[4] At the event, Julius distributed the first version of the Demb family tree, printed, of course, on a dot matrix printer. Julius had found close to 400 relatives. A paper scroll version of the Demb family tree was taped

---

[3] Julius Edlavitch is a great-grandson of Rivka and Israel Jacob Demb. His grandmother was Sarah Shulman, the daughter of Pearl Malka (Demb) Shulman. His mother was Betty (Shulman) Edlavitch.
[4] Lynne is the granddaughter of Mollie (Gruber) and Israel Herman. Her father was their son, Al Herman, and her mother Carlyn (Weinstein).

to the walls so that everyone could see it and has been circulating in the family ever since. Julius's work on the family history continued until he suffered from a brain tumor.

The following account of the Demb family story builds on Julius's earlier efforts and is informed by my many Sunday conversations with father's first cousin, Ted Fishman, as well as by the stories and photos graciously shared with me by dozens of other Demb descendants.

Figure 6 The Demb Family Tree Scroll opened with daughter Penina

***

What Did Rivka and Israel Jacob Demb Look Like?

Only two photos survive of the matriarch and patriarch, Rivka (Gruber) and Israel Jacob Demb. They both are from a later period when their children were adults and they had many grandchildren and some great-grandchildren.

The first photo, from about 1913, shows the couple seated in the center of a photo with the family of their daughter Pearl Malka Shulman. My grandmother, Pepe, is seated on the floor in the center with her elbow up on the lap of her grandmother, Rivka, who is wearing a shmata that was customary of women of her generation. Other photos of Mlynov women from the same generation show the same kind of head covering.[5] To the left of Rivka is her husband Israel Jacob, with his head covered. To the right is Rivka's daughter Pearl Malka. We shall meet the rest of the Shulman family below.

---

[5] A photo from 1918 in the Mlynov Memorial Book, p. 13, shows all the women with the shmata in the market square of Mlynov. A photo of Anna Fishman in the collection the Goldseker family shows her with the same style shmata on her head.

Figure 7 Rivka (Gruber) and Israel Jacob Demb in the middle of Shulman family, ~1913

The only other extant photo of Rivka and Israel Jacob is from a later date. It was in the collection of Ted Fishman and came originally from a postcard. In this photo, the matriarch and patriarch are quite a bit older. Lynne (Herman) Sandler recalls this same photo hanging in the breakfast room of her grandmother "Baba" Mollie Herman, but the grandchildren never knew who they were because no one ever talked about them.

Israel Jacob Demb and Rivka (Gruber) later in life. Courtesy of Ted Fishman.

***

The Wonderful Memoir of Granddaughter Clara Fram

The little information we have about Rivka Gruber and Israel Jacob Demb comes primarily from the childhood memories of their granddaughter, Clara H. Fram, recorded in the memoir she wrote later in life. How fortunate we are to have this memoir, which her descendants graciously gave me permission to post online.[6]

Clara was born Keila Rivetz in Mlynov in ˜1902. Her mother was Pesse Demb, the eldest daughter of Rivka and Israel Jacob. Pesse married a man named David Rivetz in Mlynov before 1884 when their eldest daughter was born. Clara was their youngest daughter. According to Clara's memoir, her father took the name Hurwitz in Baltimore because someone at the local synagogue in Baltimore told him "Rivetz" could not be spelled in English. Clara grew up without knowing her original surname.

---

[6] Clara Fram, "This is My Story." Available online at the Mlynov web site:
https://kehilalinks.jewishgen.org/Mlyniv/documents/Clara_Fram_This_Is_My_Story.pdf

Figure 8 Clara Fram as a young mother in Baltimore.
Courtesy of Eileen Scher.

At the age of seven, in late 1908, Clara left Mlynov with her mother, two of her older sisters, Minnie and Rose, and her paternal grandmother, Zecil. They headed to Baltimore to join her father and brother who immigrated in 1901 and 1907 respectively. In 1982, when Clara was eighty, she took an adult education class in Baltimore in which she recorded her childhood impressions of her family life in Mlynov and Baltimore as she was growing up. The memoir includes impressions of the shtetl, stories she heard growing up and memories of her grandparents and some of her cousins. Since Clara came to Baltimore at the age of 7 and wrote her memoir at the age of 80, her memories have to be taken with a grain of salt. Still, they are precious, the only first-hand memories that have been recorded of the Demb family from this early period.

Clara's memoir began circulating among descendants by the 1990s if not earlier. I found a copy of her memoir in my father's papers after he died in 2003. Attached was a copy of an email he wrote in 2002 to his cousin Ted Fishman thanking him for sending him the copy of Clara's memoir which he enjoyed.

***

CHAPTER 2

RIVKA AND ISRAEL JACOB DEMB

Clara apparently heard a story when she was growing up about the marriage of her grandparents. According to that story, when Rivka was a young girl of 11 years old, her father Moshe Gruber decided it was time for her to get married. Clara writes:

> In the town Malynow, my maternal grandmother [Rivka] had been an only child of wealthy parents; her father, Moshe Gruber, owning a brass and copper foundry, employing about two hundred laborers. When Rifka was eleven years old her father traveled to various "Yeshivohs" [centers of learning] to find the proper scholar for her to marry. From the town of Ludmir he brought a fifteen year old scholar named Israel Jacob Demb and, according to the prevailing custom, promised perpetual support for him and his growing family.

What a sweet, precious memory of the matriarch and patriarch of our Demb family. Clara most likely heard this story about her grandparents' marriage from her mother, Pesse, Rivka and Israel Jacob's eldest daughter. The story makes several salient points that are worth exploring further.

Moshe was a wealthy man with a brass and iron foundry employing two hundred men. Rivka was quite young when Moshe decided to arrange her marriage. Due to his wealth, Moshe could afford to support a scholarly husband who would study all the time. He thus went to various yeshivot to find an appropriate husband for his daughter. He brought back the 15-year-old scholar, Israel Jacob Demb, from the town of Ludmir, a town that was 71 miles from Mlynov and which appears on maps of Ukraine, today as Volodymyr and was previously called Volodymyr-Volinkskyi (see Figure 4).

***

From Family Memory To History

After the Soviet Union fell in the 1990s, researchers gained access to Russian archives. From records that have been located, we now know that the story Clara heard about her grandparents' marriage is anchored in fact but also represents certain exaggerations.

In 2020, I hired a genealogical researcher who found and translated the Russian "revision lists" (censuses) for Mlynov in the years 1850 and 1858. Russian revision lists (pronounced

"Revizskie Skazki" in Russian) are similar to US census records.[7] These revision lists record information about the number of households in towns, the names of their members, ages, genders, and relationships. These revision lists were instituted by Tsarist Russia in part as a means of allocating taxes and identifying individuals for conscription, and in part as an effort to track and manage its population. Though there was not complete uniformity in how information in the revision lists was collected, and there were various causes and motivations for mistakes and lies, each town had responsibility for gathering the information and submitting it to the Russian authorities. In some cases, the Crown rabbi in town was responsible for gathering the information.

What extraordinary luck to locate two such revisions for Mlynov in the mid-19th century, just eight years apart. In 1850, there were 48 households in Mlynov and 200 individuals living in town. By 1858, there were 64 households, and 284 individuals living in town.[8]

In both of these Mlynov revisions, there are two Gruber households. In the 1850 revision, which you can view online, the two Gruber households are listed sequentially (household #12 and #13) suggesting they were living next to each other, which in the revision lists was sometimes an indication of a familial relationship. The smaller Gruber household is #12 and the larger is #13. In 1858, the same two households are listed as household #12 and #14 with another household in between. It seems likely these two Gruber households were relatives but, if so, the original familial relationship that existed is no longer indicated in these censuses. We can guess that the two heads of households were brothers or first cousins, but that is not certain.

The smaller of the two Gruber households (#12) appears to be that of the matriarch remembered by Demb descendants as Rivka Gruber. The 1850 revision lists Rivka Gruber as age 8, which would put her birth year in 1842. Her father's name is listed as "Moshko-Leib aka Srul-Noeh." Moshko is a Russian equivalent of Moshe, confirming that this Rivka Gruber is almost certainly the one Clara Fram tells us was the daughter of Moshe Gruber. Moshe is also called "Srul-Noeh" [Yisrael Noah], a nickname which seems likely to have been his father and grandfather's names since these revision lists often call men by their patronym. We can guess therefore that Moshe Gruber was son of Srul Gruber who was son of Noeh Gruber.

---

[7] See the useful description by Joseph B. Everett, "The Imperial Russian Revision Lists of the 18th and 19th Century." Brigham Young University. Scholars Archive, 2018, and Eugene M. Avrutin, *Jews and the Imperial State: Identification Politics in Tsarist Russia*. Ithaca: Cornell, 2010.

[8] I've published the translation of the two Mlynov revision lists for 1850 and for 1858 with a family by family summary on the Mlynov web site. See https://kehilalinks.jewishgen.org/Mlyniv/Mlynov-Revision-1850.html

Fam # revision 10 / (revision 9)	Surname	Name	Father's Name	Estate	Implied Year of Birth (based on age in 1850)	Implied Year of Birth (based on age in 1858)	Previous Census Year	Age	Cause	When Exactly	Year	Age	Relation
12 (12)	Gruber	Moshko-Leib, aka Srul-Noeh	not indicated	townsman	1824	1824	1850	26			1858	34	head of the family
12 (12)	Gruber	Mordko	Moshko-Leib	townsman	1846		1850	4	died	1855	1858		son
12 (12)	Gruber	Surah	not indicated	townsman		1826	1850	not indicated			1858	32	wife
12 (12)	Gruber	Rivka	Moshko-Leib	townsman		1842	1850	not indicated			1858	16	daughter
12 (12)	Gruber	Molka-Roislya	Moshko-Leib	townsman		1854	1850	not indicated			1858	4	daughter

Figure 9 1850 revision list for family of Rivka Gruber

Family #	Surname	Name	Father's Name	Implied Year of Birth (based on age in 1834)	Implied Year of Birth (based on age in 1850)	Previous Census Year	Age	Cause	When Exactly	Year	Age	Relation
12	Gruberr* (*Gruber in 1858)	Moshko-Leib, aka Srul-Noeh	not indicated	1824	1824	1834	10			1850	26	head of the family
12	Gruberr	Mordko	Moshko-Leib		1846	1834	newborn			1850	4	son
12	Gruber	Sura	not indicated	1826	1826	1834	not indicated			1850	24	wife
12	Gruber	Rivka	Moshko-Leib		1842	1834	not indicated			1850	8	daughter

Figure 10 1858 revision list for family of Rivka Gruber

In the 1850 revision, Rivka's father, Moshko-Leib, is age 26 with the implied birth year of 1824. The same revision indicates that Moshko-Leib was 10 years old in an earlier 1834 revision (the record of which has unfortunately not been located). By implication, Moshko-Leib was living in Mlynov with his family by 1834 and it seems very plausible he born there. Indeed, it seems possible Moshko-Leib's parents were already living in Mlynov as early as 1793, when Mlynov was incorporated into Russia as part of the Second Partition of Poland.

The 1850 revision also indicates that Moshe-Leib's wife was called "Sura," a name not mentioned in Clara Fram's memoir. Sura is age 24 with an implied birth year of 1826. Unfortunately, Sura's surname at birth is not provided since the revision lists did not bother to record the original surnames of wives or their father's names. Once daughters left their father's household, Russian authorities had no interest in which household they were from.

The original Demb family tree scroll circulating in the family lists a "Moshe Leon" and "Sura" as the parents of Israel Jacob Demb. We can now assume that this was incorrect and that Moshe Leon and Sura were the parents of Rivka, not Israel Jacob Demb.

In the 1850 revision, Moshko-Leib and Sura also have another child named Mordko, age 4, indicating that Rivka was not an only child, as her granddaughter Clara remembered or apparently was told growing up. It is perfectly understandable that having spent most of her life in Baltimore, Clara may not have known that her grandmother Rivka had a sibling. In fact, it turns out Rivka had more than one, as we learn when we turn from the 1850 to the 1858 revision.

In the 1858 revision, Rivka is now listed as 16 years old, but she is still single and living with her family. Contrary to what Clara was told or came to believe, her grandmother did not get married at the age of 11. Instead, Rivka must have married Israel Jacob Demb between 1858 and 1864/1865 when their eldest daughter Pesse (Clara's mother) was born. In other words, Rivka must have been between the age of 16 (1858) and 22 (1864) when she married Israel Jacob Demb.

The 1858 revision indicates that a younger sister of Rivka's was born in 1854 named Molka-Roislya. What became of Molka-Roislya later in life is not known. Sadly, we also learn that a year later in 1855, Rivka's younger brother, Mordko, died at the age of 9.

***

Did Morko Gruber Really Die?

The cause of Mordko's death is not specified in the 1858 revision. Mortality was high in Mlynov between 1850 and 1858. Ten percent of the population died in that decade (29 of 284 people). However, the majority of deaths were heads of households (19 of the 29 deaths). Mordko is the only person listed who died under the age of 10. While he may have died of natural causes, it seems possible he was listed as deceased for another reason: to avoid conscription into the Russian military.

We know from these revisions, for example, that between 1850 and 1858, 6 young men between the ages of 10 and 19 were recruited, and the whereabouts of three boys under the age of 10 were unknown. Furthermore, in 1853–56, the Crimean War broke out involving Russia and the Ottoman Empire. The War may have evoked fears that other young boys would be recruited. It seems possible, though by no means certain, that Rivka's brother was in hiding to avoid conscription and survived.

Whether he survived or not, the appearance of the name Mordko (i.e., Mordechai) Gruber in this revision is tantalizing. There is another line of Gruber descendants from Mlynov who remember their ancestor's name as Mordechai Gruber.[9] Was it possible that perhaps Mordko Gruber, came out of hiding later and became the Mordechai Gruber remembered as the ancestor of the other Gruber line from Mlynov? Or alternatively, perhaps Mordko did die young and when Moshe and Sura had another son after 1858, they named him Mordechai after his brother who had died young.

***

Moshe Gruber's Brass and Iron factory

Clara indicates that her great-grandfather, Moshe Gruber, was wealthy from his brass and iron foundry which employed 200 men. This wealth empowered Moshe to seek a scholarly son-in-law, one who would need to be financially supported so he could study full time.

This story has the air of plausibility about it and is buttressed by two external sources that confirm the existence of some sort of iron foundry in Mlynov, though one with a smaller number of employees than Clara indicates. Both of these records refer to the existence of the foundry in 1905 when Clara was about three years old and still living in Mlynov.

The first source is a book published in Ukrainian about Ukrainian towns[10] and referred to in a Wikipedia article on Mlyniv. The essay on Mlyniv indicates there was an iron casting shop in Mlynov that had 60 (not 200) employees. During the Russian Revolution of 1905, that iron casting shop was taken over by a branch of the Russian Social Democratic Labour Party. Perhaps, at some

---

[9]There was another Gruber line that remained in Mlynov until the Shoah. Two sisters, Rachel and Sonia Gruber, both married cousins with the surname of Teitelman. They both survived the Shoah and wrote essays in the Mlynov-Mervits Memorial book. From family trees recorded by their descendants, we know that they were children of a man named Yosef Moshe Gruber. His father was called Mordechai Gruber.

The 1858 census doesn't list any Mordko [Mordechai] Gruber besides the deceased brother of Rivka. It is possible, of course, that there was a Mordechai Gruber from the other Gruber household listed in the Mlynov revision lists who was not yet born in 1858. But it also seems plausible, that a) Moshe and Sura had another son whom they named for their deceased son Mordko or b) that Morko was not deceased at all and after he came out of hiding became the ancestor of this other Gruber line.

[10] Bukhalo, H., Vovk, A. Mlyniv, *Mlyniv Raion, Rivne Oblast* (Млинів, Млинівський район, Ровенська область). The History of Cities and Villages of the Ukrainian SSR. See Wikipedia entry on "Mlyniv." Retrieved Feb. 2023.

point, we'll discover other Russian records about that foundry showing it was owned by a man named Moshe Gruber.

The second relevant source is a US immigration record from 1905 which alludes to the presence of an iron foundry in Mlynov. The record is a passenger manifest of a Mlynov young man named "Hersch Hirch" (later Harry Hirsch) (1884-1984), who traveled from Antwerp on the SS Kroonland and arrived in New York on July 18, 1905. Hersch was 22 years old and the first member of the Hirsch family in Mlynov to arrive in the US.[11]

The passenger manifest indicates that Hersch's occupation is "founder" a term that didn't make sense until I deciphered the word "iron" scrawled above. Hersch previously worked in an iron foundry. Perhaps Hersch left Mlynov because the iron foundry had been socialized during the 1905 revolution. It may also be relevant that Hersch's uncle, Daniel Hirsch, had an iron shop in Mlynov.[12]

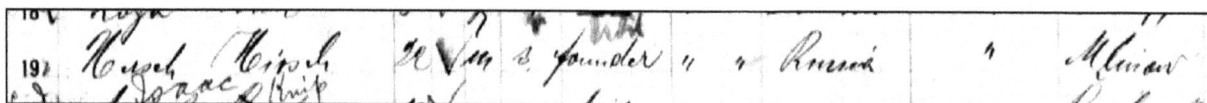

Passenger manifest of Hersch Hirsch in 1905 showing he worked in an iron foundry and his residence was Mlynow

***

Moshe Gruber and the Iron Foundry

It is worth pausing a moment to imagine why an iron foundry might have developed in Mlynov by the late 1850s when Moshe Gruber sought a husband for his daughter, Rivka. We can speculate that the foundry developed there due to the Ikva River which may have been used to drive a water wheel and to transport goods to and fro the foundry.

An iron foundry produces metal castings. Metals are cast into shapes by melting them into a liquid, pouring the metal into a mold, and removing the mold material after the metal has solidified as it cools. The industrial revolution in the 17th century produced a growing demand for iron and new techniques for refining it. Throughout the 18th century, Russia was a major exporter of iron, with the industry concentrated in the Urals Mountains.

The start of the second Iron Age is sometimes identified as 1825, as the iron industry experienced a massive stimulation from the heavy demand for railways, which needed iron rails, iron in stock, bridges, tunnels and more. Meanwhile, civilian use increased, as everything which could be made of iron began to be in demand.[13]

---

[11] See the history of the Hirsch family from Mlynov on the Mlynov website.
[12] See "A True Event in Mlynov from 96 Years Ago." Mlynov-Mervits Memorial Book, p. 175.
[13] Drawing on a number of sources including Robert Wilde, "Iron in the Industrial Revolution," Accessed Feb. 8, 2023.

Figure 11 1885 painting of an iron foundry in Copenhagen Denmark[14]

***

Moshe Goes to Ludmir

Clara's memory of her grandfather's foundry and wealth has historical plausibility. It makes sense too that Moshe's wealth was one of the reasons he wanted to find a young husband outside of Mlynov for his daughter Rivka. In 1858, when Rivka was 16 years old, Mlynov had only 13 eligible young men between the ages of 16 and 22 years old.[15] Still, she could easily have married a young man from Mervits, Dubno, or Lutsk, among other closer towns with a large percentage of Jewish residents.

We can guess that Moshe Gruber was drawn to Ludmir in particular by its reputation as a Hasidic center after the founder of the Karliner Hasidic dynasty, Rabbi Shelomoh ha-Levi, settled in Ludmir in 1786. Perhaps by 1858, Moshe Gruber already knew of the "Maiden of Ludmir," Khane-Rokhl Werbermacher (1806?–1888?), a local woman in Ludmir who became a popular

---

[14] Artist Peder Severin Krøyer: The Iron Foundry, Burmeister and Wain [shipyard]. National Gallery of Denmark. In the public domain.
[15] These statistics come from my analysis of the 1858 revision in Mlynov.

Hasidic leader known for her righteousness and wisdom. Perhaps Rivka's husband to be, Israel Jacob Demb, was even among the numerous Hasidim who gathered in her bet midrash before she left for Palestine.

From essays in the Mlynov-Mervits Memorial book (hereafter Mlynov Memorial Book), we know that at a later date the Karliner Hasidic tradition had a strong presence in Mlynov and was embraced by the second largest synagogue in town, though the largest synagogue followed the Trisk tradition and another group followed the Olyker Hasidism.[16] We don't know for sure which tradition if any that Moshe Gruber preferred.

In 1872, not long after Rivka and Israel Jacob married, the then leader of the Karliner Hasidim, Aharon (II) Perlov of Karlin (1802–1872) died just outside of Mlynov. A memorial was erected to the Rebbe's memory and folklore spang up about his death and his powers.[17] Large pilgrimages of his disciples flocked to Mlynov on the yarzheit of his death. Five of Rivka and Israel Jacob's children were already born by the time of the Rebbe's death and we can guess they grew up seeing the Rebbe's memorial, knowing the folklore about the menorah tree that grew where he died, and observing the large pilgrimages to town, just like other writers who recalled their childhood in essays for the Memorial book.[18]

Nothing further has been discovered so far about Israel Jacob Demb's life before Moshe Gruber brought him to Mlynov. As noted earlier, the Demb family tree scroll circulating in the family indicates his parents' names were Moshe Leon (Moshe Leib) and Sura, but we now know that they were Rivka's parents, not Israel Jacob's. A genealogical researcher I hired has been unable to find evidence of a Demb family in available revision census records for Ludmir (i.e., Volodymyr Volinski), though records exist for other Dembs in the area, though it is not possible to determine if they are Israel Jacob's family.

---

[16] See my summary in the "Gone But Not Forgotten," an intro to the Mlynov Memorial book and notes there, p. xi.
[17] On the folklore about the Rebbe's death remembered by Mlynov descendant Eliyahu Gelman, see "The Tree that Resembled a Menorah," Mlynov Memorial Book, p. 27.
[18] For reminiscences of the memorial and pilgrimages, see the essays by Moshe Fishman "Mlynov in the Past," pp. 54-57, and Sylvia Goldberg, "Stoliner Hasidism in Mlynov," Mlynov-Mervits Memorial book, pp. 78-81.

Yetta (Demb) Schwartz
(1870–1962)

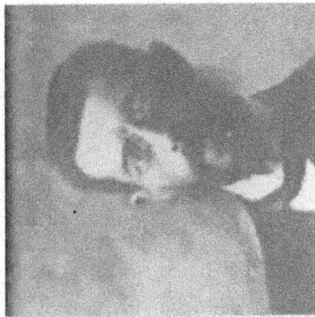

Aaron Demb
(~1876–1970)

Simha (Demb) Gruber
(~1867–aft 1913)

Hannah Demb
(? –?)

Edle Demb
(? –?)
(drown)

Pearl (Demb) Shulman
(1865–1933)

Mollie (Demb) Roskes
(~1872–1963)

Bessie (Demb) Hurwitz
(~1864–1939)

Motel Demb
(Max Deming)
(1871–1929)

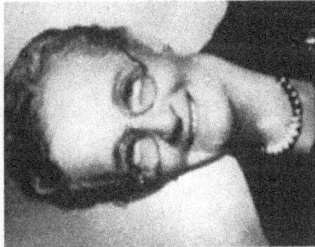

Figure 12 Collage of Demb children in adulthood
Photos Courtesy of descendants.

***

Rivka and Israel Jacob's Expanding Family: The Early Mlynov Period

After Rivka and Israel Jacob got married between 1858 and 1863/64, the first of their nine children was born. Her name was Pesse and she would become the mother of Clara, the memoirist in the family.

We know that at least seven, and probably all nine, of the Demb children were born between ˜1864-˜1880. In other words, within approximately a 16-year period, Rivka had between 7-9 children, averaging about one every other year. Since we now know that Rivka was born in 1842, she had all her children by the time she was 38. Her father, Moshe, must have been a very proud grandfather.

The above photos from descendants show the Demb children later in life as married adults in their possible reconstructed birth order. Photos of them as children no longer seem to exist.

The Demb family tree scroll gives one version of the Demb children birth order (see left column of table below). However, an alternative birth order is suggested by US immigration and naturalization records for six of the nine Demb children who came to the US between 1909 and 1925 (see right column of table below). Though riddled with inconsistencies, the US records suggest a different birth order. A detailed summary of the US records follows the description of each of these Demb individuals and their families.

Table 1 Birth Order of Rivka and Israel Jacob's Children

Birth Order of Demb Children Based on Family Tree Scroll	Birth Order and Birth Years Reconstructed from US Records
1. Pesse Demb 2. Yenta Demb 3. Simha Gruber 4. Motel Demb 5. Pearl Malka Demb 6. Mollya Demb 7. Edle Demb (drown) 8. Hanna Demb 9. Aaron Demb	1. Pesse Demb (b. ˜1864) 2. Pearl Malka Demb (b. 1865) 3. [Simha Gruber-no US records] 4. Yenta Demb (b. 1870) 5. Motel Demb (b. ˜1870/71) 6. Mollya Demb (b. ˜1872–1876) 7. [Edle Demb-no US records] 8. [Hanna Demb-no US records] 9. Aaron Demb (b. ˜1876–1880)

No family oral traditions exist about the Demb family in the years Rivka and Israel Demb's children were growing up. We can, however, now speculate about what their lives were like from essays about Mlynov life recorded in the Mlynov Memorial book. We can imagine they swam in the Ikva River that ran alongside Mlynov, that they climbed the hill near the Count's palace that children called "Mount Sinai," that they got their feet stuck in the mud on the way to cheder in the winter months, and ice-skated on the frozen pond they called a swamp in the center of town. They probably trailed after the man who was responsible for keeping the eternal light lit in the Rebbe's memorial and probably witnessed the pilgrimages to town on the yarzheit of the Rebbe's death.[19]

---

[19] See my introduction "Gone But Not Forgotten" to the Mlynov Memorial Book for references to these childhood memories.

***

CHAPTER 3

THE FAMILY OF PESSE DEMB (AKA BESSIE HURWITZ)

Pesse Demb became known later in Baltimore as Bessie Hurwitz. She is listed as the oldest child in the Demb family tree scroll and is remembered in the memoir of her daughter, Clara Fram, as "eldest of four beautiful daughters in the Demb Family."

The fact that Clara calls her mother "the eldest of four beautiful daughters" and not the oldest *child* may suggest that her brother Simha was older, but this is not certain. US records inconsistently list Pesse's birth year as 1864, 1865 and 1866.[20] She died in Baltimore on Jan. 20, 1932.[21] The earliest photo of Pesse shows her seated left with her husband David, seated right, at the 1910 marriage of their daughter Minnie to Samuel Fox in Baltimore (see below).

Pesse met her husband David Rivetz (also spelled Rivitz and Riwetz) in cheder in Mlynov, according to the memoir of her daughter Clara. The Rivetz family was living on a family compound near Mlynov and David went to school in Mlynov. Clara recounts what she learned about her parents' marriage, which was in 1882 according to the 1910 census. Clara's mother, Pesse, would have been about 17 years old at the time. Clara writes:

> As the young [Demb] family grew, my mother being the eldest of the girls, so did their grandfather's [i.e., Moshe Gruber's] so-called wealth diminish. By the time my father and my mother saw each other in Cheder, though he would have desired a scholarly bridegroom for his beautiful and accomplished Pesse, my grandfather [Israel Jacob Demb] did not object to her marrying into the Rivitz family that was well-off in their Possessia.

The story suggests that Clara's grandfather, Israel Jacob Demb, would have preferred a scholarly husband like himself for his eldest daughter Pesse. But by this time, the wealth of Israel Jacob's father-in-law, Moshe Gruber, had declined. So Israel Jacob allowed his daughter Pesse to marry David, who was not a scholar but whose family was doing well with their property, which Clara refers to as a "possessia."

---

[20] Pesse's 1909 passenger manifest lists her age as 43 with an implied birth year of 1866. In the 1910 Census, she is listed as age 45 with implied birth year of 1865. In the 1920 census, she is 56 with an implied birth year of 1864.
[21] The date of her death is given in the Jack Lewis Funeral Home Records Index posted by the Jewish Museum of Maryland http://jewishmuseummd.org/wp-content/uploads/2013/06/Jack-Lewis-records-index.pdf. Retrieved May 22, 2023.

Figure 13 Pesse (Demb) and David Rivetz (seated) 1910
Marriage of their daughter Minnie to Samuel Fox. Courtesy of Carol Engelman.

By the time David and Pesse married, the Rivetz family property was generating income from a variety of sources and Pesse went to live on the property with her husband.

> My grandfather [Mordechai Rivitz] established on his property various projects for making a living for both his daughter [Chaia] and his son [David] when they married. There was an inn where travelers could stop and be refreshed, bringing to mind, people said, the Biblical story of Abraham greeting the three strangers [angels]. There was a distillery making vodka; there was cattle, there was farming. For a number of years they all lived together, the daughter Chaia, "ruling the roost" with country strength and authority, cracking down on her quiet brother and his pretty wife [Pesse].

Clara describes this property as being in "Irslavitch," a place which has not been identified on current or older maps. We know it was close enough to Mlynov so that David could go to cheder there which is where he met Pesse Demb. The loss of this property following the assassination of Tsar Alexander II in 1881 plays an important role in the story of the Demb migration to Baltimore.[22]

Pesse and David had their first child, Gulza (or Gulzia), in 1884, according to her 1921 passenger manifest and her 1930 Baltimore census. Gulza was followed by five more siblings. Based on Clara's memoir, their birth order appears to be: Gulza, Menucha (Minnie), Yitzhak (Isaac), Ruchel (Rose), and Keila (Clara).

"There were five of us," Clara writes, "Gulza [diminutive of "Margulis"~"Margalit" in modern Hebrew], Minnie [Menucha in Hebrew], Yitzchak, our brother, all three born before my father *first* [my emphasis] left for America, at which time Gulza was six years old." Clara also remarks that "The three children, Gulza, Minnie and Yitzchak, were teenagers when my sister Rose was born; and twenty-two months later, I, Kayla, Clara, arrived."

The US records are not entirely consistent about the birth years of Pesse and David's children. Menucha (Minnie) has an implied birth year variously of 1889 (passenger manifest), 1886 (1910 and 1920 census) and 1887 (1930 census). Yitzhak's birth year is listed as 1886 (passenger manifest and 1917 Draft registration card) and 1889 (1910 census). Ruchel (Rose's) birth year is variously listed as 1900 (passenger manifest), 1899 (1910 and 1920 census) and Keila's [Clara's] as 1901 (passenger manifest, 1910 and 1920 census) and 1903 (1930 census). Her Declaration of Intention gives her birthday as May 31, 1901 which would mean she was in utero when her father left permanently for America in February 1901. Clara's memoir, however, seems to imply she was born in 1900 since she believes she was 9 months old when her father left.

Roughly, then, we can map out the story of Pesse Demb's family. She was born between 1864 and 1866. She married her husband David Rivetz in about 1882, between the ages of 16 to 18. Gulza was born in 1884, followed by Minnie ~1886/1887, Yitzhak / Isaac ~1886–1889, Ruchel/Rose ~1899/1900, and Keila/Clara ~1901.

***

Why Birth Years are Inconsistent in US Records

There are several reasons why immigrant birth years are not consistent in US records. As historians of Russian records indicate, birth dates were not recorded consistently and were not important to Jewish communities living in Tsarist Russia, though Tsarist Russia tried to capture such data in revision lists.[23]

---

[22] Tsar Alexander's son and successors were reactionary and imposed stricter rules on Jews and other minorities. Among other rules implemented, Jews were forbidden to hold property outside of towns. The loss of their property outside of Mlynov and therefore their source of income, triggered the decision by David's sister, Chaia (Rivetz) and her husband Getzel Fax, to leave for America. Most of the Dembs would follow and stay with the Fax family.

[23] See Avrutin, *Jews and the Imperial State*, p. 37.

When the immigrants came to the US, they were not always sure in which year they had been born. There were also various reasons for lying about their age to get through US customs. For example, immigrants traveling alone, like Yitzhak Rivetz, might want to appear older than they were so that US custom officials wouldn't label them as "LPC" [Likely Public Charge] and prevent their entrance. Males escaping conscription in the Tsar's army, or later the Polish army, may have listed themselves as younger or older than they were, so they would not be prevented from leaving.

Once they settled in the US, they did not always remember what age they said they were born on their ship manifest, what date they arrived, or even the name of their ship. Sometimes immigrants forgot the answers they provided in earlier census records as well. In the chaos of settling into their new homes, they sometimes didn't have records of their arrival and did not have easy access to their earlier records. For example, Clara Fram in her memoire reports that she didn't know her name was Keila Rivetz until she recovered a copy of her manifest later in life, probably in 1928 when she filled out her Declaration of Intention.

For all of these reasons, the birth years on the various records for the same individual are often inconsistent and we can't necessarily rely on the earlier records as the best and most accurate. Sometimes, immigrants felt safer to disclose information the longer they were present in the US, especially after they had been naturalized.

The summary of the US records that follows each family's description captures the immense variation in the records.

***

In the early 1890s, while Pesse and David were still having children, David Rivetz began commuting back and forth from Mlynov to Baltimore. David lived with his sister Chaia (aka Ida) and her husband Getzel Fax in Baltimore.[24] Getzel and Ida were the first couple to leave Mlynov for Baltimore, and many of the Demb and Mlynov immigrants followed them there and lived in their flats at 818 and 836 E. Pratt Street when they first landed, the latter address now on the grounds of the historic Star-Spangled Banner Flag house.

Clara's family memory is that her father David first began commuting to America "when Gulza was six years old." Since Gulza was born in 1884, David must have started his commuting in about 1890, which is when his brother-in-law, Getzel Fax, first arrived in Baltimore. Perhaps David even accompanied his sister Ida and her daughter Theresa when they first went to Baltimore to join Getzel. Their immigration record has not been located.

David must have gone back and forth several times from Baltimore to Mlynov in the 1890s. Clara recalls her mother, when reminiscing later in life about her father, frequently saying that "Whoever didn't see him get off the train in Dubno [on his return from Baltimore], has never seen a handsome man." The Dubno train station was probably opened during Russia's massive railroad boom between

---

[24] Getzel and Ida Fax appear to be the earliest Mlynov immigrants to arrive in the US and were followed to Baltimore by the majority of Mlynov immigrants.

1851 and 1875 which helped accelerate the immigration to America from the town of Mlynov since it was so close.[25]

Clara remembers that while her father was in America, her mother was called "Pesse the American" by other people in Mlynov. Talking about the location of her own home, she explains that "in the adjoining house lives Pesse the American, a name given to her because her husband keeps going to America and returning, because he doesn't want to raise his children in the 'traife' [unkosher] America."

Clara indicates that her father David left permanently for America when she was 9 months old. Since David arrived in the US in February 1901, that would place Clara's birth in 1900 (though US records say she was born in 1901). We know from his passenger manifest that "David Rewitz," age 35, a "dealer" left Bremen on Feb. 5, 1901 on the SS Koln and arrived in Baltimore on February 20. He landed a few weeks after Samuel Roskes, his brother-in-law, who married Mollie Demb, sister of his wife, Pesse.[26] Like Samuel Roskes, his destination was the home of his br. i. l. ["brother-in-law"] G. Fax at 818 E. Pratt Street. David was not reunited with his wife Pesse and his three youngest daughters (Minnie, Rose and Clara) until early 1909 when they finally arrived in Baltimore.

Manifest head of the SS Koln in Feb. 1901

David Rewitz 35, dealer, from Mlynow

Right-hand columns: headed to "br. i. l. [brother-in-law] G. Fax 818 E. Pratt St."

By the time Clara had first-hand memories in Mlynov, her older sister Gulza had already gotten married. "I have no recollection of Gulza in the house, because I was two and one-half years old

---

[25] See "The history of railroads in Russia in Photos" https://www.rbth.com/history/335244-history-of-railroads-in-russia retrieved March 28, 2023.
[26] Mollie Demb and Samuel Roskes are discussed in more detail below.

when she got married, though I remember vividly the little dresses she made for Rose and me to wear at the wedding: white pique short dresses, the yoke and cuffs trimmed with blue piping."

According to US records, Gulza got married in 1904, which seems consistent with Clara's memory as well. Gulza married a man named Leizor Mazuryk and went to live with him in Berestechko, a town 24 miles WSW of Mlynov (see map above in Figure 4). They later became Louis and Gertrude Mazer in Baltimore after they migrated in 1921 following the War. Clara believed they went to live in Berestchecko for business opportunities closer to the Austrian-Russian border. And perhaps that was one of their motivations. But Leizor was from Berestchecko and he still had family there.[27] It was not uncommon for a woman to go live in the town of her husband,[28] and it seems reasonable to assume this was one of the reasons they went to live there.

Clara has a number of sweet endearing memories of family life in Mlynov between 1904, when her older sister Gulza married, and 1908, when Clara, her mother and two sisters left for Baltimore. She recalls that her mother Pesse:

> was always occupied with her garden behind the house, where she grew potatoes, beans, carrots, radishes, cucumbers, etc. I mention these details because my mother so loved her garden, weeding and all; and it was her garden that provided much of the family's food, plus her baking every Thursday night. [P.S. Among her favorite reminiscences was, always, that giving birth to me was so easy and quick, that "she almost lost me among the cucumbers."]

I suspect Pesse felt financial pressure to raise food with her husband David living in Baltimore. To make ends meet, Pesse also took the family of the teacher, Shimeon Melammed, as lodgers into her home. "Melammed" means teacher and it is possible that this was just a nickname, as Mlynov residents often referred to each other with various nicknames, while surnames were needed only for the Russian censuses.[29]

Clara remembers listening to Shimeon Melammed teach the young boys in her home and learning Hebrew that way:

> My home, in retrospect, was far from palatial, or even comfortable. But it <u>was</u> situated opposite the synagogue. And soon I became aware of a baby in the part of the house my mother had rented to a Melamed—a Hebrew teacher and his family....In addition, the house was filled with young children, mostly boys, being taught Hebrew by the baby's father, Shimeon Melamed. It was so easy to stand by

---

[27] His sister Sura (Sarah Shifman) was still living there and married a man named Benjamin ("Ben Zion") Shifman. He arrived in Baltimore in 1913 and the rest of the family joined him in 1921.

[28] There are many examples of Mlynov women going to a husband's hometown after marriage. Mollie Demb went to Lutsk after marrying Samuel Roskes, as did Bassa Barditch, to provide a few examples. This probably aligned with notions that women were now the responsibility (if not property) of their husbands after a dowry had been paid.

[29] The essays in the Mlynov Memorial Book recall people by their nicknames often based on their parents' names, their profession or some distinguishing characteristic (e.g., "Moshe with the beard" for Moshe Goldseker, p. 111, or "Moshe the blacksmith" and "Moshe the cobber," p. 24, or Henye Arelas, meaning "Henye-Aaron Hirsch's daughter").

quietly, to listen and learn while the teacher was giving his attention to each of his students. What a thrill it was to learn to read without being taught. Back in our house, my teen-age brother, Yitzchak, taught me to write. I remember once hearing Shimeon Melamed saying to my mother, "She'll soon be teaching me."

It is not surprising that Clara, the granddaughter of Israel Jacob Demb, one of the town's scholars, also learned to read Yiddish, which was apparently not common among the women in town. One of Clara's most exciting memories was reading the Yiddish translation of the Torah on the Sabbath to the women who could not read:

> And tomorrow! It is the Sabbath. And, if you are that little girl in the household of Pesse, the American, today is the most exciting day. The Synagogue, as you know, is across the way. You watch the men entering via the main door to the left, while the women use the staircase on the right that leads to their balcony in the synagogue. And, during the service, when the men below are engaged in reading of the Torah, the women use the Yiddish translation of the Bible, call the "Teich Chumash", reading the portion of the week. But there are many women who cannot read! Never mind. They go down the staircase into the street and across the way to the house of Pesse, the American, because they know that there sits a little girl of five on the floor, as there are not enough chairs, her mother's teich-chumash on her lap, and she is reading the portion of the week in Yiddish for the women seated around her who cannot read themselves. That little girl was me!

In 1907, Clara's brother Yitzhak left for Baltimore to join their father. During this time, Clara remembers her grandfather, Israel Jacob coming to visit:

> At times, my grandmother Rifka [Demb nee Gruber] would visit us on Saturday afternoon and take us children to the nearby countryside and show us various herbs growing that she told us the Lord had put on earth for us as medicine. My grandfather [Israel Jacob Demb], when he came wanted to know what news my mother had heard from her husband, my father, as well as my brother Yitzchak who had left to join him in America.

Clara also remembers that her grandmother Rivka during this time was sufficiently well-read to even challenge her scholarly husband, Israel Jacob, at times with her knowledge.

> My grandmother Rifka Demb was especially attracted to Yiddish translations of the French novels. This could have been a relief to her husband, my grandfather, because he was known to have said once, "Blessed is the man whose wife doesn't even know the 'Alef-Bais', the Hebrew Alphabet", because she frequently took issue with him in his Biblical and Talmudic studies.

Years later in Baltimore, Clara's older sister Gulza told Clara that she and grandma [Rivka] had almost weekly arguments about the "Count of Monte Cristo" [.] Grandma was reading only on weekdays because on Shabbos she studied "Perek", and the "Chapter" – (the assigned weekly chapter in the "Ethics of the Fathers"). Gulza was begging Grandma to let her have the book for Shabbos only, but Grandma said "No" every time, and she said Gulza could have the book only when she, Grandma, was finished with it.

That Rivka in the small town of Mlynov was reading the Count of Monte Cristo is striking. The Count of Monte Cristo was an adventure novel written by French author Alexandre Dumas completed in 1844, one of the author's most popular works, along with The Three Musketeers. That a French novel had been translated and reached Mlynov by the early 1900s indicates the town was not totally isolated from larger European cultural trends.

***

Yitzhak Rivetz's Migration

David and Pesse's son Yitzhak (or Itzhik) arrived in Baltimore in 1907. He arrived six years after his father and two years before his mother and younger sisters. Yitzhak was officially the first "Demb" grandchild to arrive in America. The spelling of his name on his manifest made it difficult to locate but the destination ultimately confirmed his identity.

"Jechok Riwez," 20 years old, left Bremen on May 2, 1907 on the SS Breslau and arrived in Baltimore on May 18th. His last residence and birthplace is listed as "Blima," the "m" in Mlynov being misunderstood by custom officials through the Yiddish accent. This is not the only manifest where Mlynov shows up as "Blima." It is difficult to read all the handwriting of his destination. But his destination appears to be 836 E Pratt Street and above the address the manifest says his destination is something like: uncle ~~father~~ [David?] ~~Riwetz~~ c/0 G. [illegible]."

Manifest of SS Breslau

Manifest of Jechok Riwez, age 20

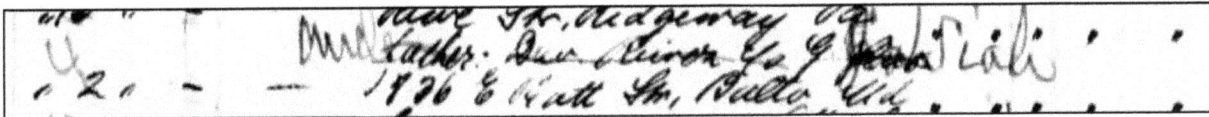

Right-hand columns of Yitzhak's manifest showing destination of uncle ~~father~~ ~~Dav.~~ ~~Rivez~~ c/o G. [Fax?] 836 E Pratt Str.

We know from Baltimore City Directories that by 1906 Getzel and Ida Fax moved from 818 E. Pratt St. to 836 E. Pratt following the Great Baltimore Fire which occurred February 7–8, 1904. As discussed below, much of the city was burned to the ground.

***

Pesse (Demb) Rivetz Heads to Baltimore in Late 1908

In late 1908, Clara's mother Pesse (Demb) made plans to join her husband and son in Baltimore. It was just about 8 years since her husband David left permanently for Baltimore and a year since her son had joined him. Pesse's younger sister, Mollie, left a year earlier to join her husband, Samuel Roskes, in Baltimore sometime in 1908. Pesse was thus the second of Rivka and Israel Demb's children to head to Baltimore.

Clara remembers this journey clearly and has a number of evocative memories about it. They traveled from Mlynov across Europe to Trieste, part of Austria at the time. Trieste was a new port for immigration that had opened and was trying to compete with the northern ports of Bremen and Rotterdam.[30] This was an unusual path for Mlynov immigrants to the US. Two other Mlynov immigrants, Meier (or Meyer) Fishman and Simon Goldberg, followed this path in April 1909 just a few months after Pesse and the children left.[31] All told the journey from Mlynov to Trieste covered 1,022 miles.

---

[30] See Aleksej Kalc, "Trieste as a Port of Emigration From East and Southeast Europe." In *East Central Europe in Exile.* Ed. Anna Zachorowski-Mazurkiewicz. Cambridge Scholars, 2013, pp. 127–140.

[31] Meyer Fishman was the brother of Moshe Fishman and Anna (Fishman) Schwartz. He married Ida Goldseker, his niece, in Mlynov, and they had one child together, Ben Fishman (who later became Ben Gresser when Ida remarried in Baltimore). His traveling companion, Simon Goldberg, has not been identified, though it is assumed he is related to either the Gelberg or Goldberg family from Mlynov that settled in New York. On the Gelbergs and Goldbergs from Mlynov, see https://kehilalinks.jewishgen.org/Mlyniv/families.html#threebrothers.

Figure 14 Map of Pesse Demb's journey from Mlynov to Trieste

In the traveling party with Clara was her mother Pesse, her paternal grandmother, Zecil (David and Ida's mother), and her two sisters, Minnie and Rose. Clara's brother Yitzhak was already in Baltimore with her father. Her eldest sister, Gulza, remained in Berestchecko with her husband until after WWI.

Clara remembers how difficult it was for her mother, Pesse, to say goodbye to her parents, Rivka and Israel Jacob, and that her other grandmother, Zecil, who was traveling with them, had to console her mother. "The things a woman does for her husband," Zecil said using a Yiddish expression. I doubt those words consoled Pesse much coming from her mother-in-law. I don't believe Pesse ever saw her parents again.

The traveling party stopped first in Berestchecko to stay with and say goodbye to Clara's oldest sister Gulza and her husband. Then they continued on their way. Clara recalls it was winter and at times they were walking through the snow and her limping grandmother had to be pulled along on a sleigh at times. They traveled through Brod, Austria and Vienna. Clara has several distinct memories of the trip. "What I remember of Brod was that there my mother brought each of us, Rose and me, a 'paletot' (French for 'warm coat') and velvet bonnet to match. Rose's outfit was red and mine was deep blue. The next notable stop was Vienna where, from a streetcar we were on, someone pointed out the place of Emperor Franz-Joseph."

Clara also remembers one terrifying experience during the journey:

It was winter and very cold. The entire area was covered with three or four days' steady snow fall. I was walking as well and as steadily as anyone in our group, I thought, since it was so cold, and it was hard to pull my little feet out of the deep snow; but I kept on. I noticed that behind me was my stout, very old Grandma on a sled being pulled by a soldier in uniform. Suddenly, I felt that on lifting my right foot out of the snow, I had left my little rubber in the snow depth, and I could go no further. I stopped, and began to cry. I don't know where he came from, but a soldier appeared and put me on his shoulders. We kept on, but my mother and the rest were not in sight. Suddenly, the soldier carrying me entered a strange, noisy room and stood me, me alone, on a table where I was surrounded by more soldiers, all talking in a strange language. It was then that I felt alone and helpless, lost in the world beyond redemption! The five or six soldiers around me could not assuage my wild fear; but my mother's timely appearance did it.

In Trieste, the traveling party waited for a month before finally getting on their ship to America. Their Americanization began almost immediately: their ship was called the SS Martha Washington. They left Trieste on January 15, 1909 and arrived in New York on February 2nd. The Riwetz travelers listed were Pesie age 43, Meniche ("Minnie") age 20, Ruchel (Rose) age 9, Keile (Clara) age 8 and mother-in-law, Lisel (also called Zecil), age 58. Their last residence was "Mlinow" and their closest relative was father/grandfather "Israel Dem."

On the second page of their manifest, they were headed, of course, to Pesse's husband Mr. D. Riwetz 836 E. Pratt Street. The handwriting also clarifies that they were "accompany[ied] by husband's mother."

Manifest of the SS Martha Washington sailing from Trieste

The Riwetz travelers on the SS Martha Washington

Page 2 of Riwetz manifest headed to husband Mr. D. Riwetz 836 E Pratt St, "accomp. By husb's mother"

Clara records only a few memories of their time on the ship. "A very vivid impression that lingers, is seeing my aged Grandmother being hoisted into a hammock for the night—no beds in the steerage, of course. And then, in the two weeks' voyage, one very stormy night, adding to the miseries engendered by the storm, a rumor was spreading that a sailor had passed through the women's section, announcing, 'Tonight you all die!' But we didn't."

Clara also had a very quaint memory from the train ride from New York to Baltimore:

> Then, the all-night train trip from New York to Baltimore. While we were sitting in the dark, dimly lit rumbling train, there suddenly appeared a man with boxes of candy. 'Welcoming presents', I thought gleefully. He put one box on my mother's lap, one box on my Grandmother's lap, one box on each of my sisters' laps, but not on mine! [handwritten note added by hand]: (I was crestfallen.) Later, however, he returned and took them all back. I felt better then.

It must have been a salesman peddling wares as they do today in the NY subways. The train finally arrived in Baltimore, "as we were alighting into the gray, early dawn, we saw in the distance one man, standing behind the gate in Mt. Royal Station, a lone solitary vigil, and I heard my mother exclaim: 'Children, there, there's your father!!!'" Clara probably couldn't recognize her father since she was just a baby or in utero when he left for Baltimore!

Not long after they arrived in Baltimore, David had rented two flats at 852 E. Pratt Street very close to the Fax family (his sister's family). Clara remembers there was no room at the place for her older sister Minnie, so Minnie slept at the home of her Aunt Mollie (Demb) Roskes around the corner at 104 Albemarle St. until her wedding which was to take place in a few weeks.

***

An Arranged Marriage in America

A marriage was arranged for Minnie to Getzel Fax's brother, Sam Fox, who was recently widowed and had two sons, Martin who was 5 and Ernest who was 2. Minnie was marrying her uncle's brother.[32] A photo of the wedding (Figure 13) shows the bride and groom, Minnie and Sam, in the center with Minnie's parents, Pessie and David, seated.

It is hard to imagine the shock that must have greeted Getzel's brother, "Solomon Fax," who arrived in Baltimore on March 2, 1904, just weeks after the devastation caused by The Great Baltimore Fire. In the fire, which burned on February 7–8, 1904, more than 1,500 buildings were completely leveled, and some 1,000 severely damaged. The fire spread across much of the city and reached all the way to the Jones Fall River which was essentially just a hop, skip and a jump away from where Getzel and Ida were living at 818 E. Pratt Street, the destination on the manifest of Getzel's brother.

Figure 15 Destruction in the wake of the Great Baltimore Fire[33]

Getzel's great-grandsons recount a family story that Getzel was up on the roof of the building with water trying to keep it from catching fire.[34] It must have been an amazing sight looking out over the burning city and watching the fire creep closer to them. It seems likely that assisting Getzel on the top of the building were Pesse's husband, David Rivetz, and her younger sister's husband, Samuel Roskes, both of whom were living with the Faxes at the time.

---

[32] Getzel was Minnie's uncle through marriage. His wife Ida was the sister of Minnie's father. The man she was to marry was Samuel Fox, Getzel's brother.
[33] The photo is by Fred Pridham - http://en.wikipedia.org/wiki/Image:Baltimore_fire_aftermath.jpg, Public Domain, https://commons.wikimedia.org/w/index.php?curid=1556388
[34] Shared with me by Charles Fax.

Figure 16 Spread of the fire to the Jones Falls River (on the right)
818 E. Pratt was just across the River.[35]

In Baltimore, Getzel's brother, Solomon Fax became Samuel Fox. Getzel's great-grandsons told me that Getzel recommended that his brother Sam adopt the surname "Fox" instead of "Fax" because the latter was more commonly the surname of African Americans. Jews arriving in America wanted to reinforce their "whiteness" in a society that discriminated more against race than religion. A 1902 Baltimore City Directory, for example, shows Getzel and Ida Fax lacking the asterisk which signified that most of the Faxes were "colored."

1902 Baltimore City Directory	*Fax Betty, 918 Harmony la *Fax Chas, lab, 108 n Vincent *Fax Chas, dentist, 914 n Eutaw Fax Getzel, mnfrs agt, 818 e Pratt Fax Ida, clothing, 818 e Pratt *Fax John, lab, 1518 Shields al Fax Myrtle, dressmkr, 602 Baker *Fax Tollie, waiter, 1025 n Front *Fax Wm H, porter, 602 Baker
1906 Baltimore City Directory	*Fax Chas, lab, 108 n Vincent Fax Gabriel F J, clk, 1349 n Gilmor Fax Geo, paper bags, 836 e Pratt *Fax Howard N, lab, 1520 n Bruce *Fax Mark C, waiter, 914 n Eutaw *Fax Wm Rev, 1215 Druid Hill av Fay Andw J, salesman, 526 n Eutaw Fay Bartley, clk, 4 e Hill

By 1906, Getzel and Ida moved a few doors away to 836 E. Pratt Street, now the grounds of the Star-Spangled Banner Flag House, a national historic landmark in Baltimore. This was the

---

[35] See https://www.youtube.com/watch?v=nCxUG65HGsc for a video illustrating the spread of the Great Baltimore Fire by Box 414 Association.

destination address of David's son Isaac in 1907 and then his wife Pesse and daughters in 1909. It was also the destination of other Demb immigrants, like Benjamin Schwartz, as we shall see.

After David and Bessie married their daughter Minnie off to Sam Fox, the newlyweds initially lived in the District of Columbia, where their first child together, Sarah Ann Fox, was born in 1910. Sarah Fox (married name Sarah Ann Kappelman Harris) was the first great-grandchild of Rivka and Israel Demb born in America. Minnie was homesick living in DC away from her family and they returned to Baltimore not long afterwards. Minnie and Sam had two additional children together: in 1911 Michael (also called Michel) Fox, and in 1914, Jack Fox.

Figure 17 "The Five Little Foxes"

Children of Minnie (Hurwitz) and Sam Fox. (standing l to r) Ernie and Martin Fox, (seated l to r) Sarah, Jack and Michael. ~1914

Courtesy of Carol Engelman

**

David Rivetz's Photo in Baltimore in the 1890s

There is only one known photo of David Rivetz from before the wedding of Minnie and Sam Fox in 1910. He is sitting next to his sister, Ida, and her husband, Getzel Fax, and their daughter Therese in Baltimore in the 1890s.

This photo came into my hands serendipitously. In 2019, I hosted a gathering of 80 descendants of Mlynov immigrants to Baltimore. Many Demb descendants were represented. A reporter for *The Baltimore Sun* took an interest in the gathering and an article covering the event appeared on the front page and in an inside spread. It was the first time since 1914, as far as I can tell, that the shtetl, Mlynov, was mentioned in Baltimore papers.

Figure 18 Photo of David Rivetz and Faxes in 1890s
(l to r) David Rivetz, Ida (Rivetz), her husband Getzel Fax and their daughter Theresa
Courtesy Marcia Goodman.

A great-granddaughter of Getzel and Ida Fax, a woman by the name of Marcia Goodman, saw the names of her great-grandparents in *The Baltimore Sun* article and got in touch with me via the reporter. When I spoke to her, she told me she was looking at a photo on the wall of her great-grandparents, Getzel and Ida Fax, and their daughter (her grandmother), Theresa, from the 1890s in Baltimore standing with a man whose identity she did not know. I knew exactly who that man was: It was Clara's father David.

16 THE BALTIMORE SUN | NEWS | SUNDAY, AUGUST 25, 2019 **FROM PAGE ONE**

AMY DAVIS/BALTIMORE SUN

Roughly a century ago, scores of immigrants moved to Baltimore from a Russian village. Many of the families attended the Lloyd Street Synagogue.

From Russia to Baltimore: Immigrants shaped city

Descendants to celebrate forebears from 1 village

By Jonathan Pitts

Howard Schwartz says he was never one for researching family history, but after his mother died six years ago, a pair of old photographs hanging on her wall piqued his curiosity.

Who, he wondered, were those serious-looking, bearded men? The women in buttoned-up dresses, the girls with the braids, the boys in knee-length trousers?

Beginning with those questions, Schwartz, a 63-year-old Baltimore native who lives in California, developed an extraordinary chronicle of a clan that emigrated to Baltimore in waves from a single village in Russia roughly a century ago.

In all, several dozen immigrants came to Baltimore from Mlynov, Russia, from 1890 to 1929 — people named Fishman and Goldseker and Shulman who, with

See RUSSIA, page 16

RUSSIA

From page 1

others from their village and their descendants, left indelible marks on their adopted city in Maryland.

The Mlynov community gave rise to many prominent citizens, including doctors, lawyers, rabbis and politicians.

One was Morris Goldseker, who came to Baltimore at 16 in 1914, went to work in a pants shop, and later became a local real estate tycoon. More than $10 million of his estate went toward the creation in 1975 of the Morris Goldseker Foundation, one of Maryland's largest philanthropic foundations.

Ellen Shulman Baker, a physician and NASA astronaut, is a member of the clan. So was Neena Betty Schwartz, a renowned endocrinologist who died last year.

At Schwartz's behest, more than 80 members of the group he calls "the Mlynov descendants" will gather in Baltimore next week for a day of remembering and honoring their forebears.

"I found first, second and third cousins, but I came to realize I couldn't make sense of my family without understanding these other families they knew," says Schwartz, who plans to present his research as part of the celebration. "So, I expanded to other people who came from the same village. And I realized that Mlynov itself was an extended family.

"This project is actually about both — a village and a family — and I'm really looking forward to getting everyone together."

In many ways, the migration of the Mlynov descendants to Balti-

COURTESY HOWARD SCHWARTZ/HANDOUT

Four generations of the Shulman family, seen in Mlynov in about 1917. Howard Schwartz's great-great grandparents, Israel Jacob and Rivkah Demb, are in the center of the middle row; Howard Schwartz's grandmother, Pauline Shulman, then 10, is seated on the floor in the center. Most of the family emigrated to Baltimore in 1921. Pauline married Paul H. Schwartz in 1923.

Figure 19 "From Russia to Baltimore," The Baltimore Sun, Aug. 25, 2019

more is a microcosm of the waves of immigrants, many of them Jewish, that came to the United States from Europe in the late 19th and early 20th centuries.

In Russia, the dominoes began falling in 1881 with the assassination of Czar Alexander II, whose policies toward the Jewish population were open-minded for the time. His son, Alexander III, a virulent anti-Semite, soon began a campaign of persecution that included new laws banning Jews from holding certain jobs, owning property and living in rural areas.

The moves sparked a massive wave of emigration. Of the 2.5 million Russian Jews who relocated to America from 1881 to 1914, most arrived via New York, but Baltimore drew such migrants by the tens of thousands.

Among them, Schwartz learned, were the "Mlynov pioneers," Getzel and Ida Fax, a young couple who arrived in Baltimore from the village in western Russia in 1890 and 1891.

According to a memoir written by a Schwartz relative in 1982, the Faxes had owned land near Mlynov. But when they lost their right of possession, Getzel grabbed "the first ticket available" to the U.S.

He found work in Baltimore and sent for Ida.

They soon moved to a rowhouse at 836 E. Pratt St., near what is now the Star-Spangled Banner Flag House. Their home, and another house at 104 Albemarle St., became landing places for the dozens of men, women and children who came from Mlynov in three major waves, the first from 1890 to 1909, the second from 1910 to 1914, and the third from 1920 to 1929.

The Dembs and Fishmans, Schwartzes and Grubers, Goldsekers and Roskes who arrived during those years helped establish a

COURTESY MARVIN SCHWARTZ AND IRENE SIEGEL/HANDOUT

Benjamin Schwartz, right, with an unknown friend. Benjamin emigrated to Baltimore from Mlynov in 1910, became a grocer, husband and father, and was murdered in 1937.

communal life in the neighborhood — a part of town that Baltimore in 1907 designated as a tenement district, where multiple families packed most of the rowhouses and kosher chicken butchers operated in the alleyways.

Many members of these families, Schwartz learned, had married each other in the old country, often within families, information he confirmed through DNA research. The pattern continued in Baltimore, and the Mlynov immi-

grants became integral to a community that worshiped at Shomrei Mishmeres HaKodesh — an Orthodox Jewish congregation that moved into the Lloyd Street Synagogue in 1905 — and gave one another lodging and work.

Newspaper clippings from the era, he found, spoke of a world teeming with activity, some of it downright comical, including the time The Sun reported that a man named Hyman Bressner "stole up the middle aisle" at the synagogue and "pulled a handful of whiskers from the bounteous beard of Mr. Abraham Bronstein, a furniture dealer." When the police were called, the paper reported, "almost the entire congregation followed them to the police station" to see Bressner pay his fines.

"There are many stories we can tell about this congregation's life," Schwartz says.

Some were tragic. On Oct. 8, 1937, Benjamin Schwartz — a brother of Howard Schwartz's grandfather, Paul H. Schwartz, and a successful merchant — was shot to death in his store in West Baltimore, a crime that triggered a manhunt.

Schwartz says he spent uncounted hours calling and reaching out online to hundreds of people for the project. Few had heard of him, and most knew little of their distant relations. Some treated Schwartz as "a stalker or internet troll" until he had a chance to establish his bona fides.

One who needed little convincing was Ted Fishman, a 92-year-old Columbia retiree whose father, Benjamin, came to Baltimore from Mlynov in 1920.

As Fishman tells it, Benjamin, then 18, happened to be standing nearby when a native who had emigrated to America and fought in World War I returned to

Mlynov and sought to bring family members to the U.S.

Benjamin volunteered to go with them, and he, too, was soon living in a rowhouse in East Baltimore.

Fishman's best friend growing up, Leon Schwartz, was Schwartz's father. Like many in the clan, the two would later move with their families to Northwest Baltimore, a sign of the community's entry into the American middle class.

"My father never forgot his good fortune, to be living in a country where he could go wherever he wanted, and no one would ask him for his papers," Fishman recalls.

It's one of the many stories Fishman plans to tell when he addresses the gathering, an event that is to include a walking tour of the old neighborhood and tours of the synagogue and the Jewish Museum of Maryland.

Schwartz, for his part, now knows the names of nearly everyone in the two pictures that catalyzed his journey. But it won't come full circle until he sees his extended family members connect, sharing photos and family stories and solidifying the connections that run from Mlynov — a Russian "shtetl" (Yiddish for a village) that became part of Poland, and now is part of Ukraine — through Baltimore and beyond.

If he'd had enough time and money, Schwartz says, he's sure he could have filled a venue the size of Camden Yards. But those who do come will be celebrating a valuable bond.

"I imagine our ancestors looking down and being amazed and moved at how many descendants are taking the time to assemble to honor them and their memories," he says. "It will be a fitting tribute."

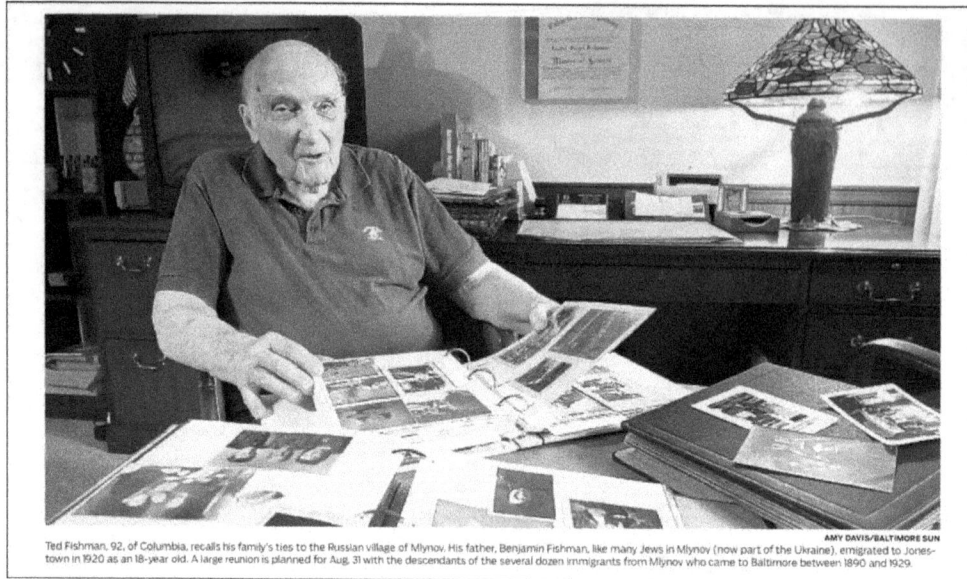

Ted Fishman, 92, of Columbia, recalls his family's ties to the Russian village of Mlynov. His father, Benjamin Fishman, like many Jews in Mlynov (now part of the Ukraine), emigrated to Jones-town in 1920 as an 18-year old. A large reunion is planned for Aug. 31 with the descendants of the several dozen immigrants from Mlynov who came to Baltimore between 1890 and 1929.

Figure 20 Ted Fishman, my interlocutor, and family historian in his 90s

***

The Rivetz Family Settles in Baltimore

Clara remembers her father "was earning about six dollars a week. He was in his early forties but looked like an old man with his long black beard a la Theodore Herzl, whose portrait graced many a Jewish home." She also "heard him tell mother how on his route where he was peddling, frequently gentile boys would try to attack him, pulling his beard and calling him 'Santa Claus.'"

Sometime between 1907 and 1910, David decided to change his surname from Rivetz to Hurwitz. In the 1907 Baltimore City Directory he is still listed as Rivetz. By the 1910 census, the family is called Horwitz and David is listed as presser in the clothing industry.

1907 Baltimore City Directory	Rivetz David, pdlr, 836 e Pratt Rivkin E F & Co (Esther F Rivkin), jewelry, 57 n Caroline Rivkin Esther F (E F Rivkin & Co), 57 n

1910 Census for David "Horwitz" and family at 852 E. Pratt Street. Pesse is now called Bessie. Minnie's name is apparently scratched out because she got married.

As noted before, Clara said that her father made the decision to change his surname after a conversation with another man at the local synagogue they were attending, called Shomrei Mishmeres Hakodesh Anshe Wolin (The Guardians of the Holy Service of the People of Volyn), now a landmark in Baltimore known as the Lloyd Street Synagogue.

In 1845 when it was built, the synagogue was the first in Maryland. It is now the third oldest synagogue still standing in the US. The German-speaking Baltimore Hebrew Congregation that originally built and occupied it had since sold the building and moved northwest out of East Baltimore. A Catholic Church occupied it for a few years (1889–1905) until it was purchased again by a congregation of immigrants who came from the area of Russia known as Volyn, which is where Mlynov was located. Clara recalls:

> My uncle Getzel Fax was the president when we arrived in Baltimore, and it was here that my father, when he was a new arrival, had casually changed his name from Rivitz to Hurwitz because a man told him that Rivitz cannot be spelled in English. "What is your name?" asked my father. "Hurwitz", the man replied. "So mine will be Hurwitz, too", agreeably said my father. I never did know our family name in Europe, and so Rose and I were entered in school as Rose and Clara Hurwitz.

Despite the beautiful Greek Revival style architecture of the building, the congregation had the etiquette of an Eastern European shul. Signs were posted reminding congregation members not to spit on the floor when they chewed tobacco during the Sabbath to alleviate their craving to smoke, which was forbidden on the Sabbath. Instead, beautiful spittoons were provided.

Bessie's husband David Hurwitz and her brother-in-law Samuel Roskes were probably both there that day in early February 1908 when an incident occurred in the synagogue that is almost better than fiction.[36] One Hyman Bressner, of 1121 E. Pratt Street, "stole up the middle aisle and pulled a handful of whiskers from the bounteous beard of Mr. Abraham Bronstein, a furniture dealer, Bond and Baltimore Streets." The incident occurred during the services: "In the midst of this solemnity, when piety and religious thoughts were uppermost in the minds of most of the members of the church, there was heard a scream.... 'You thief!' shouted Bressner, and as he did so he is alleged to have slapped Mr. Bronstein in the face with one hand and grabbed his flowing beard with the other" apparently tearing some of it off in his hand. When the police were called, "Almost the entire congregation tailed on behind to the police station, and there were about 300 persons in the building when the hearing took place." A decade later, Getzel Fax's son, Joseph, married Zelma Bronstein, a granddaughter of Abraham Bronstein, the furniture dealer whose whiskers were yanked that day.

It is uncertain exactly when Clara's father, David Rivetz, had his conversation with the other member of this congregation who convinced him to change his surname. David appears under both

---

[36] "Broke Up the Service," *The Baltimore Sun*, Feb 9, 1908 p. 20.

the Rivitz and Hurwitz surnames in the 1913 Baltimore City Directory, but after that date the surname Hurwitz or some variation thereof is stable.

Figure 21 2017 Visit to Lloyd Street Synagogue

By 1913, the Hurwitz family moved to 921 E. Lombard Street and David is listed as a tailor. Sometime the previous year, David and Bessie's son Yitzhak, now called Isaac, got engaged to Celia (also spelled Cecilia) Kramer. The application for their marriage license was submitted by Samuel Fox, the husband of Yitzhak's sister, Minnie. Isaac and Cecila's son, Howard C. Hurwitz, was born in 1913.

1912 (Feb. 13) *The Baltimore Sun*, p. 7	HURWITZ—KRAMER.—Isaac Hurwitz, 24; Celia Kramer, 21. Applicant, S. Fox, 929 West Saratoga street.

***

Clara Joins the Star-Spangled Banner Centennial

In September 1914, with news of WWI filling the newspapers, the City of Baltimore carried out a massive centennial celebration commemorating the end of the 1812 War against England and proclaiming its own special place in American Patriotism. The Dembs in Baltimore could not help but be aware of the celebration that took over the city that week, with parades, speakers, dedications and fireworks at night. How proud must David and Pesse been when their young daughter, Clara, the memoirist in our family, participated with 6,500 other schoolchildren across the city in creating a human version of the Star-Spangled Banner Flag on the grounds of Fort McHenry. Clara recalled:

> I had plenty of spare time to play "Hopscotch" or "Simon Says" with my friends on the sidewalk before the famous "Flag House" on the corner of Pratt and Albermarle [sic] Streets, where had been made the flag that flew over Fort McHenry during the War of 1812. (P.S. In 1912 [note it was 1914] there was a citywide celebration of the event on which Francis Scott Key had composed our national anthem, "The Star Spangled Banner." Hundreds of Baltimore school children were assembled at Fort McHenry, each wearing cape and hood, either red, or white, or blue. We were placed, according to the colors we wore, on a pre-constructed bleacher, so that we presented a human flag of red, white and blue. I was in one of the white stripes, as I wore a white cape and hood.) P.P.S. President Woodrow Wilson and many other dignitaries were in the tremendous audience we faced. I have a duly signed and dated picture of the scene.

Figure 22 Clara Fram in Human Flag at 1914 City Centennial

That same week, Clara and her family were very likely at the gathering at 844 E. Pratt Street when a commemorative plaque went up on the brick building adjoining the one where the Fax family lived and where Clara's father stayed in his first years in Baltimore. It was on its way to becoming a national historic landmark, the home of flag maker Mary Pickersgill, who made the massive Star-Spangled Banner flag in six weeks' time back in 1814, with her daughters and an indentured servant named Grace Wisher. In 1916, two years after Clara participated in the human flag, President Woodrow Wilson signed an executive order designating the Star-Spangled Banner music as "the national anthem of the United States" for all military ceremonies. In 1927, the home of Mary Pickersgill was purchased by the City of Baltimore and the Star-Spangled Banner Flag House Association, to become a museum.

To me, there is something very poignant about the close proximity of the Star-Spangled Banner House to the location where the first Demb descended families lived. Whatever its particular impact on them, they were inevitably engaged with American identity and the process of Americanization at the time the symbols of that identity were being further elaborated. And that very identity was in part being made where these Eastern European immigrants had made their home. How far they had come from Mlynov.

The building at 836 E. Pratt Street, where the Fax family lived and where two Demb husbands and several other Mlynov immigrants got on their feet, is no longer standing. It is now part of the grounds of the Star-Spangled Banner Flag House national landmark. In old photos of the building, one can see the adjoining building at 836 E. Pratt in which the Fax family once lived. Who knows, perhaps the kid leaning on the telephone pole in this 1910 photo, was actually Clara or one of her sisters.

Figure 23 Star-Spangled Flag House at 844 E. Pratt August 1910
Courtesy of Star-Spangled Banner Flag House Museum

The Hurwitz family remained at 921 E. Lombard until about 1917 when they moved to 1173 E. Lombard. In June that year, Isaac filled out his WWI Draft Registration Card while still living at that address. He is listed as a grocer and asks for an exemption to support "a father, mother, wife and child."

***

A Family Bar Mitzvah Makes the Papers

On November 18, 1917, a rather stunning and unusual bar mitzvah announcement appeared in society pages of *The Baltimore Sun*, p. 36. The short celebratory notice described a bar mitzvah party gathering for Martin Fox. Martin, as mentioned earlier, was the second son from Sam Fox's first marriage and one of two stepsons that Minnie (Hurwitz) helped raise.

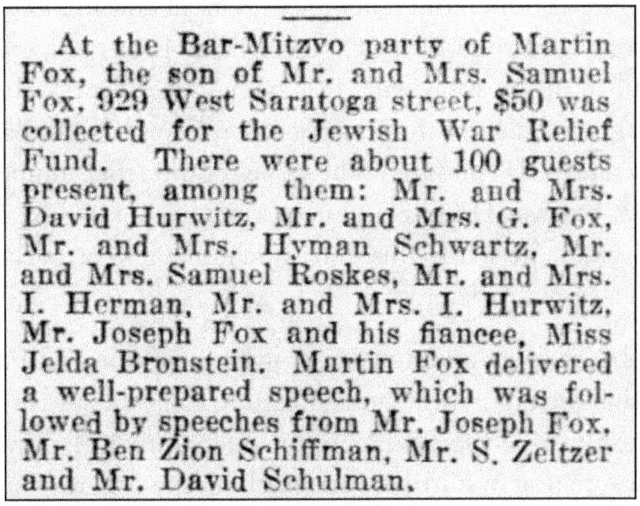

> At the Bar-Mitzvo party of Martin Fox, the son of Mr. and Mrs. Samuel Fox, 929 West Saratoga street, $50 was collected for the Jewish War Relief Fund. There were about 100 guests present, among them: Mr. and Mrs. David Hurwitz, Mr. and Mrs. G. Fox, Mr. and Mrs. Hyman Schwartz, Mr. and Mrs. Samuel Roskes, Mr. and Mrs. I. Herman, Mr. and Mrs. I. Hurwitz, Mr. Joseph Fox and his fiancee, Miss Jelda Bronstein. Martin Fox delivered a well-prepared speech, which was followed by speeches from Mr. Joseph Fox, Mr. Ben Zion Schiffman, Mr. S. Zeltzer and Mr. David Schulman.

Figure 24 Bar Mitzvah Party Announcement
The Baltimore Sun

The announcement is a fascinating window into the life of the Demb family in Baltimore at a key moment of World War I.

WWI had broken out three years earlier in the summer of 1914, but the United States had remained neutral until April 1917 when President Wilson finally succeeded in getting the US to declare war. During this period, all the Dembs in Baltimore had family back in Mlynov as the fighting on the Eastern front moved close to the shtetl and required the evacuation of the town.[37] Then early in 1917, the Tsar's government was toppled and only weeks before Martin's bar mitzvah the Bolshevik Revolution had taken place. What would this mean for their siblings, parents, wives and children who had been left behind? The War was on everyone's mind. The first compulsory draft in the US since the Civil War started the previous summer. Would the Demb immigrants, who had to register, be called up to fight?

The Baltimore family was obviously doing well and invited over 100 guests to the bar mitzvah party. The occasion was deemed important enough for the family to pay for an announcement in

---

[37] See Helen Lederer's "In Pain From the First World War," Mlynov Memorial Book, pp. 137–38 for a description of Mlynov's evacuation and https://kehilalinks.jewishgen.org/Mlyniv/mlinov_in_WWI.html#Easternfront for my discussion of the Eastern Front in relationship to Mlynov.

The Baltimore Sun's society pages. Hardly any other bar mitzvah celebration announcements are found in *The Baltimore Sun* in this period.

A slew of Demb relatives were present to celebrate Minnie's stepson. Those mentioned included Minnie's parents, Bessie (Demb) and David Hurwitz, her brother Isaac Hurwitz and his wife, Cecilia. Also present were the families of Minnie's two aunts, Yenta (Demb) and her husband Hyman Schwartz (my great-grandparents), and Mollie (Demb) and her husband Samuel Roskes. Minnie's first cousin, Mary (Gruber) Herman and her husband Israel Herman were there that day too. The other Dembs who already arrived were probably present as well.

Of course, Sam Fox's brother and sister-in-law, Getzel and Ida Fax [spelled Fox here], were present with their son Joseph Fax and his new fiancée Zelda Bronstein, granddaughter of the man whose whiskers were pulled in the synagogue. It is perhaps no surprise that Getzel and Ida's son, Joseph Fax, gave one of the speeches for the occasion. Joseph was born in Baltimore and by this time had become an attorney. He likely epitomized the hopes of the other immigrants for their children. Also giving a speech that day was David Schulman, a nephew of Tsodik Shulman, the man who married Pearl Malka (Demb). In 1921, this David Schulman went back to Europe to help the Shulmans immigrate, in a story told later.[38]

The celebratory bar mitzvah announcement, which appeared in *The Sun* on November 18, 1917 (p. 36), indicates that the family and guests raised $50 for the Jewish War Relief Fund. It is a reasonable guess that the family felt some discomfort celebrating in Baltimore while their relatives and other Jews were still suffering in Europe. Articles about the suffering of Jews in Europe because of the War appeared in *The Baltimore Sun* throughout 1916–1917 and Jewish relief efforts had been going on throughout that period. For example, Jacob Epstein, Baltimore's most prominent philanthropist, and the founder of the Baltimore Bargain House, one of the country's largest mail order firms, gave $9,000 to the war relief effort and was contributing $1,000 a month, according to an announcement on April 28, 1917 (p. 14). By March 1917, (p. 4), $70,000 had been raised for the Jewish Relief Fund in one week. Still, the fifty dollars raised at the bar mitzvah of Martin Fox was substantive in that year. In today's value, each person contributed the equivalent of approximately $240.[39]

***

The Tragic Death of Isaac Hurwitz

A year after Martin Fox's bar mitzvah, Bessie and David's son, Isaac Hurwitz, died in the 1918 pandemic often mistakenly called the "Spanish flu."

---

[38] Speeches were also given by Ben Zion Schiffman known in Baltimore as "Benjamin Shifman." Benjamin married Sura Mazuryk, the sister-in-law of Minnie's older sister, Gulza, who was still living in Berestchecko at the time.

[39] A baby carriage, for example, was advertised in the same paper for $2.98, which means $50 was approximately the value of sixteen baby carriages. On today's scale, a baby carriage might cost between $50–$200. Sixteen baby carriages today would be the equivalent to $800–$2400 today. By a rough estimate of today's standards, each person gave on average $240 dollars at the event.

The 1918 flu pandemic, also known as the Great Influenza epidemic, was an exceptionally deadly global influenza pandemic caused by the H1N1 virus. The earliest documented case was on March 1918 in Kansas, United States, with further cases recorded in France, Germany and the United Kingdom in April. Two years later, nearly a third of the global population, or an estimated 500 million people, had been infected in four successive waves. Estimates of deaths range from 17 million to 50 million, and possibly as high as 100 million, making it one of the deadliest pandemics in history.

Here lies
a man pure and upright our teacher the honored

Yitzhak son of David
Rivetz

Died 5679 20th of Tevet

(Dec. 23rd 1918)

May his soul be bound up in the bond of life.

The first cases showed up in Baltimore at the end of September 1918.[40] Isaac died on December 23, 1918, and was one of 4,125 Baltimoreans to die in the epidemic. Isaac was buried in the cemetery of Shomrei Mishmeres HaKodesh Congregation in Rosedale, Maryland (Row 7-8 Memorial ID 80691874) where many of the first Dembs are buried. His tombstone is in Hebrew lettering only with no English. Yitzhak was the first Demb grandchild to die in Baltimore.

***

The Hurwitzes in the 1920s

In 1920, David and Bessie are still living at 1303 E. Fayette Street. David is 55 and is a tailor in a shop, his wife Bessie (Demb) is now 46. They are still not yet naturalized. Their daughter, Clara,

---

[40] See The Influenza Encyclopedia article on Baltimore for an interesting discussion of the influenza in Baltimore, accessed online April 11, 2023. https://www.influenzaarchive.org/cities/city-baltimore.html

is age 19 and still living at home. Also living with them is Isaac's widow, "Ceily," age 36, and Isaac's son, Howard, age 6. In May 1921, David Hurwitz finally began his naturalization process and filled out his Declaration of Intention. Perhaps he was anticipating the arrival of his daughter Gulza who would arrive that year.

In 1920, David and Bessie's daughter, Minnie, and her husband Sam Fox are living at 929 Saratoga Street. Sam owns a grocery store. His oldest son, Ernie (from his first marriage) has gone to live with Sam's brother, Getzel, and thus appears in the 1920 census of the Fax family. Sam's second son, Martin (the one who had the bar mitzvah party), age 15, is still in the household as are the children Sam and Minnie had together: Sarah, now age 9, Michael age 8, and Jacob age 6.

Sometime before 1920, David and Bessie's daughter, Rose, married Harry Finkelstein, who was manufacturing men's clothing. They appear together with no children in the 1920 census. Their daughter Sylvia (later Sylvia Scherr) was born in 1921, Alma G (later Alma Finkelstein Lewis) was born in 1924, a son Gilbert in 1929 and another son Joel "Buddy" in 1933.

***

Gulza and Leizor's Migration

When the War ended, David and Bessie's oldest daughter Gulza and her family finally made their way to Baltimore (see manifest below). They left Antwerp on July 21, 1921 on the SS Zeeland and arrived in New York on August 1st.

"Gulcia Mazuryk" is 37, her husband "Lejzor" is 38, a merchant, and their son Mordko is 7. By this time of course their nationality is listed as Polish. Their last residence was Berestchecko where Lejzor's mother "Witia" was still living.

They were headed to Lejzor's father-in-law (i.e., Gulza's father) David Hurwitz at 1303 E. Fayette Street in Baltimore. For consistency all of them list "Beresteczko" as their birthplace, even though Gulza was born in Mlynov.

In 1930, David and Bessie are still living at 1303 E. Fayette. David is finally naturalized, though his Petition for Naturalization has not been located. Of their children, only their daughter Clara, the future memoirist in the family, is still living with them. She is a bookkeeper in a department store. While living with her parents, Clara had to initiate her own naturalization efforts in 1928 and was not able to be grandfathered into her father's naturalization status, the way women had earlier been able to do. She was 27 years old when she filled out her Declaration of Intention and her parents probably worried about her becoming an old maid.

IMMIGRATION SERVICE

List 28.

" LIST OR MANIFEST OF ALIEN PASSENGERS FOR THE UNITED

ALL ALIENS arriving at a port of continental United States from a foreign port or a port of the insular possessions of the United States, and all aliens arriving at a port of said insular possessions from a foreign port, a port of continental United States. This (white) sheet is for the listing of

S. S. ZEELAND

Passengers sailing from ANTWERP

JULY 21TH, 1921

No. on List.	HEAD-TAX STATUS.	NAME IN FULL		Age.			Sex.	Married or single.	Calling or occupation.	Able to —				Nationality, (Country of which citizen or subject.)	†Race or people.	*Last permanent residence.		The name and complete address of nearest relative or friend in country whence alien came.	Final destination.	
		Family name.	Given name.	Yrs.	Mos.					Read.	Read what language. Write.					Country.	City or town.		State.	City or town.
1	811	JAMUDIER	BASIA	26		F	S	MILLINER	YES	HEBREW	6x8	YES	POLISH	HEBREW	POLAND	KRASNOSTAW	COUSIN BENIAMIN JORYSZ, KRASNOS TAW	R.Y.	PROVIDENCE
2		JAMUDIER	NUCHIM	19		M	S		YES	HEBREW		YES	POLISH	HEBREW	POLAND	KRASNOSTAW	DO	R.Y.	PROVIDENCE
		MAZURYK	LEJZOR	38		M	M	MERCHANT	YES	HEBREW		YES	POLISH	HEBREW	POLAND	PEREBTECZKO	MOTHER WITLA MABURYK, PEREBTECZ KO	MARYL.	BALTIMORE
		MAZURYK	GULCIA	37		F	M H.WIFE		NO			NO	POLISH	HEBREW	POLAND	PEREBTECZKO	DO	MARYL.	BALTIMORE
	UNDER 16	MAZUREK	MORDKO	7		M	S	CHILD	NO	CHILD		NO	POLISH	HEBREW	POLAND	PEREBTECZKO	GR.MOTHER	MARYL.	BALTIMORE

Passenger manifest of Gulcia Mazuryk in 1921 with husband Lejzor and son Morko

STATES IMMIGRATION OFFICER AT PORT OF ARRIVAL

States, or a port of another insular possession, in whatsoever class they travel, MUST be fully listed and the master or commanding officer of each vessel carrying such passengers must upon arrival deliver lists thereof to the immigration officer.

STEERAGE PASSENGERS ONLY

Arriving at Port of ...N E W Y O R K...................................., 19......

1 AUG 1921

List ....

The entries on this sheet must be typewritten or printed.

78

75

No. on List.	Whether having a ticket to such final destination.	By whom was passage paid?	Whether in possession of $50? and if less, how much?	Whether ever before in the United States; and if so, when and where?		Whether going to join a relative or friend; and if so, what relative or friend, and his name and complete address.	Purpose of coming to United States.				Whether alien intends to return	Condition of health, mental and physical.	Whether alien had been previously reported within one year.	Deformed or crippled. Nature, length of time, and cause.	Height.		Color of—			Marks of identification.	Place of birth.	
				If yes — Year or period of years.	Where?		Length of time alien intends to remain in the United States.	Whether alien intends to return	Whether a polygamist.	Whether an anarchist.					Feet.	Inches.	Complexion.	Hair.	Eyes.		Country.	City or town.
1	NO	SELF	50	NO		FAUTHER ISSEAL GAMODIER. R.Y. PROVIDENCE.55 DOGLAS AVENUE.		always	yes	no	no	good	no	nc	5	0	FAIR	BLK	BRN	NONE	POLAND	KRASNOSTAW
2	NO	SISTER		NO		DO		always	yes	no	no	good	no				FAIR	BLK	BRN	NONE	POLAND	KRASNOSTAW
3	NO	SELF	65	NO		FAUTHER IN LAW DAVID HURWITZ. 1303 E.FAYETTE STREET.BALTIMORE MARYLAND		always	yes	no	no	good	no		5	2	FAIR	BLK	BRN	right rupture	POLAND	BERESTECZKO
4	NO	HUSBAND		NO		FATHER DO		always	yes	no	no	good	no		5	2	FAIR	BLK	BRN		POLAND	BERESTECZKO
5	NO	FATHER		NO		GR.FATHER DO		always	yes	no	no	good	no				FAIR	BLK	BRN	NONE	POLAND	BERESTECZKO

Page 2 of manifest heading to Father in Law David Hurwitz 1303 E. Fayette Street

***

Why Clara Had to Seek Her Own Naturalization

Up until the Cable Act of 1922, women's naturalization was tethered to the status of their husbands, as established by earlier laws. That's why we don't find a Petition for Naturalization for any of the Demb women until after 1922. Prior to that year, when a man received naturalization, his wife and children were grandfathered in as well. However, women who married an alien actually lost their citizenship if they already had it from their fathers or by being born in the US.

1928 Clara Hurwitz's Declaration of Intention

After women received the right to vote in 1920, they lobbied for their own naturalization process.[41] In addition, women's suffrage slowed a man's naturalization process as some judges delayed a husband's naturalization in order to verify his wife met naturalization requirements, such as speaking English. For these reasons, Congress changed the laws for women's naturalization in 1922 and women began filling out their own Petitions for Naturalization. The law exempted women from filling out a Declaration of Intention if they were already married, which explains why Clara, who was still single, filled one out.[42]

By 1930, Rose and Minnie and their respective families moved northwest to a nicer part of town and are living close to each other at 2307 and 2409 Callow Ave. Both families own their homes.

Rose has a "servant" named Nannie Wallace living in the household at the time. Her husband Harry was running a men's clothing business known at one point as De Luxe Clothing. By 1927, the business had moved to 329 W. Baltimore Street, now called the Abell Building which is a national landmark in Baltimore. Harry tragically died in a fatal car accident in June 1939.

Clara's engagement to Philip Fram was announced in *The Baltimore Sun* on June 14, 1931. He was from Texas, the son of Rabbi Abraham Fram. Their daughter Betty (married name Korpeck) was born in 1933 and their son David Hirsch Fram in 1937.

Bessie Hurwitz (the original Pesse Demb) lived long enough to see her daughter Clara get married. Bessie passed away on January 20, 1932, and her husband David died June 1, 1933. Records indicate Bessie was buried in the "Rosedale cemetery" and David in the "old Rosedale cemetery," probably of Shomrei Mishmeres Hakodesh Cemetery where their son Isaac was buried.[43]

Bessie, the eldest child of Rivka and Israel Jacob Demb, was the second of their children to pass away in Baltimore. Her death followed that of her brother Motel Demb (Max Demming) who died on January 18, 1928. Their sibling, Pearl Malka Shulman, died in March 1933.

In the collection of Ted Fishman, the photo below of Clara's three sisters is labeled "commemoration for the Mlynov ghetto liquidation in Israel Oct. 28, 1943." The label is probably intended to record the date of the liquidation, which was actually October 8–10, 1942. Another photo from the same commemoration shows Mlynov survivor, Nahum Teitelman, who arrived in Israel only in 1949, and Minnie's husband, Samuel Fox in attendance, who died in 1966.

---

[41] See Marian L. Smith, "Women and Naturalization, ca. 1802-1940," retrieved online April 27, 2023 https://www.archives.gov/publications/prologue/1998/summer/women-and-naturalization-1.html and Tanya Ballard Brown, "That Time American Women Lost Their Citizenship Because They Married Foreigners," NPR retrieved online April 27, 2023.

[42] Other Demb women immigrants in the 1920s, such as Pearl Malka Shulman, filled out a Petition for Naturalization but did not have to fill out a Declaration because she was married.

[43] The dates of Bessie and David Hurwitz's deaths and burial locations were located by Carol Engelman in the Jack Lewis Funeral Home Records Collection hosted by the Jewish Museum of Maryland. Retrieved May 18, 2023 http://jewishmuseummd.org/wp-content/uploads/2013/06/Jack-Lewis-records-index.pdf.

Figure 25 Minnie, Gulza, Rose and [Aunt] Mollie Roskes (r to l)
Courtesy of Ted Fishman

The photo was probably taken in October 1955. A passenger manifest of Gulzia Mazer in July 1955 traveling on the SS Queen Mary from New York to Cherbourg seems likely to have been the beginning of this trip. In attendance in Israel were three of the "Hurwitz" sisters, Minnie, Gulza, and Rose, along with their Aunt Mollie Roskes, who had already made aliyah in a story told later.

Figure 26 Martin Mazer and Mollie (Shindel),
daughter Betty
Courtesy of Eileen Sherr

US Records Summary for family of Bessie (Demb) and David [Rivetz] Hurwitz

1901 (Feb. 20) Passenger Manifest	David Rewitz departing from Bremen on SS Koln arriving in Baltimore Feb 20, 1901, age 35, dealer, last residence Mlynov, heading to br. i. l. [brother-in-law] G. Fax 818 E. Pratt
1907 (May 18) Passenger Manifest	Jechok Riwez (Yitzhak Rivetz), age 21 with implied birth year of 1886, sailing from Bremen on SS Breslau on May 2nd arriving in Baltimore May 18, 1907. Last residence, Blima [Mlinov] Russia. headed to uncle ~~father~~ ~~Dav Riwez~~, c/ G Fax 836 E. Pratt Str, Balto.
1909 (Feb. 2) Passenger Manifest	Sailing from Trieste January 15, 1909 on SS Martha Washington arriving in New York, Feb 2nd. Pesie Riwetz, age 43 with implied birth year of 1866, laborer, [children]: Meniche [Minnie], age 20 with implied birth year of 1889, Ruchel [Rose] age 9 with implied birth year of 1900, Keila [Clara] age 8 with implied birth year of 1901, Lisel (mother-in-law) 58, last residence Mlinow, closest relative is father / grandfather Israel Dem, headed to husband Mr. D. Rewitz 836 E. Pratt St. Baltimore. Manifest also says " accomp[anied] by his mother"
1910 (April 23) US Federal Census	For David Horwitz and his family 852 E Pratt Street, dwelling number 125, David Horwitz, head, age 43 with implied birth year of 1867, married 28 years implied year of marriage 1882, arrival year 1901, Al[ien] status, presser, clothing house; Bessie Horwitz, wife, age 45 with implied birth year of 1865, married 28 years with implied marriage year of 1882 at age of 17, 5 children and 5 alive, arrival year 1901 [incorrect]; [Children] scratched out name, Isaac 21 with implied year of birth 1889, arrival year 1908 [incorrect] no occupation, Rosie age 11 with implied year of birth 1899, arrival year 1908 [incorrect], Clara age 9 with implied year of birth 1901, arrival year 1908 [incorrect].
1910 US Federal census	For David and Pesse's married daughter Minnie (Hurwitz) and her husband Samuel Fox and two children of Sam. Residing at: 1024 First Street in District of Columbia. Samuel, head, age 28 with implied birth year of 1882, years married 6 [incorrect], immigration year 1904, naturalization PA [pending], occupation Grocery, Own store. Minnie Fox, wife, age 24 with implied birth year of 1886, years married 6 [incorrect] number of children born 2 [incorrect] children living 2, immigration year 1904 [incorrect]; [children of Sam's] Martin age 5, Earnest age 2 8/12, both born in Maryland.
1917 (June 5) WWI Draft Registration	Isaac Hurwitz, 1303 E. Fayette, date of birth June 16, 1886, alien status, Grocer, employed at 1303 E Fayette St. has a father, mother, wife and child to support. Claims exemption "yes-father mother, wife & child"
1920 (Jan. 15) US Federal Census	For David Horwitz and family, residing at 1303 E. Fayette, David, head, O[wns] M[ortgaged] age 55 with implied birth year of 1865, immigration year 1900 [incorrect], Al[ien] status, tailor in tailor shop, Bessie, age 56 with implied birth year of 1864, immigration year 1901 [incorrect] Al[ien], [Children]: Clara age 19 with implied birth year of 1901, immigration year 1901 [incorrect] Al[ien], Howard age 6 [son of Isaac who died], Ceily (widow of Isaac) age 32, year of immigration 1906, Al[ien]

1920 (Jan. 9) US Federal Census	For Minnie and husband Sam Fox 929 Saratoga St, Samuel Fox, head, O[wns], F[mortgage free], age 37, immigration year 1904, Pa[naturalization pending], owner, grocery store; Minnie, wife, age 34 with implied birth year of 1886, immigration year 1904 [incorrect], ~~PA~~ Al [still alien], [Children] Martin age 15, born in Maryland, errand boy for District Store, Sarah, 9 1/12, born in Maryland, Michael, age 8 1/12 born in Maryland, Jacob, age 6 6/12 born in Maryland [Note: Samuel's son Ernest age 12 is living with Getzel Fax, Samuel's brother]
1920 (Jan 12-13) US Federal Census	For Rose and husband Harry Finkelstein 2120 Baltimore St. Harry Finkelstein, head, age 18, year of immigration 1904, Na[turalized] in 1915, Mens Clothing, Manufacturing; Rose, wife, age 21 with implied birth year of 1899, year of immigration 1909, Na[turalized in 1915 [via her husband's naturalization]. No Children listed.
1921 (May 2) Declaration of Intention	David Hurwitz, age 55, born in Mlinow, on Oct. 25, 1866, resides 1303 E Lafayette St. Baltimore. emigrated on Rhine, last residence was Mlinow, Russia, wife: Bessie, born at Mlinow. arrived at port of Baltimore March 4, 1901 [incorrect].
1921 (Aug. 1) Passenger Manifest	For Gulza/ Gulzia Mazer, David and Besse's daughter Sailing from Antwerp on July 21, 1921, arriving in New York Aug 1. Lejzor Mazuryk (Louis Mazer), age 36 with implied birth year of 1885, merchant, last residence Beresteczko, Poland closest relative Witia Mruryk, Gulcia, wife, age 37 with implied birth year of 1884, Child: Mordko (Martin Mazer), age 7, destination, father-in-law/father, Dawid Hurwitz, 1303 E. Fayette Street, place of birth: Beresteczko
1928 (July 31) Declaration of Intention	For Clara Hurwitz, age 27, occupation Correspondent, Cons Gas and Elect Co, color white, complexion Fair, 5'2", 105 lbs, color of hair brown, eyes blue, born in Mlynov Poland, May 31st 1901, resides at 1303 E. Fayette St, Baltimore. Emigrated from Trieste Austria on SS "Martha Washington" last residence was Mlynow Poland, not married. arrived at port of New York on March 1909.
1930 (April 10) US Federal Census	For David Hurwitz and family: 1303 E. Fayette St. Dwelling number 204. David "Herwitz," head, O[wner], Home value $2,000, age 64, age at marriage 19, Na[turalized] Retail Merchant, Groceries, Bessie Herwitz, age 64, age at marriage 19, Na[turnalized], Clara Herwitz, age 27 with implied birth year of 1903, Na[turalized], Book Keeper, Dept Store
1930 (April 2) US Federal Census	For family of Gulza, David and Bessie's daughter 1644 Ellsworth St. Louis Mazor, head, R[enting], Home Vaue $3750, R[adio] age 50, marriage age 24, born in Poland, Store, Grocery business; Gulzia, wife, age 46 with implied birth year of 1884, marriage age 20 with implied year of 1904, born in Poland, [Child] Merton [Martin], age 17, born in Poland.
1930 US Federal Census	For Minnie and Sam Fox and Family residing at 2307 Callow Ave. Samuel Fox, head, O[wned home] Home value: $8,000, age 46 with implied birth year of 1884, year of immigration 1904, Na[turalized], Dealer in Real Estate; Minnie, wife, age 43 with implied birth year of 1887, year of immigration 1908 [she arrived in 1909]; Children: Sarah age 20 born in District of Columbia, Michel, son, age 19, born in Maryland, helper in restaurant, Jack son, age 17 born in Maryland, clerk in State Police Department.

1930 [April 5] US Federal Census	For Pesse and David's daughter, Rose and her husband Harry Finkelstein and family. Residing at 2409 Callow Ave. Harry B. head, O[wns] home, home value $4,500, age 38, marriage age 27, born in Russia, year of immigration 1906, Na[turalized] Manufacturer of Clothing; Rose L. wife, age 30 with implied year of birth 1900, age at marriage 19, born in Russia, year of immigration 1909 [correct], Na[turalized], [Children] born in Maryland, Sylvia B., age 9, Alma G. age 6, Gilberg I age 1 and servant Nannie Wallace, Neg[gro] age 29 born in Virginia.
1935 [June 21] Petition for Citizenship	For "Clara Hurwitz Fram" Place of residence 938 Whitelock St. Baltimore, occupation Housewife, born in Mlynow, Poland on May 31, 1901, race Hebrew, Declared my intention July 31, 1928, name of husband Philip, married on Oct 11, 1931 at Baltimore. He was born in Lithuania, entered the US in Boston in 1905. Children Betty Iris, born Aug 29, 1932 in Baltimore. My last residence was Mlynow, Poland, emigrated to US from Trieste Italy [was Austria at the time] entered NY under name Keile Riwetz on Feb. 2, 1909 on the vessel Martha Washington. Witnesses: Sarah A. Fox (her niece) Assistant Buyer at 2307 Callow Ave and Robert Lavenstein, Clothing Manufacturer 2401 Callow Ave.

***

Chapter 4

The Family of Simha (Demb) Gruber

Simha Gruber is remembered as the oldest son of Rivka and Israel Jacob Demb. Since Simha did not come to the US, we have no US records indicating his year of birth. Simha's descendants have only a few oral traditions and a few hints about his life in his children's immigration records.

The family tree scroll lists Simha as third in the birth order after the daughters, Pesse and Yenta. However, as previously noted, Clara Fram in her memoir describes her mother Pesse as the "eldest daughter" (not as the eldest child). It seems conceivable that Simha may have been older than Pesse, though this is by no means certain and was not how the birth order was reported when the family tree was first made.

Why the Gruber Surname?

According to oral traditions among his descendants, Simha was given the surname "Gruber" (his mother Rivka's maiden name) to avoid conscription into the Russian army, because "only one son was taken from each family." Listening to an old recording of the 1992 Demb family reunion, I heard someone say that Simha was adopted by a Gruber family to avoid conscription and that's why he had the Gruber name. If so, I suspect the adopting family might have been one of his mother's cousins in the other Gruber line we know was living in Mlynov.[44] There is no way to verify if this story about Simha's surname is true, especially since the effort to avoid conscription has been used somewhat indiscriminately as a catch-all explanation among Jewish immigrants for a wide range of name changes in earlier generations.[45]

We do know from the 1850 and 1858 revision lists (censuses) now translated for Mlynov that Mlynov boys were being conscripted during that time. In the 1850 census of Mlynov there were 48 households and 200 living individuals. The revision lists indicate 5 individuals were "recruited," 5 were "on the run," and 5 had "escaped." In 1858, 6 were "recruited," but none were on the run, and none listed as escaped.

There is evidence, therefore, that Mlynov young men were being conscripted in this period and Rivka would have known about it and probably knew some of the boys involved. However, it also appears that the risk of conscription was significantly reduced between 1850 and 1858. This

---

[44] As noted earlier, the 1850 and 1858 censuses show another large Gruber household in Mlynov. We also know there were Grubers in Mlynov and Mervits remembered as ancestors by Rachel (Gruber) Teitelman and Sonia (Gruber) Teitelman, survivors who contributed to the Memorial Book. See above footnote 9.

[45] See, for example, the interesting essay and caution by Dan Leeson, "Military Conscription in Russia in the 19th Century." https://www.jewishgen.org/infofiles/ru-mil.txt retrieved online April 2023.

brutal practice of conscripting young Jewish boys as a means of Russifying them and converting them to Christianity was implemented by Nicholas I who was Tsar starting in 1825.[46] The Cantonist system, as this conscription program was called, began with a proclamation in 1827. Boys as young as seven were conscripted for 25 years of service. In fact, Clara Fram, our family memoirist, reports that her paternal grandfather (David's father) was conscripted at a very young age and only released after 15 years.

In 1855, Tsar Nicholas I died, and his son Alexander II became Tsar. The new Tsar abolished the brutal Cantonist policy with a decree on August 26, 1856. Simha's mother, Rivka Gruber, you may recall, was 16 years old in the 1858 census. She would have known that the new Tsar had abolished the conscription policy of his father. She married Israel Jacob Demb sometime between 1858 and 1864 when Pesse was born. If Simha was the oldest in the family and was older than Pesse, that would mean he was born between 1858 and 1864. Even if the practice of conscription had subsided, Rivka knew about the practice and plausibly took precautions by giving Simha her own birth name of Gruber. Or, perhaps the whole story is a bubbe meise!

***

Simha Gruber's Family
In the Demb family tree scroll, Simha's wife's name is "Chava (Eve)," and three children are listed in this birth order: Malia Gruber (married name Mollie Herman), Nathan Gruber and Samuel Gruber. Confirmation that Simha was one of the older children of Rivka and Israel Jacob is suggested by the birth year of his daughter, Mollie. According to US records, Mollie was born in ~1882 in Mlynov before any of Rivka and Israel Jacob's other grandchildren.[47]

Overlapping Generations

It is interesting to note that Rivka and Israel Jacob's first grandchild (Simha's daughter Mollie Gruber) was born within a couple years of Rivka and Israel Jacob's youngest child, Aaron Demb. Childbearing years extended so long that the birth of the next generation overlapped with the previous one. Similarly, Clara's older sister, Gulza, got married when Clara was just 2 or 3 years old. And Pepe Shulman was probably about 6 when her niece was born.

---

[46] See "Conscription of the Jews," pp. 13-34 in Michael Stanislawski, *Tsar Nicholas I and the Jews*. Philadelphia: Jewish Publication Society, 1983. See also "Cantonist" in Wikipedia.

[47] Pesse's oldest child, Gulza, was born in 1884. Pearl Malka's eldest daughter, Nehuma, was born in about 1887. Yenta's eldest child, Benjamin, was born in 1891, and Motel's eldest, Sylvia, was born in 1900.

Not much is known about Simha or his family life before the migration of his three children to Baltimore. According to family oral traditions, Simha's wife, Chava, died when their daughter Mollie was 13 and he remarried a woman named Chaindel.[48] This account would place Simha's remarriage in about 1895.

A photo remembered by descendants as the "hoola-hoop photo" is believed to be of Simha with his second wife Chaindel. Someone wrote on the reverse side indicating a son and daughter-in-law and grandchildren are in the photo. This is the only known photo that has survived of Simha and we have no knowledge of what became of the members of his second family. I suspected that perhaps the son and daughter-in-law behind Simha are his son Nathan with his wife, Gitel, and their two eldest daughters, Jennie and Doris, who were born before Nathan migrated to Baltimore. But his great-granddaughter doubts the identification.[49]

The little bit of information that we have about Simha's life comes from hints in the passenger manifests and naturalization papers of his sons discussed below.

A photo of Simha with a second wife and son. Courtesy of Tamara Kirson

[48] This information comes from a written narrative shared with me by Mollie's granddaughter, Lynne (Herman) Sandler.
[49] In a recollection below, Nathan's daughter, Doris, says she never met her father Nathan's parents. But if the baby is Doris in this photo, she would not have remembered this occasion. A great-granddaughter of Nathan notes that his wife was taller than him in a later photo and doesn't believe this looks like Nathan. This photo also could not be of Simha's other son, Sam and wife, because he had only one child before leaving Europe.

***

Mollie (Gruber) Herman

Simha's eldest daughter, Mollie Gruber, was born in 1882 or 1883 according to US records. She is called Malia or Madig in some records and remembered by descendants as Baba Malka or Maltza. Mollie married a man named Israel Herman (called Israel Erbman in some records). They probably married in 1899 before their oldest daughter Jennie / Jean (Zlate) was born.

According to the family narrative, Mollie didn't get along with her stepmother and left home. It is not known where the Gruber family was living at the time, though Mollie went to Berdichev where she worked in a dress factory sewing sequins onto dresses. It is possible the whole family was in Berdichev together at this time. From her brother Nathan's immigration records, we know that their father, Simha, was living in Berdychiv in 1912, and we know that their brother Samuel fell in love with and married a woman from Berdychiv before 1913. In any case, Mollie was back in Mlynov by the time she and her husband Israel Herman had their first daughter, Zlate (Jennie/Jean).

There are conflicting records about the birth location of Mollie's husband Israel Herman. His 1911 US Border Crossing record lists his place of birth as Dubna [Dubno] Russia. His 1912 passenger manifest lists his birthplace as "Russia, Plotsk" [Lutsk?]. In his 1920 Declaration of Intention, however, he indicates he was born in "Mlinow, Russia Poland" and his 1923 Petition for Naturalization similarly indicates he was born in "Malinow, Poland." Israel's brother, Isaac Herman, who came to the US is also listed as born in Mlynov in some of his records.

It seems likely then that Israel Herman was born in Mlynov but said "Dubna" in his 1911 passage, either referring to the District in which Mlynov was located or the larger nearby town because its name was more easily recognizable. When people from the East Coast ask me today where I live, I often say "Marin" or "San Francisco" which are both more familiar than my city, San Rafael.

The earliest record of Mollie and Israel's family is a 1911 census of England and Wales. The family had been living in England at the time for a few years on a journey that they made from Mlynov through Austria and eventually to Baltimore.

In the 1911 census, the couple has 5 children although only four are still alive. Israel Herman, the father, is age 30 and a cabinet maker and "Mary" (Mollie) is 28. They have been married for 12 years according to the record, placing their marriage in 1899. They are living at 10 Davis Avenue Hunt St, Mile End New Town Brixton.

The birthplaces of their children testify to the family's trek across Europe. Their eldest daughter "Jane" (married name Jennie Bernstein) is age 10 and was born in Mlynov according to her father's 1923 Petition. The second daughter Sarah (later Sarah Newman) is age 5 and was born in Austria, suggesting that by 1906 the family was already out of Russia. Their son Hyman (later Albert) is age 2 and was born in London indicating they had arrived in London by 1909 at the latest. A daughter Rebecca (married name Betty Davidson) age 1 was also born in London.

1911 Census for family of Israel Herman and Mary (Gruber)

A photo shows the family around 1913 with children (l to r) Jennie, Albert (Hyman), Betty and Sarah.

Figure 27 Israel Herman and Mollie (Gruber)
Courtesy of Miriam Berkowitz

A written narrative in the family fills in some details from the period before they reached England including the death of one of their children.[50] According to this narrative, Israel was drafted into the Tsar's army. In 1906, the couple and their two eldest children left on the Q.T. so Israel could avoid conscription. Israel and Mollie traveled across Europe. Sarah was born in Toprev, Austria in 1907 (later part of Czechoslovakia and called Toplice). According to this family account, another son named Herschel died of a fever and by falling off a bed (or both) while the family was in Toprev. The daughter, Sarah, was told that her father was so depressed that he decided they should leave. He went ahead to Paris but didn't like it there and headed to London, where he earned enough as a cabinet maker to send for his family.

Not long after their census in England, Israel headed to Baltimore via Canada. He sailed on the SS Uranium and arrived in Halifax, Nova Scotia on November 1, 1911. The ship left Rotterdam but he likely picked it up in Southhampton. He is listed as Israel "Erbman," a carpenter. From Halifax, Israel headed to Montreal via the Canadian Pacific Railway, which appears as C.P.R. on one of his records. A record of his crossing from Montreal to Buffalo, New York, indicates he took his US examination on Nov. 27th and that he was headed to 104 Albemarle Street in Baltimore, the address of his wife's Aunt Mollie (Demb) and her husband Samuel Roskes. Many of the Demb and Mlynov immigrants were getting their start at the Roskes apartment which was just around the corner from where the Fax family lived (more on them below).

1911 Israel Erbman border crossing record

---

[50] I want to thank descendant Lynne (Herman) Sandler in particular for sharing these writings and oral traditions about Israel and Mollie's trek across Europe.

Figure 28 Mollie and Israel with family circa 1922
Courtesy of Miriam Berkowitz.

1. Mollie (Gruber) Herman
2. Israel Herman
3. Jennie (Herman) Bernstein
4. Jennie's husband, Michael Bernstein
5. Sarah Herman
6. Al (Albert/Hyman) Herman
7. Betty Herman
8. Joe Herman
9. Sally Herman
10. Sylvia (Jennie and Michael's daughter)
11. Buddy Bernstein (Jennie and Michael's son)

Mary and the children followed Israel to the US in 1912. The family departed Liverpool on August. 3, 1912 on the SS Campania and arrived in NY on August 11th. Mary is 30, Jane (Jennie) is 11, Sarah age 6, Hyman age 4 and Rebecca 2. They headed to 104 Albemarle St. where Mollie's husband, Israel, was living with the family of her Aunt Mollie (Demb) Roskes. In Baltimore, Mollie and Israel had two additional children, Joseph in 1913 and Sadie (married name Sally Chancey) in 1915.

Manifest of SS Campania sailing from Liverpool

1912 Manifest of Mary and the children

In Baltimore, Israel continued work as cabinet maker and then bought a secondhand furniture store where he did refinishing. Eventually Israel bought a downtown grocery store and eventually sold that and bought another uptown, when he also began dabbling in real estate.

In the 1920 census, Israel and "Mary" Herman are living at 1636 McHenry St. Israel is listed as 42 and as store keeper of his own store; Mary is 38. Their eldest daughter Jennie is no longer living with them. She has married Michael Bernstein and appears in the 1920 census in the home with his family at 6th St NW, in the District of Columbia. Their first child Sylvia (married name Kaplowitz) was born in 1920, followed by Mishel ("Buddy") in 1921 and Marion (married named Esterson) in 1925. For their part, Israel and Mollie and the rest of the children are living at 1915 Clifton Ave through most of the 1920s and the family appears to have a business called the Clifton Lamp co.

In 1929, Israel went back to Mlynov with his wife's Aunt Yenta (Demb) Schwartz. Photos from that trip show Israel and Yenta with one of the Shulman families that did not survive the Shoah. According to Israel's descendants, he went back to assist some family members migrate, but they refused to leave.

Israel and Yenta Schwartz appear on the same returning passenger manifest, though Israel is listed with other US Citizens and Yenta appears on a page with other aliens who had permits to return. Their ship, the SS Aquitania, left Cherbourg, France on Sept. 21, 1929 and arrived in New York on Sept 27. Israel was 49.

Figure 29 Israel Herman (seated right) and Yenta Schwartz (seated center)

Yenta and Israel are with the Miller/ Meiler[51] family in Mlynov. Courtesy Ted Fishman

In the 1930 census, Israel and Mary "Hillman" and five of their children are living at 2309 Wichita Ave. They own a home valued at $7,000 and they own a radio, as the census informs us. Israel is 50 and said to have married at age 23. His occupation is listed real estate agent. "Mary" is 45 and said to have married at age 18. Sarah is 23, Albert 22, Betty 20, Joe 16, and Sadie 15.

The Wichita Ave home became a gathering place for family as recounted in this personal remembrance of one of Mollie's granddaughters.

---

[51] The eldest daughter of Pearl Malka (Demb) and Tsodik Shulman was Nehuma Shulman (standing center). She married Saul (or Shaul) Miller (also spelled variously as Meiler Mejler and perhaps Malar) (seated left). Standing with them are their two daughters, Tamar (standing left) and Nina (standing right). The spelling "Miller" appears in the family scroll and in Tsodik's obituary. The spelling "Meiler" appears in a handwritten note by Ted Fishman on the photo of them in Mlynov and the spelling "Mejler" appears on the manifest of Simon Shulman from 1922. I suspect Saul may have been related to Yussel "Malar" who married Esther Gelberg / Goldberg from Mlynov.

***

Remembrances of Baba (Maltza Herman) [Mollie Herman]
By Lynne (Herman) Sandler[52]

I want to speak of a time gone by-a time of family gatherings and cousins clubs, of matriarchs, of holiday get-togethers and Sunday afternoons, of politics and Zionism and war stories, and of cousins with secrets and special games. We drank from jelly glasses and Yahrzeit glasses, ate wonderful food from mismatched dishes-brisket or flanken and kasha, cooked with onions and gravy and wonderful flavors; chicken and homemade luchshen soup, homemade gefilte fish with "real" horseradish, chicken eggs and chicken feet, schav and dairy meals: blintzes with fruit, sour cream, homemade borscht; desserts of cakes that will never again be duplicated because their recipes were never recorded.

It was in Baltimore, during the 40s and 50s that I grew up. The matriarch was my grandmother, "Baba" - Mollie (Malka or Maltza) Herman. The meeting place was her home on Wichita Avenue.

Figure 30 Home of Mollie Herman on Wichita Ave

As you walked in the house, you could look straight back into the breakfast room. The furniture in the living room was dark and well-worn, and it included a large tv and a radio, and lots of brass pieces from Russia: mortars and pestles, plus a samovar. From the entrance hall you could see the breakfast room, where we ate our Friday night Shabbos dinners, where the table and chairs

---

[52] As noted previously, Lynne is a granddaughter of Mollie (Gruber) and Israel Herman, and the daughter of their son Al (Albert) Herman.

were of lighter wood. The walls held pictures of the family, but the back room really had lots and lots of pictures from the old country. The grownups never talked about them. The people in the photos were old, and the women wore babushkas. Even the children looked like little old men and women. We (the young cousins) delighted in these pictures of "the old people" and often made up stories about them or just looked at them and laughed. It's only recently that I learned the names of these family members [i.e., Rivka (Gruber) and Israel Jacob Demb]. The dining room was large, and when the table was open, it held lots of family, but the kids always ate in the breakfast room on Sundays. We liked it that way, and it made more room for the adults.

My family had dinner there every Friday night, from the time we moved to Baltimore after Zayde died, until I went to college when Baba was sick and unable to prepare the big dinners she had cooked for so many years. But what I remember from those earlier years was that when I came in on Fridays, Baba would be sitting at the counter in the kitchen, on her high stool, making a cake or chopping something. When she made cakes, she measured with her hands or with an eggshell or a glass. Those cakes were wonderful, not always the same, and no one could ever capture just how she made them. The house always smelled of chicken soup and matzo balls, roasted chicken, gefilte fish. Everything was homemade.

First Baba's gefilte fish (and it was the real meaning of gefilte - stuffed). The fish skin was on the outside, and the fish cake on the inside. Homemade horseradish too, never from a jar - white or red, made with beet juice. Next came the chicken soup with matzo balls unless there was luchshen (noodles) often made by Mima Mollie [Roskes]. Usually the balls were light as could be, but when they had a hard center, we ate them anyway. In the spring, the soup had the little egg yolks that came in the chickens which my brother and I loved. My brother, who was born in 1944 when I was 4 years old, was named for Zaydeh. He received the name Israel Gerald but became Buzzy at about the time he entered kindergarten.

Then came the meal-usually chicken (sometimes roasted but frequently just soup chicken with some watery ketchup on top, baked in the oven). When we were really lucky, we had meat-probably flanken, with potatoes at the bottom of the pot, along with the schmaltz.

For dessert, the teapot was put on [the stove] and yahrzeit glasses came out for the tea-but sometimes we used real China cups. I usually did my favorite thing: getting out the dessert dishes-pink and green depression glass plates, and Baba served her delicious cake.

Uncle Nathan [Gruber] was always with us, except for the times when he and Baba stopped speaking to each other. He lived on the top floor. When they would come to our house for occasional meals, we always served them on glass plates because our house wasn't kosher, and Baba was insistent that Nussen be served first. I learned that I was named for his late wife Gertrude, but I never knew anything about her and when I asked my mother, she said that when I was born she was told that one of my names had to be for Gertrude. Sad that I never knew much about her. My cousin Trudi Kadish (Lando) was also named for her. My middle name is Gertrude (Hebrew: Leah Gittel).

And Baba always looked the same. She was involved in what she was doing; cooking for her family was so natural to her. She smelled just like the food she cooked–it seemed as if her perfume must have been essence of chicken fat, carp, or onions. She was a big woman, and she looked old for as long as I can remember. She was about 70 when she died, which must have made her in her early 50s during this time period. Her hair was gray and a little wavy. She wore flowered aprons, and plain, shapeless dresses. Her arms were large, and the skin was soft and fleshy. She spoke with a Yiddish accent, and frequently lapsed into Yiddish expressions. I didn't speak Yiddish nor did any of the cousins, and neither did my mother, but when my father or any of his siblings was around, she used Yiddish. I remember when Baba studied to get her American citizenship because I helped to quiz her on some of the subjects, and we were both so excited when she passed the test.

Baba was truly the matriarch of the family. Widowed suddenly when she was only in her 40s, she rose to power when her home became the central meeting place for "the family". She was a founder and officer of the Maryland Free Loan Society,[53] an organization which provided interest-free loans to Jews struggling to "make it" in the new land. Softspoken she was not - her words were law. She spoke with knowledge and authority. She was a good person, believing wholeheartedly in Jewish values, but she had a sharp tongue and knew how to use it. She had six children, two boys and four girls, plus another son who died in early childhood, and she had her favorites–the boys. She even had her favorites amongst her grandchildren, and we kids knew it, but we accepted the fact that the males were more special to her than the females.

If Friday nights were reserved for her son Al and his family (and occasionally her daughter Betty and family), then Sundays were for the whole mishpacha–called lantsmen. Somehow the house expanded on Sunday afternoons to accommodate aunts, uncles, cousins, second cousins, great aunts, rabbis, friends, and whoever else wanted to visit Maltza. And she cooked–when, I don't know, but there was always a lot of food.

More of the stringy meat, kasha cooked with onions and gravy, potatoes with onions and gravy, vegetables, fruit, and real strudel. Or it could be a dairy meal, with what seemed like hundreds of blintzes, enough that sometimes we'd have to send out for more sour cream. The house would be filled with people, talking, laughing, arguing, and laughing again. Politics, Palestine, the war, Russia, were some of the topics I heard discussed. But the kids weren't interested in what the grownups were doing. We were having our own fun, running around upstairs when there were no tenants, or playing in the basement with the windup victrola. We sometimes had fun with the older cousins when they would play with us. The other good thing was that we got to drink soda with our meals.

My only regret is not asking questions about where they came from and how they managed in their new country.

---

[53]The Maryland Free Loan Society began as the Mlynov Verein, a group of Mlynov immigrants who got together socially and to raise money. See the essay about the Verein by Eta [Goldseker] Fishman, "Jews from Baltimore Assisted their Home Shtetl Mlynov," Mlynov Memorial Book, pp. 505-506. The Jewish Museum of Maryland has many records from the Mlynov Verein.

***

Nathan Gruber

Nathan Gruber was the second child of Simha Gruber. Nathan's US naturalization papers indicate he was born in Mlynov [in the district] of Volin, in 1885, though the month varies from May–July. He followed his sister Mollie to Baltimore three months after she and the children arrived.

"Nussen" (Nathan) Gruber left Bremen on November 10, 1912 on the SS Neckar and arrived in Philadelphia on Nov. 22nd. Nathan was not traveling alone. There were several other Mlynov immigrants on the ship with him including his Aunt Yenta (Demb) Schwartz, her husband Chaim and their two youngest sons (one of whom was my grandfather), as well as Chaim's sister-in-law, Sarah (Fishman) Schwartz and her children, and her nephew Morris Fishman, who is listed next to Nathan on his manifest.[54]

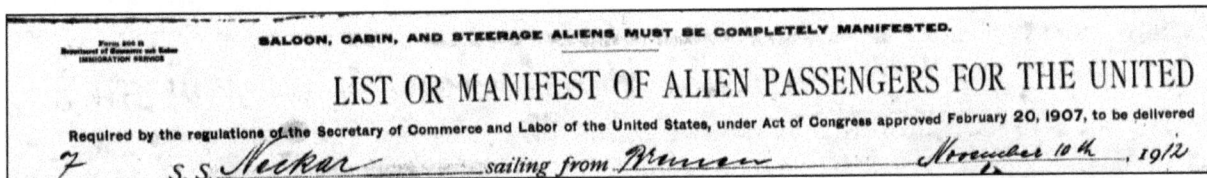

Manifest of the SS Neckar sailing from Bremen on November 10, 1912

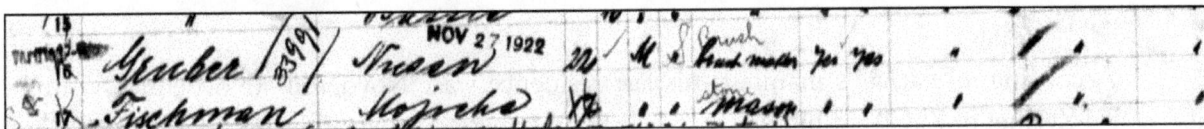

Nussen Gruber, age 22, brush maker, traveling next to a friend from Mlynov, "Mojochs Fischman"

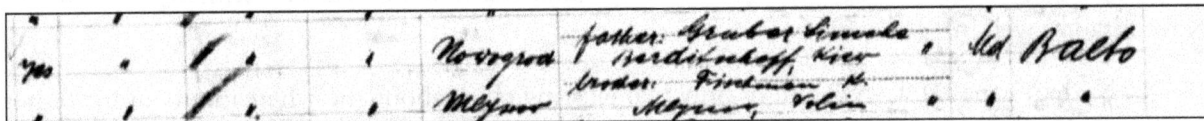

Nussen's last residence Novogrod and his closest relative "father: Gruber, Simcha in Barditecheff, Kiev"

On page 2 of Nussen's manifest we can see he was headed to his "br. i. l." [brother-in-law] Israel Herman at 106 Albemarle St. Balto, Md." This address was abutting the Roskes address at 104

---

[54] Yenta (Demb) Schwartz was the sister of Nathan's father, Simha. She was traveling with her husband Chaim Schwartz and sons Norton and Paul. Their son Benjamin was already in Baltimore. Sarah (Fishman) Schwartz was married to Israel Schwartz, Chaim's brother. Morris Fishman, who is next to Nathan, was son of Sarah Fishman's brother David Fishman.

Albemarle. His friend Mojochs (Morris) Fischman is headed to his "cousin Scwarz Israel at 1152 E. Lombard Str."

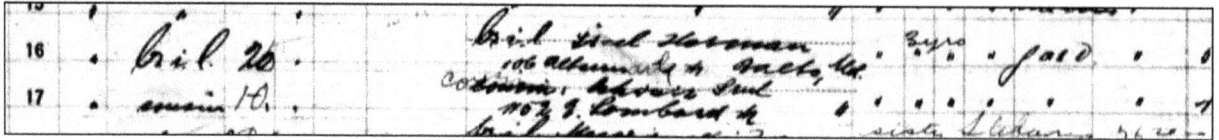

Page 2 of Nathan's manifest: headed to br. i. l. [brother-in-law] Israel Herman at 106 Albemarle Str

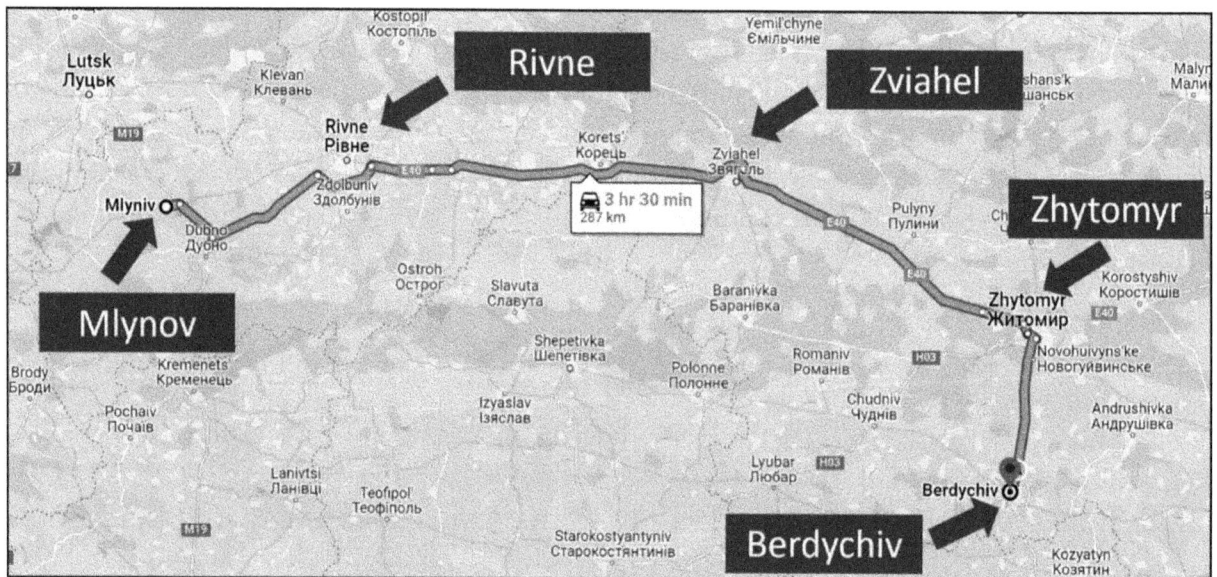

Figure 31 A map of Zviahel (Novohrad) and Berdychiv in relationship to Mlynov

According to Nathan's manifest, his last residence was "Novogrod" (Novoghrad Volinski also called Zviahel or Zhvil). In his later naturalization papers, Nathan indicates that his wife Gitel Garfinkle (married name Gertrude Gruber) was born in Novoghrad Volinski. We can thus speculate that Nathan was visiting Novoghrad Volinksi before ~1908 when their first daughter Jennie (Jennie Feinberg) was born. Their second daughter Doris (married name Doris V. Fishman) was born in Novoghrad as well in 1910.

Nathan's manifest gives one of only two existing clues about the whereabouts of his father Simha Gruber. His "father Simha Gruber in Berditcheff, Kiev" is listed as his closest relative in his last location. On current maps, Berdychiv, Ukraine is about 257 miles east / 5.5 hours driving today from Mlynov. It is due south of Zhytomyr and you would pass through Novoghrad Volinski (Zviahel) on your way from Mlynov to Berdychiv.

Nathan was separated from his wife and daughters for eight years by the intervention of WWI. In the meantime, he settled in Baltimore, and became Nathan Gruber. His brother Samuel arrived in Baltimore not long after. Nathan remained a brush maker in Baltimore and in 1914 and 1915 was living at 104 Albemarle Street, with his Aunt Mollie (Demb) Roskes.

1914	ˮ ᴸᵘˡᵘ ᴿ ᵈʳᵉˢˢᵐᵏʳ 826 n Mount h do " Myer B com trav h 808 Newington av " Nathan brushmkr 104 Albemarle " Reuben A plumber h 1929 Lansdowne " Saml tailor 104 Albemarle " Werner ctr 1095 Somerset
1915	ˮ ᴸᵘˡᵘ ᴿ ᵈʳᵉˢˢᵐᵏʳ 826 n Mount h do " Myer B com trav h 808 Newington av " Nathan brushmkr 104 Albemarle " Reuben A plumber h 1929 Lansdowne " Saml tailor 104 Albemarle " Werner ctr 1095 Somerset

By September 12, 1917, when Nathan filled out his Draft Registration Card, he describes himself as a laborer working in the Dry Dock at Locust Point in the Baltimore harbor. As we shall see, his occupation is significant for an incident that occurs two years later. His address is now listed as 205 Albemarle. His wife, Gitel, is still back in Russia.

September 12, 1918
Nathan's Draft Registration Card

Nathan began his naturalization process in November 1919 probably in anticipation of his family's arrival. His Declaration indicates he is living at 102 Albemarle Street, is 34, and now lists himself as a grocer. By January 9, 1920, the day of the US Federal Census, Nathan has moved to 2300 Ettinger Street and has several lodgers. He is no longer at the Dry Docks and his occupation is now listed as a proprietor of a grocery store.

12		2300	236	244	Gruber	Nathan	Head	1	O	M	M	W	34	M	1913	Pa	1917		6/0
13					Barker	Eva	Lodger				M	W	25	M	1915	Pa	1918		4/0
14					"	Ida	Lodger				F	W	20	M				NKO	40
15					"	Beatrice	Lodger				F	W	18	X					40
16					"	Ruth	Lodger				F	W	3	X					

1920 US Federal Census for Nathan Gruber on Ettinger St. His wife and children arrive six months later.

A real estate transaction captured in *The Baltimore Sun* suggests that perhaps the Ettinger property or one nearby was sold to Nathan by his brother-in-law, Israel Herman.

Jan. 31, 1920, *The Baltimore Sun*, p. 16	Aliceanna, 12.6x70. g.r. $30..................... 0 Israel Herman to Nathan Gruber, s.w.s. Etting st., nr. Baker. 12x66, g.r. $36.................. 5

***

Recollections by Nathan's daughter Doris (Gruber) Fishman[55]

My mother Gittel Garfinkle was born in Russia in a small village, like our suburbs in Baltimore, in Novograd Volynska Gubernia. This village in Yiddish was called "Sissla". We lived with our maternal grandparents but never knew our paternal grandparents [i.e. Nathan's parents Simha Gruber and Chava].

We lived in a one story spacious house, which was called a "kretchma". Kretchma means the gathering of folks of the village who came together to meet their neighbors and discuss the issues of the day. This room was used as a "commoradia" place: it was actually the entrance to the house. It was a long narrow corridor room with benches on each side of the wall. My grandparents held synagogue services in the main and largest room in the house. The floors through the entire house were earthen and painted an ochre color. I remember my mother using a broom like brush, which she dipped into a bucket containing water and a reddish ochre mixture.

The entire house was heated by a stove built into the walls of the kitchen from floor to ceiling. The lower chamber of the stove held the wood and was called a "pripechik" or hearth and was where the cooking and baking was done. On the top of this hearth, set towards the wall, was the baking oven where bread was baked and where "russel fleish" was cooked over night (cholent). We had a barn and a hayloft and two cows.

My mother has three brothers. Alex was killed in the First World War and became an unknown soldier, never to return home. Baruch lived in the vicinity with his wife and children. After the war, we never heard from him again. The other brother (mother could not remember his name) lived closer to us and did not have any children. He used to mill flour or grain for the

---

[55] Quoted with permission from Nathan's granddaughter, Louise Marine, who also provided a number of photos.

community and earned his livelihood this way. The mill was attached to the back of his house and the grain was milled by a horse going around and around to crush and grind the wheat or any other grain.

My mother married Nathan Gruber who lived in a shtetl called Mlynov, which was quite a distance from Sissla. My mother was a beautiful woman and only saw my father once [before they were married?], but he had a photograph of her before they became engaged. Their marriage was hurried because the First World War (1914) had already started.[56] His real last name was Aven, but in order to escape induction into the Russian army he changed it to Gruber. By making the change, the Army could not locate him quickly and therefore they could get married.[57]

We all lived with our grandparents. My sister Jenny was almost a year old when my parents heard rumors that the war was going to break out near our village. My father crossed the border to avoid the draft and try to get to America. As soon as he was able to earn enough money to go to America, he promised to send for Mother, my sister Jenny and me (I was called Dora).

I imagine it was difficult for my mother when my father was gone. After the First World War broke out there were difficult times for us. There were pogroms going on in the big city, Novograd Volynsk, and our shtetl was experiencing looting and taking over of property. The army took over our cousins, Zena and Paula Litt's house. The house was semi-detached to ours and became the officer's headquarters. In some ways, this was a blessing because the officers protected us from being molested. My mother was a very beautiful woman.

Several times my family and many people in the community were ousted from our homes and made to walk for miles like, "bezenkis" until we were rescued and returned to our homes. My mother worked like a man to take care of us and the grounds.

My father went to Baltimore where his sister [Mollie Herman] lived, as did other relatives from Mlynov. My father worked in a brush factory. With the help of the Tucker family,[58] who were "lanzalite" (friends) my father brought a grocery store and saved up enough money to send for us. When Mr. Israel Lerner[59] made a trip to Russia to bring back people to America we were on his list. He arrived with an army trunk and we put everything we owned that could fit in it. He then took us to Kiev and then Warsaw where he put us on a ship called the "Imperator". It had four smoke stacks and was very crowded. We were on the ship for many days.

---

[56]This recollection doesn't quite align with records. Nathan left for Baltimore in 1912 before WWI was on the horizon and after his two eldest daughters, Jeanne and Doris, were already born.

[57] This memory appears to be a distorted version of the tradition in the family that Nathan's father, Simha Demb, had his named changed to Simha Gruber to avoid conscription.

[58] Samuel and Sarah Tucker and five children also lived at 104 Albemarle Street in the 1910 census which is probably how Nathan Gruber met them. Samuel Tucker was listed at that address in the 1905-1909 City directories. While living there a son, Myer Tucker, age 12, drown in the harbor when he was at play on the piers in the harbor (*The Baltimore Sun*, July 14, 1910, p. 12).

[59] Itzhik Lerner went back to Mlynov in 1920 and helped his mother and siblings make their way to America. Also traveling with them were two other Mlynov families. See more below "Itzik Lerner Returns to Mlynov" pp. 206ff in the discussion of Aaron Demb and the journey of his wife Bessie to America.

Gittel (Garfinkle) Gruber with daughters, Doris standing,
and Jean seated ~1916
Courtesy of Louise Marine

When we came to Baltimore, we stayed with Mima Roskes [Nathan's Aunt Mollie] on Albemarle Street. We were fed and given clothes. The next day we went home to 1300 Etting Street [probably 2300 Etting], the grocery store where Mrs. Tucker helped Daddy run the business. We were now told to call ourselves Jean and Doris. We attended School #21 and later School #49. My father sold the Etting Street property and bought a house at 1900 Kennedy Avue. My sister Sylvia was born and then I attended Eastern High School. My sister Jean dropped out of school and went to work to help the family.

***

The Migration of Nathan's wife and children

WWI intervened between the time that Nathan Gruber arrived in Baltimore and his wife and daughters could leave. Nathan's wife, "Gitla," and his two daughters departed Southampton on July 3, 1920 on the SS Imperator and arrived in New York on July 12th. As discussed above in Doris's recollection, they were assisted by another Mlynov man that Nathan knew living in Baltimore. His name was Isadore (Itzik) Lerner.

Nathan probably already knew Itzik Lerner from Mlynov though he was about 5 years younger. Itzik Lerner was born in Mlynov and had followed his father Joseph Lerner to Baltimore in December 1913. At the time, Itzik's father, Joseph, was staying at 106 Albemarle St. with Israel Herman who is listed as his nephew in Lerner's passenger manifest. This is the same address where Nathan was staying when he arrived in Baltimore as well. If Nathan didn't know him already, he got to know him on Albemarle Street. In January 1920, Isadore made plans to go back to Mlynov to help get his mother and siblings to Baltimore.

As discussed in more detail below, Itzik also assisted the families of two other Mlynov husbands, Aaron Demb and Isaac Marder, who were also in Baltimore and had been separated from their families during WWI. Aaron Demb, of course, was the youngest child of Rivka and Israel Jacob Demb. He arrived in Baltimore in 1914 and was also separated from his wife and children during WWI. It is apparent that Itzik Lerner was coordinating with the Mlynov husbands who had been stranded in Baltimore and who lived at 102 or 104 Albemarle Street. Nathan, being one of those men, must have asked Itzik to also assist his wife and daughters make their way to Baltimore as well.

The last residence of Nathan's wife, "Gitel," and their daughters is listed as Rowno and perhaps they came West from Gitel's hometown near Novoghad to meet up with Itzhik Lerner and the other travelers, though Doris's memory is that Itzik Lerner picked them up in a truck and took them to Kiev and then Warsaw. Either way, they probably listed their last residence and birthplace as Rowno to avoid further inconsistencies or questions in customs while coordinating with Itzik and the other families he was helping.

On the manifest, "Gitla" (Gitel) is 36, Zenia (later Jean Feinberg) is age 10 and Dora (later Doris Fishman) is 8 years old. Gitel's closest relative in Rowno is "Shesl Miller," who is remembered in the Shulman family as "Shaul Miller/Meiler," the man who married Nathan's first cousin Nehuma Shulman, daughter of Pearl (Demb) and Tsodik Shulman (more on them below). This Meiler family would not survive the Nazi invasion in 1942.

The manifest lists Gitel's destination as "husband 102 Albemarle Street," the address where Nathan had been living with the family of his Aunt Mollie (Demb) Roskes. Gitel apparently did not yet know that he had already moved to Ettinger Street, which is where he appears in the 1920 census. Gitel and her daughters had not seen Nathan in nine years by the time they finally arrived. Ten months later their daughter Sylvia was born in May 1921. She was 11 years younger than her sister Doris.

Manifest of the SS Imperator, sailing from Southampton

Manifest of Gitla and daughters, Zenia (Jennie) and Dora

Right-hand columns showing their last residence as Rowno and closest friend there Shesl Miller

Page 2 showing destination "Husband Nathan Gruber, 102 Albenarce [Albemarle] Street"

***

The Mystery of Nathan's Naturalization Process

A mystery surrounds Nathan's naturalization process. He is the only Mlynov immigrant who filled out his Declaration of Intention twice (once in 1919 and a second time in 1924), even though the first one was still valid.

Why did Nathan fill out a second Declaration in 1924? Did he forget he had already done so?

I suspect that Nathan was hiding the fact that he had lived at 102 Albemarle Street which was the target of a raid during the Red Scare in 1919, just weeks after he filled out his first Declaration with the address of 102 Albemarle Street.

Following WWI and the Bolshevik Revolution, fear of communists and anarchists spread across the US leading to a series of Federal raids to arrest suspects.[60] Often the suspects arrested were immigrants who were involved in various labor unions; some were Jewish immigrants. A number were even deported like the famous Emma Goldman, who was deported on December 21, 1919, even though she had already become an American citizen.

In the fall of 1919, the Red Scare precipitated the Palmer raids, a series of arrests which reached Baltimore.[61] A Federal raid took place in Baltimore on December 13, 1919, and 14 persons were arrested across the city. It was big news locally.

Those arrested were involved in an anarchist group called the Union of Russian Workers, a group that espoused unification of Russian workers in the US and Canada to battle against

---

[60] See for example, Robert K. Murray, *Red Scare: A Study in National Hysteria, 1919-1920*. New York: McGraw Hill, 1964 and Christopher M. Finan, *From the Palmer Raids to the Patriot Act*. Boston: Beacon Press, 2007.
[61] See Vernon L. Pedersen, *The Communist Party in Maryland, 1919-1957*. University of Illinois, 2001.

capitalism and forces of authority. Among those arrested were a Russian Jewish immigrant, Morris Isaac Berezin, age 31, who was living nearby at the time in East Baltimore at 2123 East Pratt St.[62]

The two Declarations of Nathan Gruber, Nov. 20, 1919 and May 7, 1924

Four of those arrested lived on Albemarle Street and one of them, Stefan Panko, was living at 102 Albemarle Street, the same address where Nathan was living when he filled out his first Declaration of Intention in 1919. An article the same day indicated that the agents had also searched through the Baltimore Dry Docks and Shipbuilding Company looking for subversive materials. Four of those arrested worked at the Dry Docks. Nathan listed himself as a laborer at the Baltimore Dry Dock when he filled out his Draft Registration card in September 1918, only a year earlier.

[62]"Red Suspects Grilled," *The Baltimore Sun*, Nov. 15, 1919, p. 20.

14 ALLEGED REDS TAKEN

Suspects Believed To Be Active In Russian Union.

FOUR OF NUMBER LOCKED UP

They Will Be Given Hearings Soon And May Later Have To Face Deportation Proceedings.

Fourteen alleged members of the Union of Russian Workers fell into the net spread here yesterday by Federal officials.

According to agents of the Department of Justice, they are persons who have been instrumental in spreading Russian propaganda among mill, plant and shop workers here. Those taken, it is said, assistants to the ringleaders who were caught in the round-up on November 8.

Of the 14 arrested, one is a woman. She is the wife of one of the alleged under-secretaries of the Russian Workers. Four were locked up in Western Police Station.

The 14 arrested are:

JOHN FECHUK, 37 years old, 909 Fawn street.

JOHN KUFEL, 40 years old.

HELEN KUFEL, his wife, 25 years old, 1714 Fleet street.

NICHOLAS KLEINSCHECK, 30 years 428 South Paca street.

ALEXANDER SCZERBA, 116 Albemarle street.

ANDRE SCHECH, 116 Albemarle street.

GREGORY OPORKO, 927 Hanover street.

IGNATZ YATZUK, 40 Albemarle street.

ANDRE STAROUN, 101 South Exeter street.

STEFAN PANKO, 102 Albemarle street.

IGNACY KLINCHUK.

MICHAEL WASKEWICZ.

IGNATZ FECHIK.

Woman Said To Be Leader.

Helen Kufel, who is the first woman to be apprehended on the charge here, is said to be one of the leading spirits in the cause of the Russian Union Workers. For months she was associated with the leaders of the union, and at their meetings, according to Special Agent Doyas, she fired the men with her singing of Russian soviet songs. She was a seamstress and in the shop where she worked she diligently spread the doctrine of soviet government. Federal agents attended the meetings where Mrs. Kufel sang.

When she was arrested she smiled at the special agents who searched her house. She showed no surprise and to one of the interpreters she expressed the hope that she would not be separated from her husband "when the Government put her in prison." She was separated, however, for the couple occupy different cells at Western Police Station.

Ten Suspects Seized.

Ten other suspects were taken to the office of William Doyas, chief of the local office of the Department of Justice. Mr. Doyas expressed the opinion last night that all of the 14 will be held pending a hearing before United States Immigration Commissioner B. M. Stump. Those held, it is said, are scheduled for deportation.

Agents Have 200 Names.

Four of the fourteen were employed at the plant of the Baltimore Dry Docks and Shipbuilding Company, others were

(Continued on Page 12, Column 5.)

Figure 32 A Red Scare raid strikes 102 Albemarle St.
The Baltimore Sun, December 13, 1919, p. 18

Nathan had reasonable grounds to worry that if he continued his naturalization process his address might trigger suspicions with authorities and even deportation. Since he was living at that address when he filled out his first Declaration of Intention from 1919, he may have filled out a second Declaration of Intention after he had a new address, to avoid any association with the man who was arrested during that raid.

Nathan finally filled out his Petition for Naturalization in 1926 and was finally naturalized November 8, 1926. I imagine he breathed a sigh of relief when he was finally a citizen. The certification below with his photo was printed later in 1953.

By 1930, the family was living at 1900 Kennedy Street in Baltimore. Nathan at this point owned his home with a $6,000 value as well as a radio (which the census that year recorded as a significant metric). He was a proprietor of a grocery. All three daughters were still in the household. His daughter Jean was a librarian for the City of Baltimore. Dora was 18 and a stenographer for a decorator. Sylvia was still only 9 years old.

Nathan Gruber's Naturalization Certificate
Courtesy of Louise Marine

Jean married Harry Feinberg on May 3, 1934 in the District of Columbia and they had three children (Robert, Charlotte Isabelle Feinberg-Brody, and Trudi Cohen). Jean passed away in 1992.

Doris V. married Benjamin J. Fishman who was born in Mlynov in 1910 and a cousin of the other Fishman line from Mlynov. Benjamin arrived with his mother as a boy of about 11 in Baltimore in May 1921. It seems likely that Doris met Benjamin through all the Mlynov relatives and friends of her father. They had a lot in common coming to the US after being separated from their fathers by the War.[63]

---

[63]This Benjamin J. Fishman was the son of Joseph and Ida Fishman and grandson of Malka and Nathan ("Nuti") Hyman Fischmann. A Fishman family tree handwritten by his cousin Benjamin "Bennie" Fishman (who married Clara Shulman) indicates they were third cousins. According to that tree, Benjamin J.'s grandfather, Nathan Hyman Fishman, was a brother of Berel Dov Fishman, who was the father of Moshe Fishman, Meyer Fishman, and Sarah (Fishman) Schwartz. Nathan Hyman Fishman and his wife Malka had five children including Joseph Fishman the father of this Benjamin J. Fishman who married Doris V. Gruber. Nathan Hyman ("Nuti Fischmann") arrived in Baltimore 1911 with Israel Schwartz and Usher (Harry) Teitelbaum and stayed at 836 E. Pratt Street with the Fax family. His son Joseph Fishman followed in Aug 1912. Joseph was separated from his wife and son during WWI. Benjamin J. and his mother left Le Havre, France on the SS Rousillon and arrived in New York on May 2, 1921.

Figure 33 Nathan, Sylvia, Gertrude Gruber

Figure 34 Wedding of Doris's daughter Linda Fishman

(l to right) Julian Lapides (Linda's husband) Nathan Gruber, Linda (Fishman), Linda's grandfather, Joseph Fishman

Benjamin J. Fishman, wholesaler

By DeWitt Bliss
Staff Writer

Benjamin J. Fishman, a retired wholesaler and founder of an international organization of stamp collectors, died Wednesday of cancer at his home in Mount Washington.

Mr. Fishman, 83, retired in 1973 as the owner of Benjamin J. Fishman & Co. Inc., which sold bedroom, bathroom and dining room linens, and similar goods.

He had started in the business in 1927 as a bookkeeper for Abraham Baumblatt and bought the company from Mr. Baumblatt's estate in 1944.

During World War II, he also worked as an inspector at the American Hammered Piston Ring Division of the Koppers Co.

In 1978, he founded the Israel Plate Block Society, and was president of the group and co-editor of its journal at the time of his death. He sold his collection of American plate blocks and first-day covers to buy his first home.

David Lebson, treasurer of the organization of collectors of blocks of stamps containing the plate number and co-editor of the journal, described Mr. Fishman as a "helpful, considerate and gentle man who was dedicated to the society."

"He was always willing to share his knowledge or his services," Mr. Lebson said.

Benjamin J. Fishman was an avid stamp collector.

He also marveled at Mr. Fishman's memory, explaining that he would not take a list of coveted stamps to a show, like most collectors. "He would carry it in his head," Mr. Lebson said.

Mr. Fishman was also a founder, in 1945, of the League Chapter of the Labor Zionist Organization of America and was its first president.

Mr. Fishman was born in Mlynov, Russia, in 1910. He and his mother came to Baltimore in 1921 to join his father, who came here in 1912.

He graduated from the Baltimore Hebrew High School in 1926 and two years later from the Baltimore Hebrew College and Teachers Training School, now the Baltimore Hebrew University.

In 1933, he graduated from the Baltimore City College Evening School.

Mr. Fishman was a life member of the Society of Israel Philatelists, a former president of its Baltimore chapter and a member of the American Philatelic Society and the Baltimore Philatelic Society.

He also was a member of the Jewish Historical Society of Maryland and the Beth Am Congregation.

For 30 years, he was a member of the Summit Country Club.

A painter of still lifes and a few landscapes, he also used his talent for calligraphy in making award-winning displays of his stamps for exhibitions.

He traveled eight times to Israel and toured the United States, Canada, Europe, the Caribbean and North Africa.

Services were scheduled for 11 a.m. today at Sol Levinson & Bros. Home, 6010 Reisterstown Road, Baltimore.

He is survived by his wife of 60 years, the former Doris Vera Gruber; two daughters, Linda F. Lapides and Nancy F. Bloom, both of Baltimore; and a grandson.

The family suggested memorial contributions to the Jewish Historical Society of Maryland.

Obituary of Doris's husband, Benjamin J. Fishman who was from Mlynov. The Baltimore Sun, Oct. 15, 1993, p. 95.

***

Samuel Gruber

Samuel Gruber was the third child of Simha (Demb) Gruber and was also born in Mlynov. US records suggest his birth year variously as 1889, 1891, 1892, and 1893. His 1921 Declaration of Intention indicates his wife Bessie (Gospin) was born in "Bardechov, Russia" (Berdychiv), suggesting he was there with his father and brother in 1912 the year his brother Nathan's manifest indicated Berdychiv was his last residence. Samuel's 1930 US Census indicates he was age 18 when he married, suggesting he was in Berdychiv and married Bessie by ~1910. We can guess that business purposes took the two Gruber sons and their father to Novohrad and Berdychiv.

According to family stories overhead by their granddaughter growing up, Samuel and Bessie had a child before Sam fled to Baltimore so as not to be conscripted into the Tsar's army.[64] Sam hid in barns on his way to the port and reached Baltimore with the help of money sent by his brother Nathan. Sadly, their child died of starvation before Bessie could join him in the US later that year. This may explain why Bessie was able to join him before WWI, in contrast to Nathan's wife and daughters who missed the window and had to wait until after the War.

Sam left for Baltimore on January 10, 1913 from Bremen on the SS Brandenburg. He is listed as "Schapsy" Gruber, age 21, and like his brother, a brush maker. He arrived in Baltimore on

---

[64] Reported by Arlene (Kirson) Polangin, daughter of Sam and Bessie's daughter, Jean (Gruber) Kirson.

January 31, 1913. His last residence and birthplace listed is Mlynov, suggesting that he may have moved back to Mlynov from Berdichiv before leaving. His father Simha is listed as his closest relative in Mlynov, suggesting that he too had returned to Mlynov by 1913. This is the last trace we have of Simha (Demb) Gruber, the eldest son of the matriarch and patriarch Rivka and Israel Jacob.

Samuel's destination is his brother Nathan Gruber at 104 Albemarle Street, the address of their father's sister, Aunt Mollie (Demb) Roskes.

Manifest of the SS Brandenburg sailing from Bremen January 10, 1913

Manifest of SS Brandenburg - Schapsy Gruber 21 brush maker

Right-hand columns of manifest: last residence Mynov, closest relative father Gruber Simcha, Mlynov Volyn Russia

Page 2 of Samuel's manifest: headed to brother Gruber Nathan 104 Albemarle Str, Balto Md.

As we shall see, a number of other relatives and friends settled for a time at the Roskes residence at 104 Albemarle Street.

***

Samuel's Wife, Bessie (Gospin) Gruber Arrives

Nine months after Sam arrived in Baltimore he was joined by his wife Bessie, who followed his route and even took the same ship as Sam across the ocean. "Basie Gruber" traveled from Bremen on October 9, 1913 on the SS Brandenburg and arrived in Baltimore on Oct. 23rd. She is age 23 with an implied birth year of 1890; her last residence is Odessa and her closest relative there was her "mother Gospin [A. or R.] in Odesa."

It seems that Bessie must have headed to Odessa from Berdychiv after Sam left for America. Her passenger manifest lists Odessa as her birthplace as well, though Sam's Declaration of Intention in Baltimore lists her birthplace as Berdychiv. It seems likely that Berdychiv was her birthplace but she wrote Odessa to align her birthplace with her last residence. Bessie's destination is her "husband Gruber Sch 104 Albermarle Str" in Baltimore.

Bessie appears to be traveling with another woman named [Frdokia?] Shwetz [Shwartz?] from Odessa, who perhaps was a girlfriend. She was headed to someone named Schwartz in Baltimore.

Manifest of SS Brandenburg sailing from Bremen on Oct. 9, 1913

Basie Gruber's manifest showing her age 23 and her mother in Odessa

Destination is husband Gruber Sch 104 Albemarle Str.

In Baltimore, Sam and Bessie had five children: Jean (married name Jean Kirson) 1915-1984, Ida (married name Ida Goldstein Gaylor) 1916-1999, Nathan 1917-1989, Morris 1920-1980, and Vera (married name Vera Mendelsohn) 1924-2003.

Sam and his brother Nathan are still living at 104 Albemarle Street in 1915. That same year Sam and Bessie's eldest daughter Jennie (later Jean Kirson) was born. According to Jean's daughter, Arlene Polangin, her mother's name was shortened to Jean to avoid the frequent confusion with her first cousin Jeannie (daughter of Nathan), though Nathan's daughter also appears as Jeanne in some records. A second daughter Ida (later Goldstein/ Gaylor) was born in 1916.

1915 Baltimore City Directory for Nathan and Samuel Gruber.	" Nathan lab 104 Albemarle " Olive F dressmkr 826 n Mount h do " Reuben A pipeftr h 1929 Penrose av " Saml tailor 104 Albemarle

Figure 35 "The sandwich photo"
Courtesy of Tamara Kirson

1. Mollie (Gruber) Herman
2. Nathan Gruber
3. Nathan's wife Gertrude (Garfinkle)
4. Samuel Gruber
5. Samuel's wife Bessie (Gospin)
6. Jean Gruber
7. Ida Gruber
8. Morris Gruber
9. Nathan Gruber
10. Vera Gruber

Samuel filled out his WWI draft registration card in 1917. He lists his address as 117 S. Bond St. and like most Mlynov immigrants requested an exemption, his reason: "ill health." A son Nathan was born in 1917, another son Morris in 1920, and a daughter Vera (later Mendelsohn) was born in 1924. It is not clear why Samuel called his son "Nathan" when his brother Nathan was still alive.

The 1920 Census shows the family is living at 1746 Ashland Ave. Sam still has an alien status and did not pursue his naturalization until 1921 when he filled out his Declaration of Intention on November 9th of that year. A large hiatus intervened before he continued his naturalization process, possibly because Sam's grocery was placed under temporary injunction for violating the Volstead Act, informally known as Prohibition, which had become law in 1920.[65] He was not the only Mlynov-born grocer to violate Prohibition and get in trouble with the law for that reason.[66]

***

Sam Gruber Runs Afoul of Prohibition

Though Maryland was the 6th state to ratify the 18th amendment, the state was never able to muster legislation to enforce Prohibition. The result was that enforcement was done by the Federal government only and not by local enforcement.[67] Baltimore, in particular, was viewed as a center of resistance to Prohibition and was considered a "wet" city. Still, there were a number of arrests during the decade in Baltimore for the manufacturing and consumption of alcohol and at least four of these arrests touched relatives from Mlynov, as we know from news accounts published in *The Sun*.

A series of crackdowns on Baltimore establishments making or selling liquor began in the early 1920s. One enforcement sweep, in March 1924, which was targeted against "the big, commercial violators" and sent two persons to jail, also slapped a temporary injunction against Sam Gruber and his store operator, Abe Miller. The injunction was applied to 827 N. Calhoun Street where Sam and the family were also living. In 1922, Sam and Bessie were listed as grocers at that address.

On May 23, *The Evening Sun* reported that two new permanent injunctions were signed, one of which applied to the "Dwelling at 827 North Calhoun street: Abe Miller, operator: Samuel

---

[65] In January 1919, the Eighteenth Amendment, prohibiting "the manufacture, sale, or transportation of intoxicating liquors" within the United States, was ratified and would become the law of the land a year later in January 1920. The amendment did not make it illegal to possess or consume alcohol in private residences but only in public establishments. In contrast to its reluctance about suffrage, Maryland was the sixth state to join thirty-six other states that ratified this constitutional amendment. In October 1919, following ratification, Congress passed the "National Prohibition Act," more commonly known as the "Volstead Act," specifying how Prohibition would be defined and enforced in the land. In early January 1920, the Supreme Court declared constitutional both the Eighteenth Amendment and the Volstead Acts, setting the stage for their implementation starting January 16, 1920.
[66] The first Mlynov born grocer to run afoul of Prohibition was Isadore (Itshik) Lerner, the same man who had helped Nathan's wife and children migrate to the US. His grocery was raided on Sept. 4, 1921 (*The Baltimore Sun*, p. 8). Isaac Marder's grocery was raided on April 5, 1922. He pleaded guilty on June 2, 1922 and was fined $250.
[67] See Walsh, *Baltimore Prohibition: Wet and Dry in the Free State*, pp. 11-12. On the use of alcohol in Baltimore during this time, see pp. 88ff. On enforcement by the Fed, see p. 90, and enforcement against big commercial violators, see p. 90.

Gruber, owner." The article indicated that "the dwelling on Calhoun Street also can be occupied while under injunction if a $1,000 bond is posted." This was quite a lot of money at the time. We do not know whether Sam posted the bond, and perhaps, the inability to do so explains the family's multiple moves to two new addresses shortly after this date.

Injunctions

Two permanent injunctions were signed by Judge Morris A. Soper in the United States District Court yesterday for violation of the Volstead act. This brings the total of places permanently enjoined in Baltimore to 86. One hundred and eight temporary injunctions have been issued, making a grand total of 194.

According to court records the places permanently enjoined yesterday were:

Harmonie Cafe, 414 West Fayette street: George Burkhardt, Sr., his sons, George, Jr., William M. and Charles Burkhardt, and Frederick Foster, operators; Harmonie Building Company, owner.

Dwelling 827 North Calhoun street: Abe Miller, operator; Samuel Gruber, owner.

The Harmonie Cafe premises can be reopened under $1,000 bond for purposes other than as a place for sale of near-beer or soft drinks. The dwelling on Calhoun street also can be occupied while under injunction if a $1,000 bond is posted.

The Evening Sun, May 23, 1924, page 52

The announcement of the injunction against Sam and Abe Miller appears again in *The Baltimore Sun* on May 28. The good news is that Sam was granted a temporary rather than permanent injunction. Perhaps the fine had been paid.

The Prohibition violation apparently involved a grocery store or bar that Abe Miller was operating at the Gruber's 827 Calhoun address, since Sam and Bessie had a grocery store there in 1922. They may have purchased the property from Samuel Fox (husband of Sam Gruber's first cousin, Minnie), since a record of a transaction appears in *The Baltimore Sun* in August 1922.

Sometime in 1923, the Baltimore City Directory makes clear they moved their grocery store to a new address at 1341 W. Lafayette Street, while their home remained at 827 Calhoun, where the raid took place. Apparently, their operator Abe Miller was still operating at 827 Calhoun, even though they now had a grocery on Lafayette.

Abe Miller, the operator of the grocery, does not appear to have been deterred by the arrest. He is still listed in the city directory at 827 Calhoun in 1928 and 1930 after the Grubers left this address and moved on. He is arrested several more times for violating Prohibition after they apparently terminated their business relationship with him.

2 Are Jailed And 3 Fined For Liquor Violations

Four More Temporary Injunctions Granted Under Volstead Act.

Five more violators of the Volstead act pleaded guilty yesterday in United States Court, two being sent to jail and three fined.

Besides receiving a term of 60 days, John J. O'Connell forfeited his automobile. He was arrested on Washington Boulevard with 35 gallons of alcohol in the car. Tuzie Lifkin got three months for having on his premises on South Broadway materials for the manufacture of intoxicating liquor. For having liquor in their possession George H. Yaeger and Charles Berger each were fined $200 and Joseph Diggs $50.

Four more temporary injunctions were granted. They were against Abe Miller, Samuel Gruber and the premises, 827 North Calhoun street; James E. Donnelly, John H. Donnelly and 4110 Frederick avenue; Harry Wolf, Wolf Becker and 1028 Pennsylvania avenue, and William E. Brown, Thomas R. Hicks, Elizabeth Warner and 1612

The Baltimore Sun, March 28, 1924, p. 3

The Baltimore Sun, Aug. 29, 1922, p. 14	John Battaglia to Luciana del Acqua, s.e.s. Belair rd., nr. Brehm's lane, g.r. $75........ 5 Samuel Fox to Sam Gruber, s.e. cor. Lafayette ave. and Calhoun st., g.r. $97.......... 5 Robt. A. Fryer and wife to Wm. J. Miller and
1922 Baltimore City Directory	" Nathan* (Gert) grocer 2300 Etting h do " Olive F dressmkr 805 Appleton " Rose R The News 800 w Franklin " Ruben (Elbertia) pipeftr h 1929 Penrose " Saml clk 800 w Franklin " Saml (Bessie) grocer 827 Calhoun h do
1923 Baltimore City Directory	" Nathan (Gitre) gro 1347 Myrtle av h do " Olive F drsmkr 805 Appleton " Rose C sten 800 w Franklin " Rubin A (Alverta) pipeftr h1929 Penrose av " Saml (Bessie) gro 1341 w Lafayette av h827 n Calhoun
1924 Baltimore City Directory	" Nathan (Gertrude) gro 920 Cathedral h do " Olive F drsmkr 805 Appleton " Rosa C sten 2027 Madison av " Rubin A (Alverta) pipeftr h1929 Penrose av " Saml (Bessie) cigars 110 e Lexington h1644 Appleton

By the 1930 Census, Sam and Bessie moved the family to 795 Saratoga Street in Baltimore. The family was renting the property for $70.00. Sam is 38, Bessie, 39. The record indicates Sam was 18 and Bessie 19 when they first married. Sam and Bessie still have not been naturalized and are still listed as "AL," aliens. Their eldest daughter Jennie is now 15, Ida 14, Nathan 12, Morris 10 and Vera 4 and "9/12." All the children were citizens having been born in Maryland.

BARBER AND GROCER HELD UP BY BANDIT

Former Robbed Of $5 In Shop In Presence Of Two Customers

LATTER LOSES $17

Samuel Gruber Reports Gunman Forced Son To Empty Cash Register In Store

A barber and a grocer were held up in their establishments last night, and both told the police that the bandit who robbed them was a thin, well-dressed young man of about 25.

There were two customers in Fred Zeiler's barber shop at 1116 Carroll street when a bandit entered at 9 o'clock. At pistol point he forced Mr. Zeiler, Otto Nenzeh, of the 1500 block McHenry street, and Leonard Jenkins, of 1243 Carroll street, to a corner of the shop and then took $5 from the barber's pockets. He searched the cash register and, finding nothing, fled.

Grocery Store Held Up

An hour and a half later a bandit walked into the grocery of Samuel Gruber at 795 West Saratoga street. Mr. Gruber was in the rear of the store and his 15-year-old son Nathan was behind the counter.

The bandit asked for "the boss" and Nathan called his father. The robber pressed a gun against Mr. Gruber's side, forced his son to scoop $17 from the cash register and, after taking the money, fled.

Baltimore Sun, Dec. 02, 1932, page 3.

In 1932, the grocery at Saratoga was robbed by a well-dressed young man. Nathan was in the store at the time when the bandit demanded to see the "boss." When Sam appeared, the robber held the gun to his side and demanded that Nathan give him the $17 in the cash register. Sam was not the only Mlynov-born grocer in Baltimore to be robbed. Five years later his first cousin, Benjamin Schwartz was robbed and killed in his grocery store, in what produced one of the largest manhunts in Baltimore in more than 15 years (discussed later).

Not long after this robbery, Sam and Bessie's daughter, Jean, captured a cute moment in family life, submitting a funny comment by her younger sister Ida to a column that *The Evening Sun* ran on witticisms of children.

Children's Bright SAYINGS

One evening while having company I was telling my friend that our cat had kittens and I remarked how very white their fur was. My little sister, who was listening, said:

"No wonder they're so white, they were born in a flour barrel."

JEAN GRUBER,
795 W. Saratoga street.

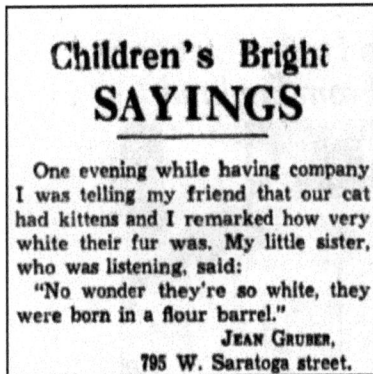

The Evening Sun, April 13, 1934, p. 32

By 1935 the family left Baltimore for the District of Columbia. There in 1937, Sam and Bessie's two eldest daughters both married. Ida married Louis Goldstein (later Gaylor) on February 28, 1937, and Jean married Julius Kirson six months later on August 22, 1937. In the 1940 census in the District of Columbia, the family is living at 4506 Georgia Ave NW. The census record indicates that Sam's naturalization is finally pending.

In February 1944, a memorable photo of the family appeared in the Washington *Evening Star* Bessie and her daughters were crowded around a radio waiting to hear her two sons, who were meeting up in England during the War. A photo of the two sons was set on top of the radio.

One of her daughters remarked that they had never seen their mother speechless before. Bessie was tied up in knots ever since she received a telegram that her two sons, who were somewhere in England, were meeting up and going to speak on a broadcast arranged by the BBC.

Her son Morris had been overseas for two years, and she hadn't spoken to him in that time. Her son, "Nat," left for overseas only a few weeks before; his finance Miriam Holzman was present and was twisting her engagement ring as they waited to hear the two boys speak.

Bessie's husband, Sam, was in the store but had taken a radio with him in case he couldn't make it home in time. Eventually, the boys were brought on the air and got to say their names. No time had been left for them to say anything else. Still the family was still excited to have heard their voices. They had not heard Morris's voice in over two years.

Mother Sticks Close to Radio to Hear Voices Of 2 Soldier Sons in Broadcast From England

Family Gets Thrill As Brothers Are Introduced on Air

By FRANCES LIDE.

The mother, Mrs. Sam Gruber, twisted a handkerchief in her hands and walked restlessly about the house—but within earshot of the radio.

She kept glancing out the window, hoping that her husband would come in soon, but she didn't have much to say to the womenfolk about her. There were a lot of them—her three daughters, the fiancee of one of her sons, her 4-year-old granddaughter and several neighbors who had come in.

"I never saw Mrs. Gruber before when she didn't have anything to say," one of them remarked.

But the mother had been like that since the afternoon before when she received the telegram. The telegram that said her two sons "somewhere in England" were to be included on a broadcast arranged by the BBC servicemen's program, "American Eagle in Britain."

One of the boys, Morris, has been in England about two years, one of his sisters said. He's a corporal and will be 24 in April.

Nathan, who is 26 and a sergeant, has been overseas only for a few weeks.

The family received several letters from both of them Friday, but the boys hadn't managed to get together when the last letters were written—10 days earlier.

One of the sisters pointed to an enlarged snapshot over the radio. "That was taken the last time they were together—two and a half years ago, I guess," she said. "They were both home on furlough."

Nat's fiancee, Miss Miriam Holzman, who lives with his family in the corner house at 315 Oglethorpe street N.W., twisted the diamond ring on her finger. Mrs. Gruber patted her freshly marcelled hair—this was an occasion, though her boys wouldn't see her—and went to the telephone to confer again with the boys' father. He might be able to make it, she reported, but if he couldn't come home, he'd taken a radio to the store. Saturday afternoon was such a busy time.

The Grubers gather around the radio. Seated, left to right: Mrs. Sam Gruber, the mother; Mrs. Louise Goldstein, a sister; 4-year-old Arlene Kirson, a niece, and Miss Vera Gruber, a sister. Standing are Miss Miriam Holzman (left), fiance of Sergt. Nathan Gruber, and Mrs. Julius Kirson, a sister. On the radio are pictures of Sergt. Nathan Gruber (left) and Corpl. Morris Gruber. —Star Staff Photo.

Figure 36 Gruber family by the radio
The Evening Star, February 27, 1944, p. 20

Then Mrs. Gruber looked at the clock and hastily pulled up a hassock to the radio. It was almost 5:30—time for the program to start. A British announcer's voice was heard. Mrs. Gruber beckoned her children to come closer.

First there was interviews with four boys from as many States. But the group didn't hear much that was said. They were waiting for Morris and Nat.

Then there was a "musical break," and more boys from more States. Finally the announcer carried his audience to a "brother's dinner." The Grubers were tense. Almost before they knew it, the emcee was calling on two brothers from Washington. He asked them to give their names, and their voices came in clearly. "Corpl. Morris Gruber." "Sergt. Nathan Gruber."

That was all they had a chance to say, but as far as their family was concerned the program was over as the announcer continued to make the rounds at the brother's dinner.

Mrs. Gruber needed her handkerchief now. And almost in a single gesture the girls reached for theirs, too.

Finally the mother could speak again. "That was the first time I've heard Morris' voice in two years," she said. "And now they are together."

Somebody rushed to the telephone to check with the father. "It sounded swell," he reported. "I'm sorry they didn't say anything, but they sounded swell."

That's just like Mr. Gruber, a neighbor remarked. "He's always so calm—never gets excited."

Figure 37 Wedding of Nathan Gruber, son of Samuel and Bessie.
Courtesy of Tamara Kirson and Arlene (Kirson) Polangin

1. Samuel Gruber
2. Bessie (Gospin) Gruber
3. Morris Gruber
4. Vera (Gruber) Mendelsohn
5. Nathan Gruber, groom
6. Miriam (Holzman), bride
7. Ida (Gruber) Gaylor
8. Louis Gaylor
9. Jean (Gruber) Kirson
10. Julius Kirson
11. Arlene (Kirson) Polangin

Gruber, 82, operated food store chain

Silver Spring, Md. (Special) —Funeral services for Samuel Gruber, a retired food store owner, were held yesterday at the Danzansky funeral establishment in Washington.

Mr. Gruber died Saturday at the Bel Pre Health Center in Silver Spring after a long illness. He was 82.

He was born in Russia and came to Baltimore in 1910. Mr. Gruber and his family opened a chain of food stores that bore their name.

Retired in 1950

In 1936, he moved to Washington where the family continued in the food business. Mr. Gruber retired in 1950.

He was past president of the Odd Fellows and was a founder of the District Mutual

Building Association and the Ideal Loan Association.

Mr. Gruber also helped organize the Agudath Achim Synagogue and was a member of the Argo Lodge of B'nai B'rith and the George Washington Lodge.

He was active in the United Jewish Appeal, the Hebrew Home of Greater Washington, and the Jewish Community Center.

Mr. Gruber is survived by two sons, Nathan and Morris Gruber, both of Silver Spring; three daughters, Mrs. Jean Kirson, of Silver Spring, Mrs. Ida Taylor, of Wheaton, Md., and Mrs. Vera Mendelson, of Rockville; 13 grandchildren and 2 great-grandchildren.

Obituary of Samuel Gruber, The Baltimore Sun, June 9, 1973, p. 12

***

US Records Summary for Children of Simha (Demb) Gruber

US Records for Mollie (Gruber) Israel Herman

1911 Census of England and Wales	Census for Mary Herman (Mollie Gruber) and husband Israel Herman. Living at 10 Davis Avenue Hunt St, Mile End New Town Brixton. Israel is age 30 with implied birth year of 1881 and Mary is 28, implied birth year of 1883. Israel is listed as a cabinet maker. They have been married 12 years with implied year of marriage in 1899. They had five children and 4 are still alive: Jane (later Jennie Bernstein) age 10 with implied birth year of 1901, born in Russia, Sarah (later Sarah Newman) age 5 born in Austria, Hyman (later Albert) age 2 born in London, and Rebecca (later Betty Davidson) age 1 born in London. [Family oral tradition records that the child who died was named Herschel and he died in 1907 in a story told in the narrative above.]
1911 (Nov. 1) Canadian Passenger manifest	Line 11. Israel "Erbman," age 29, implied birth year 1882. Departed Rotterdam, Netherlands [no date given] on SS Uranium and arrived on Nov. 1, 1911 in Halifax, Nova Scotia. Destination Montreal. Listed as carpenter travelled inland on C.P.R. [railroad]
1911 (Nov. 27) US Border Crossing from Canada to US	Entering in Buffalo, NY: Israel Erbman, place of birth Dubna Russia, age 29, Cabinet maker, last permanent residence Toronto, wife Malia Erbman, 516 Oxford Street, London, England. Destination: Baltimore, Md, uncle S. Roskes 104 Albemarle St. "seek work" Date of landing: Halifax, Nov. 1, 1911, 3rd Uranium. Dates 11/27/11 in Buffalo, N. Y.
1911 Manifest of Alien Passenger Applying for Admission at Port of Buffalo.	Line 16. Israel Erbman age 29, implied year of birth 1882, cabinet maker. Hebrew from Russia, last permanent residence, Toronto. Nearest relative: wife Madig Erbman, 316 Oxford st. London, England. Destination: Baltimore, Md. Page 2: destination (uncle) S. Roskes, 104 Albemarle St. Balt. Md., birthplace Dubna. Seaport of Landing: Halifax, Date of landing 11/1/11. Name of SS: Uranium. Date of examination: Nov. 27.

1912 (Aug 11) Passenger Manifest	Line 13. Manifest of Mary "Herman" and children. Departed Liverpool on Aug. 3rd, 1912, and arrived in NY on August 11. Mary, age 30, with implied birth year of 1882. Friend in London Mrs. Solomon 314 Oxford St. Stepney, London 6. Destination; Baltimore, MD, [Page 2] Destination; Husband Israel Herman 104 Albemarle St. Baltimore Maryland. Place of birth: Russia, Plotsk [Lutsk?]. The children: Jane [Jennie] age 11 birthplace same as mother, Sarah age 6 birthplace same, Hyman age 4, born in London, Rebecca age 2 born in London.
1920 US Federal Census	Herman family. Living at 1636 McHenry Street, Baltimore. Israel age 42, implied birth year of 1878, O[wns home] mortgage F[ree]. Mary age 38 with implied birth year of 1882. They are all listed as migrating in 1911. Israel's occupation is store keeper and owns store. Their naturalization is pending (PA). The children are listed as Sarah, age 12, born in Austria, Hyman age 11, born in England, Rebecca age 11 born in England, Joseph age 6 born in Maryland and Sadie (later Salley Chancey) age 5 born in Maryland. Daughter Jennie has already married Michael Bernstein and moved out of the house (see her 1920 Census summary)
1920 (Nov. 24) Declaration of Intention	Israel Herman, age 39, hardware merchant, born in "Mlinow, Russia Poland" on April 6, 1881, living at 1915 Clifton Ave. Emigrated to US from Toronto on "(Railroad unknown)"; wife's name Mary, born at "Mlinow, Russia Poland." I arrived at port of Buffalo on Nov. 20, 1913.
1920 US Federal Census	Jenny (Herman) Bernstein. Now married to Michael Bernstein. Living with husband's family at 6th St. District of Columbia, N. W. Jenny is listed as "daughter-in-law" age 20. Immigration year 1912. Na[turalized] in 1919 [probably through her marriage to Michael, who was already naturalized]. Michael age 33, Immigration year 1895, NA[turalized] 1900.
1923 (Feb 27) Petition for Naturalization	Israel Erbman also known as Israel Herman, 1915 Clifton Ave, Baltimore. Real Estate Agent. Born April 6, 1881 at Malinow, Poland. Arrived in the US from Toronto, Canada on or about the 27th of November 1911 at the port of Buffalo on the Michigan Central Rairoad. Wife's name: Mary, born on May 30th, 1883 at Malinow, Poland. I have 6 children: Jennie birthdate Oct. 30th, 1900 Mlinow, Poland [lives at 906 Whitelock], Sarah Marian birthdate March 26, 1907 in Austria, Hyman Aug. 6, 1908 London England, Rebecca May 20, 1910, London, Joseph June 14th 1913 Baltimore, and Sadie Feb 21, 1915. Signed Israel Erbman. Witnesses: Benjamin Schwartz, Real Estate Agent, 2116 E. Fayette St, and Samuel Fox, Real Estate Agent, 2307 Callow Ave.
1930 (April 7) US Federal Census	Israel "Hillman" residing at 2309 Wichita Ave, Baltimore, age 50, Owns home, value $7,000, age at marriage 23 with implied year of 1903, Mother Tongue for all the family listed as "English", year of immigration 1912 [actually 1911], naturalized, occupation: real estate agent. Mary age 45, age at marriage 18 with implied year of 1903, year of immigration 1913 [actually 1912]; Children: Sarah age 23 born in England, occupation: chemist in hospital, Albert [previously Hyman] 22, born in England, occupation: owner of Hardware Store, Betty age 20, born in England, Joe age 16 born in Maryland, Sadie 15 born in Maryland. See daughter Jennie's census below.
1930 (April 12) US Federal Census	For family of daughter Jennie (Herman) Bernstein. 122 Biddle Street, Baltimore. Listed as Mary J. Bernstein. Age 29 (implied birth year 1901, age at marriage 18. Born in England [actually Russia] Language English. Immigration year 1910 [actually 1912], Na[turalized]. Husband Michael Bernstein, Rents home, value $60, age 42, age at marriage 31, born in Russia, immigration year 1895, owns grocery store. Children: Sylvia (later Kaplowitz) age 9, born in Maryland, son Mishal ("Buddy") age 8, born in Maryland, Marion (later Esterson), age 4, born in District of Columbia.

1940 (April) US Federal Census	2309 Wichita Ave, Baltimore. Israel Herman, age 60, Education 8th grade, NA[turalized], real estate, owns business. Mary age 57, AL[alien]. Children all out of the house.
1950 US Federal Census	Mollie Herman and brother Nathan Gruber Residing at 2309 Wichita Ave, Mollie Herman, head, age 66, widowed, Nathan Gruber, brother, age 66, widowed.

US records Summary for Nathan Gruber and family

1912 (Nov. 22) Passenger Manifest	Line 16. Nusen Gruber, departing Nov. 10, 1912 from Bremen, Germany, on the SS Neckar arriving in Philadelphia on Nov. 22nd. Age 22 with implied birth year of 1890. Occupation brush maker, last residence Novogrod [Novoghrad Volinski]. Nearest relative in country of origin: father Gruber Simha Berditcheff, Kiev, headed to Baltimore. Page 2: He is headed to br.i.l [brother-in-law] Israel Herman 106 Albemarle St., Baltimore Md. Born in Melynow. Nathan is on the same ship with the family of his Aunt Yenta (Demb) Schwartz and her husband Chaim and their two younger sons. See their record above. They are on a different page of the same manifest. Also on the same ship is Chaim's sister-in-law, Sarah Fishman and her kids. Her nephew, "Mojochs Fischman" (son of her brother David Fishman) is listed next to Nathan Gruber on the manifest.
1919 (Nov. 12) Declaration of Intention	First Declaration of Intention. Nathan Gruber, age 34, Grocer, born in Mlnov, Russia, on June 16, 1885, resides at 102 Albemarle St. Emigrated to US on "Neckar," my last residence was Novogradvalynsk, my wife Gitel resides at Novogradvalynsk, he arrived at port of Philadelphia, on Dec. 15, 1912.
1920 (Jan 9) US Federal Census	2300 Etting Street, Baltimore. Nathen Gruber owns his unit with a mortgage. He is 34, immigration year 1913 [incorrect], his naturalization is PA [pending] as of 1919. His birthplace Volin [=Volyn District] Russia, occupation is proprietor of a Grocery store. He has a number of people lodging with him with an illegible surname that looks like Brooke.
1920 (July 12) Passenger Manifest	Nathan's wife Gitla Gruber and children. Sailing from Southhampton, England, on July 3, 1920 on the SS Imperator and arriving in New York on July 12. Gitla age 30, last residence Rowno, closest relative Shesl Miller [remembered in family as Shaya Meiler/Malar who married Nehuma Shulman daughter of Pearl (Demb) Shulman]. Headed to husband Nathan Gruber 102 Albenarce [Albemarle] Street. Place of birth Rowno. Children Zenia [later Jennie Feinberg] age 10, Dora [later Doris V. Fishman] age 8.
1924 (May 7) Declaration of Intention	Second Declaration of Intention. Nathan Gruber, age 38, a grocer, born in "Mlinowe Russia on May 16, 1885. Living at 1233 E. Pratt Str. Baltimore, Md. Wife Gertrude, she was born at Novograd Volinsk [Novohrad-Volynsky also called Zviahel], Russia. I arrived at Philadelphia Sept. 15, 1913 [incorrect]
1926 (June 29) Petition for Naturalization	For Nathan Gruber. Nathan Gruber 1900 Kennedy Ave, Baltimore Maryland, Grocer, born July 16, 1885 at Mlinow, Russia, lists correct immigration information. Married to Gertrude, born 1883 at Novogradvolinsk, Russia now resides with me. Children Jennie (later Jennie Feinberg) born Sept. 13, 1908, Novogradvolinsk; Doris (later Doris V. Fishman) Feb. 5th, 1910 in Novogradvolinsk; Sylvia May 1, 1921 in Baltimore Maryland. Signed by brother-in-law Israel Herman, merchant 1915 Clifton Ave and Samuel Fox, Real Estate Broker, 2307 Clifton Ave.
1926 (Nov. 8th)	Nathan Gruber, age 40, Children Jennie, 18 years, Doris 16, Sylvia 5.

Order of Admission for Naturalization	
1930 US Federal Census	1900 Kennedy Street, Baltimore. Nathan Gruber, owns home, $6000 value, R (owns a radio set)age 44, age at marriage 22, year of immigration 1913 [incorrect] Na[turalized], Proprietor Grocery, wife Gertrude, age 44, age at marriage 22, immigration year 1913 [incorrect] Na[turalized]. Children: Jean, age 20, born in Russia, librarian City of Baltimore, Doris age 18, born in Russia, stenographer for Decorator, Sylvia age 9 born in Maryland.
1940 (April 23) US Federal Census	Residing at 1900 Kennedy Ave. Nathan Gruber, head, age 54, born in Russia, Na[turalized], same house in 1935, Store Keeper, Groceries, Gertrude wife, age 54, born in Russia, Al[ien] Sylvia daughter, born in Baltimore
1950 US Federal Census	Mollie Herman and brother Nathan Gruber Residing at 2309 Anoka Ave, Mollie Herman, head, age 66, widowed, Nathan Gruber, brother, age 66, widowed.

US Records Summary Samuel Gruber and family

1913 (Jan 31) Passenger Manifest	Line 10. Schapsy Gruber, age 21 implied birth year 1892, Brush maker, Sailing from Bremen, Jan. 10, 1913 on SS Brandenburg arriving Baltimore Jan. 31, 1913. His last residence and birthplace is Mlynov/Mlynow, Russia and his closest relative is father Gruber Simcha in Mlynov, Volyn, Russia. He is headed to brother Gruber Nathan 104 Albemarle Str Baltimore Maryland.
1913 (Oct. 23) Passenger Manifest	Basie Gruber traveled from Bremen on Oct. 9, 1913 on the SS Brandenburg and arrived in Baltimore on Oct 23, 1913. She is age 23, implied birth year of 1890, her last residence is Odessa and the closest relatives is mother Gospin [A. or R.) in Odesa. She is headed to husband Gruber Sch 104 Albermarle Str Balto. Odessa is listed as her birthplace.
1917 (June 5) WWI Registration Card	Samuel Gruber 117 S. Bond St. Date of birth: 1891. Alien. born Malinov Wolina [=Volyn] Russia, Store keeper, wife and two children exemption requested: ill health
1920 (January) US Federal Census	Lives at 1746 Ashland Ave, Samuel Gruber, O[wns home] has M[mortgage], age 27, with implied year of birth as 1893, Immigration year 1912 [incorrect], alien status, Retail Merchant, Garment. Wife Bessie [Gospin], 27 implied birth year 1893, Immigration year 1914 [incorrect], alien status. Children; Jennie (later Jean Kirson) age 5, born in Maryland, Ida (later Ida Goldstein Gaylor) age 3 born in Maryland, Nathan age 1 born in Maryland
1921 (Nov. 9) Declaration of Intention	Sapsey Gruber also known as Sam Gruber, age 31, scar on forehead, born Mlynow, Russia, on Dec. 21, 1889. Resides 1746 Ashland Ave, Baltimore. Emigrated from Bremen, Germany on vessel Brandenburg, my last foreign residence was Bardechov, Russia [Berdychiv, Ukraine] wife Bessie. She was born in Bardeave, Russia [Berdychiv, Ukraine]. arrived Dec 18, 1911 [incorrect]
1930 (April 5) US Federal Census	Lives at 795 Saratoga Street, Sam Gruber Renting home $70, age 38 with implied birth year of 1892, age at marriage 18 with implied marriage year 1910 [he was not yet in US], ~~Russia~~ Poland, Immigration year 1912 [incorrect], alien status, Grocer owns business; wife Bessie age 39 with implied year of birth 1891, age at marriage 19, ~~Russia~~ Poland, immigration year 1914, alien status; [children]: Jennie (later Jean Kirson) age 15 born in Maryland, Ida (later Ida Goldstein Gaylor) age 14 born in Maryland, Nathan age 12 born in Maryland, Morris age 10 born in Maryland, Vera (later Vera Mendelsohn) 4 and 3/4 born in Maryland.
1940 (April 9) US Federal Census	Lives at 1618 8th Street District of Columbia, Samuel Gruber, head, Rents, home value $80, age 48, lived in Baltimore in 1935, Naturalization PA (pending), Store keeper, Store, wife

	Bessie, age 48, alien status. Children: [Jennie and Ida out of the house], Nathan 21 born in Maryland, Morris 19 born in Maryland, Vera B age 14 born in Maryland
1940 (April 4) US Federal Census	Home of Jennie (Gruber) Kirson. Married Julius Kirson, Aug. 22, 1937 Julius Kirson, 4506 Georgia Ave NW, District of Columbia, head, age 29, place of birth Dist of Col. lived in same place in 1935, store manager Liquor Store, wife Jean Kirson, age 25, place of birth Maryland, lived in same place in 1935, Children: Arlene age 3 [months] born in Dist of Col.
1940 (April 10) US Federal Census	Home of Ida (Gruber) Goldstein. Married Louis Goldstein 28 Feb 1937. Living at 762 Princeton Place NW, District of Columbia. Louis Goldstein (lodger) age 23, born in Maryland clerk in retail grocery store, wife Ida B[eatrice] lodger, age 24, born in Maryland, both lived in same place in 1935.

***

CHAPTER 5

THE FAMILY OF PEARL MALKA DEMB AND TSODIK SHULMAN

Pearl Malka Demb (~1865-1933) was born in Mlynov. She is one of my two Demb great-grandmothers.[68] Her married name became Pearl Malka Shulman.

Pearl Malka Demb is listed as the third of Demb daughters in the family tree scroll. However, Clara Fram in her memoir remembers her "Aunt Pearl" as the "second daughter" of Israel Jacob and Rivka. This order seems to fit the US records which list Pearl as born in 1865 according to her passenger manifest and Petition, making her older than the next daughter, Yenta.

Figure 38 Pearl Malka Demb, nephew David Schulman, husband Tsodik Shulman
date uncertain[69]

---

[68]Her youngest daughter Pepe was my paternal grandmother.
[69] David was born in 1879 and appears to be 40 something in this photo which would make this photo about 1921 or later after he went back to Mlynov to help the Shulman family migrate (story below). He looks a lot like he does in his 1920 passport application to return to Europe. However, Pearl looks younger here than she does in a large photo which was probably about 1913. So it is unclear when this photo was taken.

"Pearl Malka," as she was later remembered in the family by descendants, married a man by the name of Tsodik Shulman. His birthdate is listed as April 12, 1863, on his and Pearl's Petition for Naturalization, though his 1921 manifest suggests he was born earlier in 1861. (My brother Richard and another descendant, Richard Brodsky, were named after Tsodik).

"The Shulmans" were the only family of cousins that Clara mentions in her memoir from her Mlynov period. She recalls:

> There was a Russian school somewhere in the area. Frequently, our cousin Hertz Shulman, a youth of about seventeen, a student in that school, would stop in our house to study, memorizing his work, while walking back and forth in the room with his book. We knew he was the son of my Aunt Pearl [Pearl Malka Demb] and her distinguished husband [Tsodik Shulman] whom my grandfather [Israel Jacob Demb] was delighted to have marry his second daughter. This man had arrived in Mlynow from Lithuania, well educated, rolling his R's when he spoke Yiddish; an emancipated, proud Jew, resembling one's image of Tolstoi, and possessing books in Hebrew and Russian, as well as Yiddish translations of French novels. He also subscribed to a Yiddish newspaper, and would talk to my grandfather about his uncle, the famous Hebrew writer, Kalman Shulman.

Clara recalls that her grandfather, Israel Jacob, would have preferred that her own mother Pesse had also married a scholar, so he was delighted when his second daughter, Pearl Malka, married a learned man. According to Pearl's 1930 census, she married when she was 20 (in 1885) and this fits with the birth of their first child Nehuma in 1887. They had seven children by 1905, when Pearl Malka was about 40.

***

A Note About Tsodik's Uncle, Kalman Schulman (1819–1899)

Tsodik Shulman had an illustrious pedigree. His uncle, Kalman Schulman, is well-known as one of the prominent "maskilim" (literally "enlightened ones") in Russia who was learning European languages and reading the science, literature and philosophy of Western tradition.

One scholarly article[70] describes Kalman as "the most prolific popularizer of universal and Jewish history during the reign of Alexander II." He wrote, adapted and translated almost thirty books and many more articles at his own initiative and under the aegis of the Society for the Promotion of Enlightenment among the Jews. All were written in Hebrew which Schulman believed should be diligently preserved and fostered.

He belonged to the Vilna circle of moderate maskilim and he earned his living teaching Hebrew in the secondary school attached to the rabbinic seminary. Thousands of his books were

---

[70] See "Kalman Schulman: The First Professional Popularizer." In Shmuel Feiner, *Haskalah and History: The Emergence of a Modern Jewish Historical Consciousness.* Oxford: The Littman Library of Jewish Civilization, 2004.

sold. Thanks to his strongly religious approach, his books found their way onto the bookshelves of even non-maskilic [non-modern] homes.

Kalman Schulman's uncle was Naftali Hirtz Schulman (?–1830 Amsterdam) whom one scholar considers an early Maskilic [modern] writer in Eastern Europe.[71] It seems possible that Tsodik named his own son Harry (Naftali Hertz) after this Shulman ancestor.

***

No one is sure what brought Tsodik Shulman to Mlynov. One of Pearl and Tsodik's grandsons, Ted Fishman, speculates that Tsodik was in the Russian army and came through Mlynov where he met and fell in love with the beautiful Pearl Demb. But we have no proof of that. And since hearing this speculation, I discovered that Tsodik had a sister, Sarah (Shulman) Steinberg who was living in Mlynov and eventually followed two of her children to the States leaving behind a daughter and granddaughter back in Mlynov.[72] The presence of Tsodik's sister in Mlynov suggests that more of the Shulman family settled there than we previously knew.

Tsodik is remembered in the family as a manager of the forest for the local nobleman, the Count. Clara has another endearing memory of her visit to the Shulman home on the edge of the forest. Clara writes:

> A visit with my Shulman cousins in their forest home was always exciting. Their father was the important manager of the entire forest. My recollection of their beautiful mother, my mother's sister, was that she wore a sweeping "pin-yar" (peignoir) and was generally reading books.

> I was about four or five years old on this particular visit when I found myself in the custody of their servant girl together with my three cousins [the youngest three, Sarah, Clara and Pepe] between the ages of four to seven. The girl was to take us into the woods and tell us some stories. One of the stories appeared rather strange to me. It was about what mamas and daddies do with each other, and she vividly illustrated on her own body how they go about it. There was no daddy in my house [i.e., her father David was in America], so why not wait for another story, a prettier one, I thought.

> It wasn't until I was in the sixth grade in Baltimore that some of my chummy classmates, in their own way, clarified that confusing tale I heard in the woods.

---

[71] See Chapter 4 of David E. Fishman, *Russia's First Modern Jews: the Jews of Shklov*. New York: New York University Press, 1996. On the relationship to Kalman Schulman and Naftali Hertz, see the short essay "Naphtali Herz Schulman" on the Ohio State University Website. Retrieved March 3, 2023.

[72] On how I discovered that Tsodik's sister was from Mlynov, see my essay, "The Search for Simon Steinberg." https://kehilalinks.jewishgen.org/Mlyniv/Ravings_of_a_genealogist.html#SimonSteinberg

The photo below on the left is of the three youngest Shulman daughters (from left to right: Pepe, Chaika and Sura), possibly around the age when they learned about the birds and the bees with their cousin Clara. Pepe appears to be holding a bunch of flowers, which perhaps she collected in the fields near their home. In the photo on the right, possibly between 1915-1919, Pepe (left) and Chaika (right) with unknown person in the back. They appear to be standing near a bridge and it looks like water, perhaps the Ikva River, behind them.

Figure 39 Youngest Shulman daughters
Courtesy of Karen Passero

The beautiful photo of the Shulman family below probably comes from the period just before WWI, taken in circa ˜1910-13. We have seen it before because it is one of only two photos of Rivka and Israel Jacob Demb. Pepe (my grandmother) sits in the front center with her elbow up on the knee of her grandmother Rivka. She appears to be about 6-7 years old. Her birth year was listed variously as 1904, 1905, 1906 according to US records. Israel and Rivka's great-granddaughter, Tamar Meiler, sits in the very front. The Shulman family does not appear to be as strictly religious as the previous generation. Neither Pearl nor Tsodik have their head covered. It appears the two eldest Shulman daughters, who are married and standing in the back, have their hair tied, but not covered (though it is difficult to tell if they are wearing wigs).

Figure 40 The Shulman Family ~ 1913
Courtesy of Pam Berman

1. Israel Jacob Demb
2. Rivka (Gruber)
3. Pearl (Demb) Shulman
4. Tsodik Shulman
5. Nehuma (Shulman)
   Miller/Meiler/Mejler
6. Nehuma's husband Saul
   Miller/Meiler/Mejler
7. Liza (Shulman) Koszhushner
8. Liza's husband, Shia (Shaya)
   Koszhushner
9. Shimon (Simon) Shulman
10. Harry (Ertz) Shulman
11. Sara (Sura) Shulman
12. Clara (Chaika) Shulman
13. Pepe Shulman
14. Tamar Meiler (daughter of Saul and
    Nehuma)

Based on US records, the birth years of the Tsodik and Pearl's children appear to be as follows.

Table 2 Children of Pearl Malka (Demb) and Tsodik Shulman

Nehuma Shulman (1887-˜1942)	Born March 14, 1887 according to Tsodik's 1928 Petition for Naturalization and Pearl's 1929 Petition for Naturalization. Married Saul (Miller, Meiler , Mejler [or Malar?]). They had two daughters: Tamara and Nina. The family perished fleeing from the Nazis in 1942. It is believed they perished at Babi Yar.
Liza Shulman (1889- ?)	Born Aug. 20, 1889 according to Tsodik's 1928 Petition for Naturalization and Pearl's 1929 Petition for Naturalization. Married Shia or Shaya/ Shia Koszhushner. Family fled to Russia and survived there in Kyiv. After the breakup of the Soviet Union, their children were reunited with US first cousins in early 1990s.
Simon (Shimon) Shulman (1890-1970)	Born Nov. 6, 1890 according to his father and mother's Petitions, and 1890 according to his 1922 passenger manifest, his Declaration of Intention, and his and wife's Petitions of Naturalization. Married Edith Fixman ("Alta Ides Szulman"). Came to the US in 1922 with Edith. His records say he was born in Staro-Bikhov (Stary Bykhov), but this was probably a lie to deal with customs for reasons in the narrative below. He was probably born in Mlynov like his siblings.
Harry Shulman (also called "Ertz" and "Naftali Hertz") (˜1893-1964)	Born Dec. 25, 1894 according to his father and mother's Petitions, 1893 according to his passenger manifest, 1894 according to his wife's 1927 Petition, and 1896 according to the 1930 census. Married Yetta (Eta) Perelson just before migration in 1921. Arrived in Baltimore in 1921, traveling with his parents, sisters and friend Paul Settleman. He came under the identity of his brother Simon Shulman and gave his identity to Paul Settleman.
Sara (Sura) Shulman (˜1898-1988)	Born Sept. 5, 1898 according to her father's and mother's Petitions, 1899 according to her 1921 passenger manifest, and 1896 according to the 1930 census. In Baltimore, married Pesach Zutelman/Settleman from Mervits. Pesach or "Uncle Paysie" pretended to be Harry Shulman in the 1921 passage of the Shulmans to America. He retained the Shulman name in America to avoid issues in his naturalization process.
Clara (Chaika) Shulman (˜1903-1990)	Born in 1903 according to her passenger manifest, May 27, 1903 according to her husband Ben Fishman's 1925 Petition, May 1st 1904 according to her father's 1928 Petition, May 27th 1902 according to her mother's 1929 Petition, and 1905 according to the 1930 Federal Census. In Baltimore married Benjamin Fishman who was also from Mlynov. Ben arrived in 1920.
Pepe (also called Pauline) Shulman (˜1905-1985)	Born in 1905 according to passenger manifest, Sept. 14, 1906 according to the 1928 Petition of father; Oct 18, 1904 according to her mother's 1929 Petition, 1907 according to 1930 Census. In Baltimore, married first cousin Paul Schwartz who also was from Mlynov. He was the son of Yenta [Demb] and Chaim Schwartz. Paul arrived with his family in 1912. Pepe arrived in 1921 with her family.

***

The Shulmans Between 1909 and 1921

Not much is known about the Shulman family life between 1909 and 1921 when they left for Baltimore. There is a family oral tradition that they were evacuated to Novohrad Volynski during WWI. We can imagine how terrifying this experience might have been for the kids from an essay written by Helen Lederer for the Mlynov Memorial Book. Helen (called Chultzie Gelberg then) was born in Mlynov in 1903, about the same age as Pepe and Clara Shulman. Helen was probably 11 or 12 when they were evacuated. She vividly recalled:

> It was during the time of the first World War. A cold winter day, a burning frost, a deep snow. The Germans are getting closer to our town Mlynov. All of us are taken out of our homes. The soldiers intrude into the synagogue sanctuary and pack us inside, like sardines. We are lying in great anxiety—not knowing what to expect. 2:00 a.m. An angry wind howls, like devils dancing. A banging is heard. Soldiers are standing with guns. They order everybody to go out into the street.
>
> The soldiers have brought wagons, which are standing there: "Pack what you can on the wagons, and you—walk." The horses can barely drag themselves in the deep snow. Women and children shlep after the wagons on the way to Varkevetsh. Everybody's hands are busy grabbing provisions for the children to eat. My mother, Gitl (Pesye Khoylye's daughter), has four small, crying children shlepping along with her. Also my Aunt Soreke (Pesye Khoylye's daughter) is going, carrying something in both hands, with her little girl Dvoyrele. After having walked a few versts, Soreke looked around - the child is not there!... She screamed; there was a commotion; Soreke ran back. The soldiers with their rifles drove on and said that the Austrians use searchlights on us; they will see her walking, and they will shoot. Soreke crept back and found Dvoyrele in the snow, passed out![73]

***

The Shulman Daughters At the End of Town

After the War ended in 1919, the Shulmans apparently returned to Mlynov. Memories of them living at the end of town are recalled in an essay Samuel Mandelkern later wrote about his efforts to organize self-defense in Mlynov following the end of the War.[74] It was probably 1918-1920 after the Bolshevik Revolution when units of the Tzar's armies were still in the countryside and were plundering and raping in small towns like Mlynov. Mandelkern helped convince the elders to allow the young people to organize defense, purchase rifles and engage in military drilling. In the course of describing these efforts, he several times mentions the Shulman family and the three youngest daughters.

The first mention follows an incident where the defenders scared off a calvary unit that was raiding the town. Mandelkern writes that the unit retreated down "Shulman street." This was the street that the second unit of defenders was responsible for guarding: "The role of the second unit was to guard the road that began from Yoel Goldseker to the Shulman house, after that the house

---

[73] Helen Lederer, "In Pain from the First World War." In *Mlynov-Mervits Memorial Book*, pp. 137-139.

[74] The following quotes all come from the essay by Shmuel Mandelkern, "Self-Defense in Mlynov," in the Mlynov Memorial Book, pp. 108-135.

of Muti Lieberman. Since this road was short, the duty of this unit was also to keep an eye on the town center…"

Mandelkern describes this same street as the "road to Rivne." He continues: "There, a large unit gathered, and the place they were stationed was the home of Mr. Tsodik Shulman. It is possible that this came about because of…the daughters of Shulman, Sorke, Chaika, and Pepe; all of them live today in the United States."

Mandelkern goes on to clarify that the Shulman house was a desired location for training in part due to its strategic location and in part because the young men were attracted to the three youngest Shulman daughters. It is worth quoting him in detail.

> Another maneuver which we initiated nearly every evening, and was no less important than the first [was as follows]: since we definitely knew that 90% of our friends didn't know how to use a rifle, and the men on reserve duty were almost afraid to hold a rifle in their hands, so much so that the wives of these men would warn their husbands when they left for guard duty: "Yukal, for God's sake, be careful with the rifle." – therefore, out of caution, we would go out each and every evening, in separate units of about 20 men, to the field by the road towards Uzhynets' and Sloboda, by the house of Mr. Tsodik Shulman, and train there in the handling of rifles, shooting practice and the like. This activity was also accompanied by song, and the noise of the shooting and song made an impression on the people of the villages mentioned above and they thought that in Mlynov – who knows how many soldiers and defenders are there.

> The location of training mentioned above was chosen for several reasons: 1) the field opened toward the surrounding villages, 2) [we could visit] in the meantime with the beautiful daughters of Shulman: Sarah-keh, Chiya-keh and Pepe, who live in America to this day, 3) the house of R. Tsadok and Pearl Shulman was the only house in Mlynov that was beloved by all the Mlynover youth, thanks to their support for youth engaged in cultural activities and such. Therefore, it was unanimously agreed that the maneuvers should be done close to their house, in order to bring the girls out of their isolation, since this house was the last at the end of the town.

> Each evening, the shooting practice would begin at 8 and ended at midnight – no trivial thing on behalf of those who lived in the house. And thus because of three things: defense, the [location of] Shulman's house, and Shulman's daughters, some men from Dubno, who also feared for the Jews of Mlynov, would visit us in Shulman's house, at night no less, for a meeting, tactical instruction, and the main purpose was the encouragement of our men.

Based on Mandekern's comments about the Shulman home, we can now approximate where on an old map they lived at the east end of town.

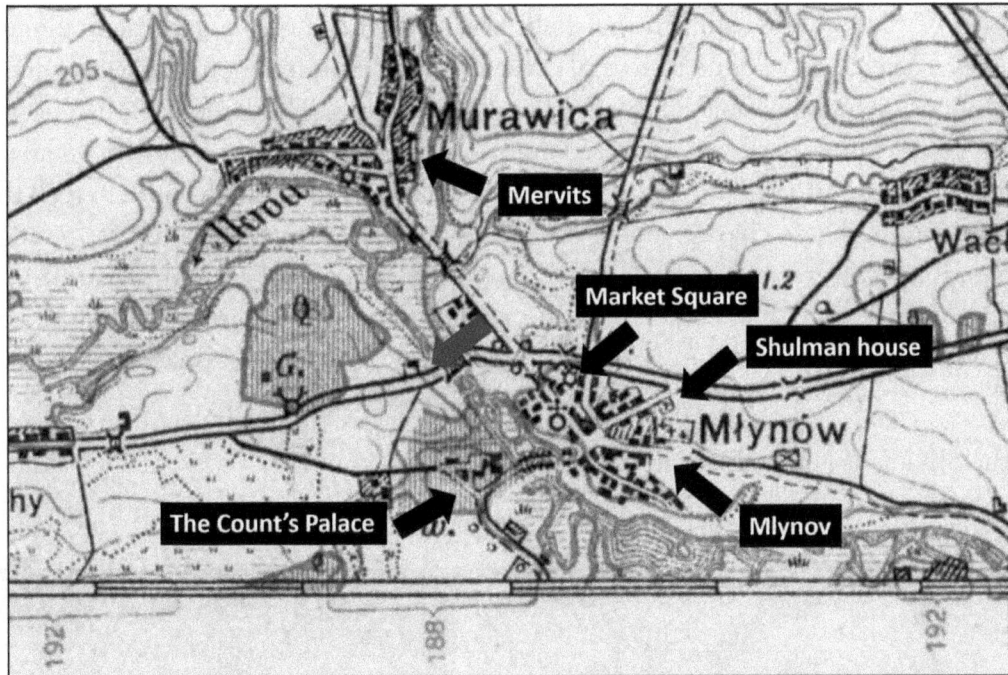

Figure 41 Approximate location of Shulman home in Mlynov

***

The Shulman Library

The Shulman home was remembered as one of the favorite hangouts for young people in town and had a special reputation. Ted Fishman told me that his father Benjamin who married Clara Shulman always called the Shulmans "cold cuts" in Mlynov, by which he meant "upper crust." He used to say that but for the Shulman library a "lower class" boy like himself never would have gotten to know his future wife, Clara Shulman.

Another young man who lived in Mlynov at the time, named Aaron (Berger) Harari, still recalled the Shulman library later in life from the period of his youth before making aliyah to Palestine in the 1930s. He opens his essay on "Culture, Education, and Social Life in the Small Town" in the Memorial Book (pp. 61-64) with reflections on the Shulman home:

> After the First World War, when most of the residents returned from their locations of exile as refugees and the small town had recovered from its destruction – the house of Shulman served as a cultural (tarbut) center in the town. This was a meeting house for all those seeking culture (tarbut). There was the library where they rehearsed plays and in a large-covered patio next to the house, performances were held. Since all of them were absorbed and influenced by Russian culture, the language spoken was peppered with Russian, and most of the books in the library were in Russian, and a few in Yiddish; there was not a trace of Hebrew books.

After WWI, a cultural shift in the shtetl began towards Zionism and the Shulman library lost its lustre. The change was due to several causes. It was becoming more difficult to get into the US due to increasing xenophobia and tighter immigration laws. The Balfour Declaration in 1917 endorsed a "Jewish Homeland" and increased momentum of the Zionist movement. Finally, Mlynov became part of Poland in 1919 and Polish nationalism also inspired Jewish youth to seek their own nationalist solution. These changes made the Shulman home less compelling for young people whose commitments were shifting to Hebrew and "Eretz Yisrael" (the Land of Israel). As Aaron Harari recalled, "The club, that centered on the Shulman house, was far from Zionism; and those that shied away from Russian culture, in the club mentioned above, were forced to look for another hangout."

In 1921 the Shulmans left for Baltimore.

Figure 42 Three Shulman sisters ~ 1920
Clara Shulman (far left), Ben Fishman (third from left) Pepe Shulman (front right), Sarah Shulman (back right). The Ikva River in the background. Courtesy of Ted and Saul Fishman.

***

The Shulmans Migrate to the US in 1921

Given the insecurity of life in Mlynov after WWI, and the growing shift away from the Russian language and towards Hebrew and Zionism, it isn't surprising that the Shulman family decided to make their way to America. By this time, Pearl Malka already had 4 siblings in Baltimore (Pesse, Yenta, Mollie and Aaron). Tsodik's grandson, Ted Fishman, speculates that Tsodik may have lost his position in charge of the forest when the Count had to flee Mlynov after the Bolshevik revolution.

One of Tsodik's nephews, David J. Schulman, came back from the US to help his uncle and their family make their way to America. David was the son of Tsodik's brother, Eli. David arrived in the US in 1901 and was sent to Three Rivers Wisconsin by the Hebrew Immigration Aid Society which sponsored him.[75] David saved some money and then brought his wife Anne Blumencrantz to join him. They lived in the Milwaukee, Wisconsin area until about 1919 when Prudential Life insurance company he worked for moved him to Baltimore for two years and then to a bigger office in Philadelphia.[76]

David's purpose in returning to Europe was to help his uncle's family with their migration as well as the sister of his wife Annie Blumencrantz and some of her orphaned nieces and nephews.[77] The Blumencrantzes were living in Kovel and ended up traveling to the US with the Shulmans.

In November 1920, David filled out a US passport application to return to "France, Poland and all necessary countries" to assist his sister and other [inlaws?]. He also included a letter saying he wanted to locate his father and sister near Warsaw.

Meanwhile the Shulmans prepared for their trip. Tsodik and Pearl's son Harry apparently wanted to bring his future wife, Ita (later Yetta) Perelson, with them to the States. According to family oral traditions, Ita's parents wouldn't let their daughter leave without being married. So Harry and Ita quickly tied the knot.

Ita's naturalization petition from 1927 under her name Yetta Shulman indicates their marriage date was May 5, 1921. They left for America 10 days later from Antwerp. Oral tradition reports that they got married at the home of David Schulman's in-laws, the Blumencrantzes, in Kovel, which is 110 km (68 m) north of Mlyniv. It is not known why they married there, but it was on the way to Warsaw where they probably headed to get their immigration papers before heading East to Antwerp, the port from which they left.

---

[75] Based on a letter his son Sol Schulman wrote to Frank Settleman. Shared with me by Irv Settleman.

[76] While David Schulman lived in the Wisconsin area, the daughter and son of Tsodik's sister, Hannah Steinberg, arrived in the US and lived with him for a time. Their names were Rose Steinberg (married name Rose Berger) and Simon Steinberg. They settled in Chicago.

[77] See prior note.

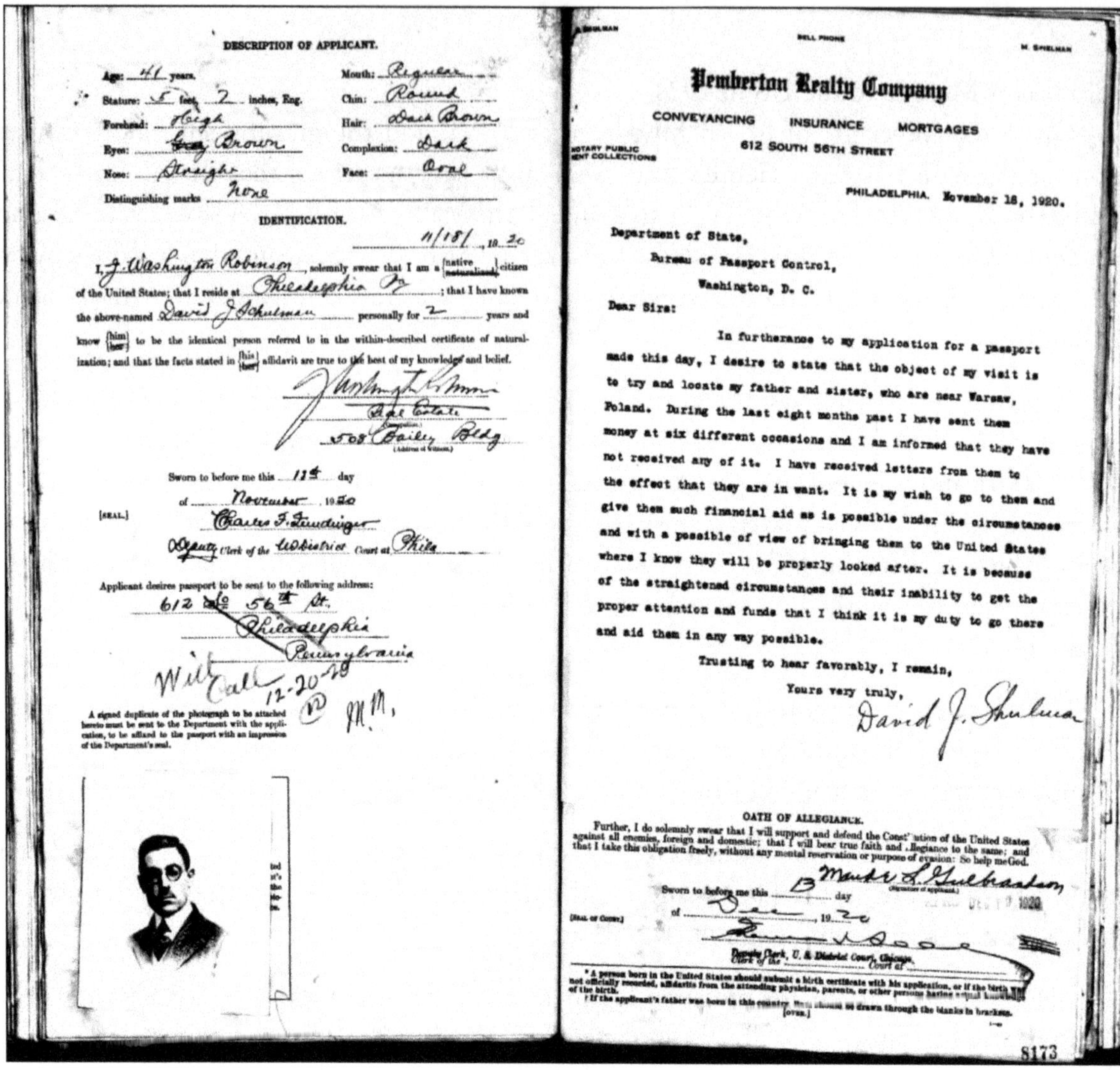

DESCRIPTION OF APPLICANT.

Age: 41 years. Mouth: Regular
Stature: 5 feet, 2 inches, Eng. Chin: Round
Forehead: High Hair: Dark Brown
Eyes: Brown Complexion: Dark
Nose: Straight Face: Oval
Distinguishing marks None

IDENTIFICATION.

11/18/, 1920

I, J. Washington Robinson, solemnly swear that I am a native citizen of the United States; that I reside at Philadelphia Pa; that I have known the above-named David J Schulman personally for 2 years and know him to be the identical person referred to in the within-described certificate of naturalization; and that the facts stated in his affidavit are true to the best of my knowledge and belief.

J Washington Robinson
Real Estate
508 Bailey Bldg
(Address of Witness.)

Sworn to before me this 13th day of November 1920
[SEAL.] Charles F. Lundinger
Deputy Clerk of the U.S. District Court at Phila

Applicant desires passport to be sent to the following address:
612 So 56th St.
Philadelphia
Pennsylvania

Will Call 12-20-20

A signed duplicate of the photograph to be attached hereto must be sent to the Department with the application, to be affixed to the passport with an impression of the Department's seal.

Pemberton Realty Company
CONVEYANCING INSURANCE MORTGAGES
612 SOUTH 56TH STREET
NOTARY PUBLIC
RENT COLLECTIONS

PHILADELPHIA. November 18, 1920.

Department of State,
Bureau of Passport Control,
Washington, D. C.

Dear Sirs:

In furtherance to my application for a passport made this day, I desire to state that the object of my visit is to try and locate my father and sister, who are near Warsaw, Poland. During the last eight months past I have sent them money at six different occasions and I am informed that they have not received any of it. I have received letters from them to the effect that they are in want. It is my wish to go to them and give them such financial aid as is possible under the circumstances and with a possible of view of bringing them to the United States where I know they will be properly looked after. It is because of the straightened circumstances and their inability to get the proper attention and funds that I think it is my duty to go there and aid them in any way possible.

Trusting to hear favorably, I remain,
Yours very truly,
David J. Shulman

OATH OF ALLEGIANCE.

Further, I do solemnly swear that I will support and defend the Constitution of the United States against all enemies, foreign and domestic; that I will bear true faith and allegiance to the same; and that I take this obligation freely, without any mental reservation or purpose of evasion: So help me God.

Sworn to before me this 13 day of Dec 1920

Deputy Clerk, U. S. District Court

8173

Figure 43 1920 Passport Application of David J. Schulman

The "Szulmans" left Antwerp on May 25, 1921 on the SS Lapland and arrived in Philadelphia on June 10th. Next to them on the manifest were the Blumenkrantzes (see manifest below).[78] The manifest lists "Codyk" as age 60, "Perla" age 56, "Pepa" age 16, "Sura" age 22, "Chaja" age 18, "Ita" (Harry's new Yetta Shulman) age 21. Their last residence was Rowno and they were headed to "son/brother" D. Szulman in Philadelphia.

[78] Traveling with the Shulmans were Frima Blomencrantz (later Fruma Moss 1886-1963), Avrum (Albert, Abe, Arthur Blum 1908-1981), Szmul (Samuel Blans 1910-1998) and Frima's nieces, Anna (Blum Feter, 1908-1999), Chaja (Helen Blum Settleman, 1902-1993). I want to thank Jay Nusholtz a Blumencrantz descendant for sharing his insights and knowledge with me.

LIST OR MANIFEST OF ALIEN PASSENGERS FOR THE UNITED

ALL ALIENS arriving at a port of continental United States from a foreign port or a port of the insular possessions of the United States, and all aliens arriving at a port of said insular possessions from a foreign port, a port of continental United This (white) sheet is for the listing of

List 96   S. S. LAPLAND   Passengers sailing from   ANTWERP   26th MAY 19 21

No. on List.	Family name	Given name	Age Yrs. Mos.	Sex	M/S	Calling or Occupation	Read	Read what language	Able to Write	Nationality	Race or people	Country	City or town	The name and complete address of nearest relative or friend in country whence alien came.	State	City or town.
1	SZULMAN	GODYK	50	M	M	LABBER	yes	648 POLISH	yes	POLISH	HEBREW	POLAND	ROWNO	FRIEND I. KARTOWEL	PA.	PHILADELPHIA
2	SZULMAN	PERLA	34	F	M H WIFE		yes	1648	yes	Polish	Hebrew	Poland	ROWNO	do	PA.	PHILADELPHIA
3	SZULMAN	FEPA	16	F	S	NONE	yes		yes	Polish	Hebrew	Poland	ROWNO	do	PA.	PHILADELPHIA
4	SZULMAN	SURA	22	F	S			2648	yes	Polish	Hebrew	Poland	ROWNO	do	PA.	PHILADELPHIA
5	SZULMAN	CHAIM	18	M	S			3648		Polish	Hebrew	Poland	ROWNO	do	PA.	PHILADELPHIA
6	SZULMAN	ITA	21	F	S	LABBER	yes	4648	yes	Polish	Hebrew	Poland	ROWNO	do	PA.	PHILADELPHIA
7	BLOMENKRANZ	PERLA	36	F	WD M WIFE		yes		yes	Polish	Hebrew	Poland	KOWEL	do	PA.	PHILADELPHIA
8	BLOMENKRANZ	AYNER	13	M	S	NONE	NO	NONE	NO	Polish	Hebrew	Poland	KOWEL	do	PA.	PHILADELPHIA
9	BLOMENKRANZ	BORUH	11	M	S	NONE	NO	NONE	NO	Polish	Hebrew	Poland	KOWEL	do	PA.	PHILADELPHIA
10	BLOMENKRANZ	JOSEP	9	M	S	NONE	NO	NONE	NO	Polish	Hebrew	Poland	KOWEL	do	PA.	PHILADELPHIA
11	BLOMENKRANZ	CHAJA	16	F	S	LABBER	yes	HEBREW	yes	Polish	Hebrew	Poland	KOWEL	do	PA.	PHILADELPHIA
12	BLOMENKRANZ	ANA	18	F	S	NONE	NO	NONE	NO	Polish	Hebrew	Poland	KOWEL	do	PA.	PHILADELPHIA
13	BLOMENKRANZ	ZALMEN	27	M	S	LABBER	yes	HEBREW		Polish	Hebrew	Poland	KOWEL	do	PA.	PHILADELPHIA

The manifest of the Szulman family traveling with the Blomenkranz family from Antwerp

STATES IMMIGRATION OFFICER AT PORT OF ARRIVAL

States, or a port of another insular possession, in whatsoever class they travel, MUST be fully listed and the master or commanding officer of each vessel carrying such passengers must upon arrival deliver lists thereof to the immigration officer.

STEERAGE PASSENGERS ONLY

Arriving at Port of ...., 19......

List 28

The entries on this sheet must be typewritten or printed.

230

Page 2 of the manifest showing they were headed to son, and brother D. Szulman.

Rowno was listed as the birthplace of the Shulmans. Tsodik's nephew, David, is listed on a different page of the manifest along with travelers who were already US Citizens.[79]

The Shulman manifest is full of obfuscations and even outright lies, indicating that the family was worried about making it through Polish and US customs. Pearl and the children were born in Mlynov, not Rowno, and Tsodik was probably born someplace in Lithuania, possibly in an area that stayed part of Russia after Mlynov became part of Poland. The family probably was living in Rowno before leaving and didn't want to introduce any complexity by listing their various birthplaces. Why they chose to list I. Kartopel in Kowel as their closest relative/friend and not someone in Mlynov or Rowno is a mystery.

On page two of the record, the manifest misleadingly states they are heading to the address of "son" and "brother" D. Szulman in Philadelphia. As indicated previously, David was in reality Tsodik's nephew, not his son. The manifest also passes off Ita as a daughter, rather than their new daughter-in-law.

Even more surprising, Ita's husband, Harry Shulman (called Ertz or Naftula Hertz), does not appear with the other Szulman travelers (on List 28). His name appears far away on another page of the manifest (List 9) along with the name of his brother, Symon Shulman. Why are they not listed together with the rest of their family?

It took some time to work out that Harry was involved in the biggest fabrication of all and it seems probable that his separation from the rest of the family was to keep his sisters and new wife from exposing the lie accidentally.

Manifest of the SS Lapland List 9

Brothers Syman and Naftula on list 9 of the SS Lapland, separated from the rest of the family

Their destination is their "brother" David Szulman in Philadelphia

---

[79] David Szulman is on the first page of the listings for United States Citizens traveling on the SS Lapland.

Figure 44 Harry Shulman ~ 1913

Courtesy of Karen Passero

Figure 45 Simon Shulman

The Big Switch on the Shulman Manifest

Although the manifest lists both brothers, Syman and Naftula Szulman, we know that Simon was not in fact on the ship with them. According to a short memoir written by Simon's wife Oula (called Edith Shulman in later records), Simon was studying to be a pharmacist in Berdychiv when they first met and fell in love. He was there in 1917 when the Bolshevik Revolution took place, and the drugstores were nationalized. The two of them could not get back to Poland until 1922. When they finally were allowed back to Poland, Simon learned that his parents and siblings had already left for America. They contacted his parents in Baltimore and his parents helped him and his wife Edith make their way to the US in 1922. A manifest below of Simon and Edith arriving in 1922 confirms the story.

So, who then was traveling with Harry Shulman in 1921, if not his brother Simon? We know from family oral traditions and naturalization records that a young man named Pesach Zutelman/ Settleman, who was from the neighboring town of Mervits, pretended to be a Shulman son and traveled with them to America. Pesach was already in love with and possibly betrothed to the Shulman daughter known as Sura (Sarah) Shulman.[80] He and Sarah Shulman married six

---

[80] Pesach is mentioned a few times in the Memorial book as conducting a choir (p. 62) and being in Mervits when his brother returned from yeshiva after being held during WWI (p. 93).

months after they arrived in the US, on Jan 17, 1922, in the District of Columbia. I remember him as my [great] "Uncle Paysie."

Part of the coverup, then, was that Simon was not on the ship with his brother Harry. A deeper dive into the records shows another deception at play. Identities were also swapped. Pesach took Harry Shulman's identity (i.e., Pesach became Naftula Szulman) and Harry took his brother Symon's identity. I assume this switch was intended to further facilitate the deception in some way. Perhaps Harry could pass more easily as Simon than Pesach could.

That the swap in identities took place becomes evident when we look at these young men's later naturalization records. In his Declaration of Intention from October 1921, Harry lists himself as "*Shimon* Hertz Shulman" picking up the name of his brother "Shimon" (Symon). Pesach, for his part, lists himself as "Naftuli Shulman also known as Paul Zutelman" on a Declaration of Intention from July 1923. He signed the document "Naftuli Shulman," which was Harry's Hebrew name. Then again on his 1930 Petition for Naturalization, Pesach describes himself as "Naftula Zulman," here perhaps intentionally adding cover by blending Shulman with Zutelman to get Zulman. Then he signed his name "Paul Shulman" and his birth surname of Settleman is scratched out. From this point forward Paul retained the Shulman last name.

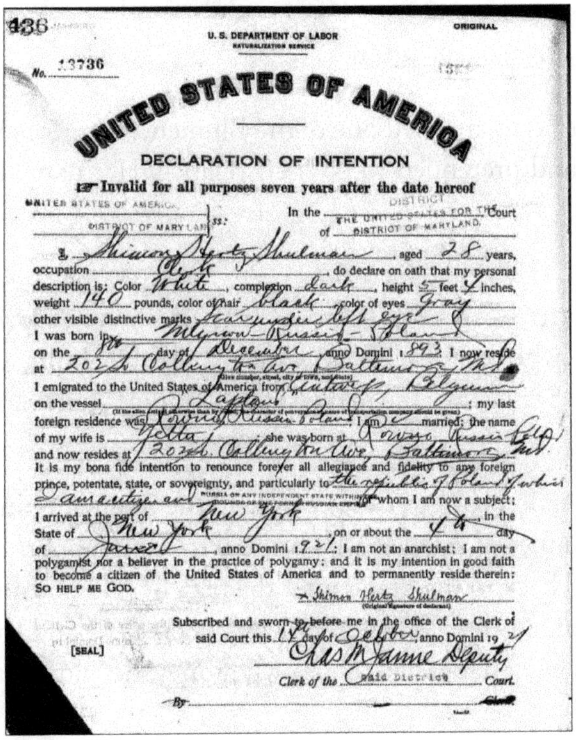
436

U. S. DEPARTMENT OF LABOR
NATURALIZATION SERVICE

ORIGINAL

No. 13736

UNITED STATES OF AMERICA

DECLARATION OF INTENTION

Invalid for all purposes seven years after the date hereof

UNITED STATES OF AMERICA, DISTRICT OF MARYLAND, ss: In the DISTRICT Court of THE UNITED STATES FOR THE DISTRICT OF MARYLAND.

I, Shimon Hertz Shulman, aged 28 years, occupation Clerk, do declare on oath that my personal description is: Color White, complexion dark, height 5 feet 4 inches, weight 140 pounds, color of hair black, color of eyes Gray, other visible distinctive marks Scar under left eye. I was born in Mlynow Russia-Poland on the 8th day of December, anno Domini 1893. I now reside at 202 S. Collington Ave, Baltimore, Md. I emigrated to the United States of America from Antwerp, Belgium on the vessel "Lapland"; my last foreign residence was Rovno Russia Poland; I am married; the name of my wife is Yetta; she was born at Rovno Russia Poland and now resides at 202 S. Collington Ave, Baltimore, Md. It is my bona fide intention to renounce forever all allegiance and fidelity to any foreign prince, potentate, state, or sovereignty, and particularly to the republic of Poland of which I am a citizen and RUSSIA OR ANY INDEPENDENT STATE WITHIN BOUNDS OF THE FORMER RUSSIAN EMPIRE of whom I am now a subject; I arrived at the port of New York, in the State of New York, on or about the 4th day of June, anno Domini 1921; I am not an anarchist; I am not a polygamist nor a believer in the practice of polygamy; and it is my intention in good faith to become a citizen of the United States of America and to permanently reside therein: SO HELP ME GOD.

Shimon Hertz Shulman
(Original signature of declarant)

Subscribed and sworn to before me in the office of the Clerk of said Court this 14th day of October, anno Domini 1921

[SEAL]

Chas M Janne Deputy
Clerk of the said District Court.

By ______ Clerk.

Figure 46 Harry Shulman's Declaration posing as Shimon Hertz

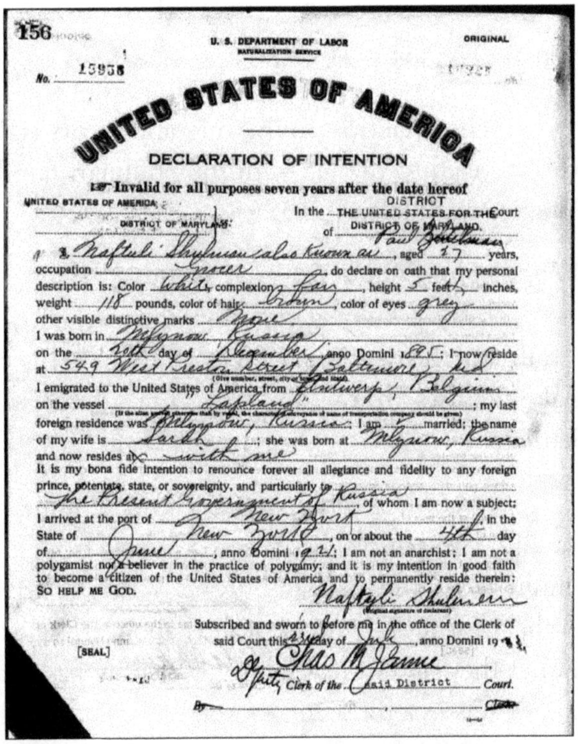
156

U. S. DEPARTMENT OF LABOR
NATURALIZATION SERVICE

ORIGINAL

No. 15938

UNITED STATES OF AMERICA

DECLARATION OF INTENTION

Invalid for all purposes seven years after the date hereof

UNITED STATES OF AMERICA, DISTRICT OF MARYLAND, ss: In the DISTRICT Court of THE UNITED STATES FOR THE DISTRICT OF MARYLAND.

I, Naftuli Shulman also known as Paul Zutelman, aged 27 years, occupation Grocer, do declare on oath that my personal description is: Color White, complexion fair, height 5 feet 4 inches, weight 118 pounds, color of hair brown, color of eyes grey, other visible distinctive marks None. I was born in Mlynow Russia on the 20th day of December, anno Domini 1895; I now reside at 549 West Preston Street Baltimore, Md. I emigrated to the United States of America from Antwerp, Belgium on the vessel "Lapland"; my last foreign residence was Mlynow, Russia; I am married; the name of my wife is Sarah; she was born at Mlynow, Russia and now resides at with me. It is my bona fide intention to renounce forever all allegiance and fidelity to any foreign prince, potentate, state, or sovereignty, and particularly to the Present Government of Russia, of whom I am now a subject; I arrived at the port of New York, in the State of New York, on or about the 4th day of June, anno Domini 1921; I am not an anarchist; I am not a polygamist nor a believer in the practice of polygamy; and it is my intention in good faith to become a citizen of the United States of America and to permanently reside therein: SO HELP ME GOD.

Naftuli Shulman
(Original signature of declarant)

Subscribed and sworn to before me in the office of the Clerk of said Court this 23rd day of July, anno Domini 1923.

[SEAL]

Chas M Janne Deputy
Clerk of the said District Court.

By ______ Clerk.

Figure 47 Paul Settleman's Declaration posing as Natali Shulman

***

The Switch Continues with Frank Settleman

There was one more bait and switch that flowed from this original swap in identities. Since Pesach Zutelman entered the US as Naftula Shulman, his brother Frank Settleman was able to assume Pesach's identity when it was his turn. Frank could not use his own identity because he had previously been forbidden to enter the US under his own name, according to the story I heard from his son. He then proceeded to Buenos Aires like other Mlynov young men to figure out how to get into the US and avoid the tightening quotas.[81]

Frank left Buenos Aires on the SS Vandyck under his brother's name "Pejsach Zutelman" and landed in New York on Dec. 22, 1923. When he submitted his Declaration of Intention on August 30, 1926, he did so under the name of "Pejsheh Zutelman also [known] as Frank Settleman."

By this time, Frank was already living with his brother and sister-in-law in Baltimore. Four years later, he is still there in the 1930 census and the identity charade continues. Paul is listed as the head of household but his brother Frank is listed as his "brother-in-law."

1930 census in which Frank Settleman pretends to be a brother-in-law of his brother Paul Shulman

The final twist in this migration story is that Frank married one of the Blumencrantz women who traveled to the US with the Shulman family and pretended to be their relative. Her name in America was Helen Blum.

A Funny Story About David Schulman

I don't know if this story, like so many of the stories I've heard, is true. It is about David Schulman, the nephew of Tsodik Shulman, the one who went back to Mlynov to help the Shulmans make their way to the US. It was told to me by Irv Settleman, the son of Helen (Blum) and Frank Settleman.

According to Irv, before David Schulman headed back to Europe to help the Shulmans and the Blumenkrantzes, he accepted money from a number of families who wanted to send support to families who were back in Europe. When he arrived back in the States after the trip, he had nothing to show for it. When questioned about it, he explained that "he had been pickpocketed," and the money they gave him was gone. When he was asked what happened to his own money, he said, "that money was in a different pocket."

---

[81] See the further discussion of Julius Deming who made his way to the US via Buenos Aires.

The story has the feel of apocrypha, though its source has some credibility since Irv's mother, Helen, was on the ship with the Shulmans. Irv is a funny guy, and it is often hard to separate what is fact from fiction when he tells a story. Irv was born in 1932 in Baltimore.

Although David Schulman apparently did very well in the insurance and then real estate business, Irv tells me he was a poor man later in life in Baltimore. Perhaps this story developed from that period.

***

The Real Simon Shulman Arrives

As noted above, Harry Shulman took his brother Simon's identity and he gave Pesach Settleman his own identity. The real Simon Shulman and his wife finally arrived in 1922. "Szymon Judel Szulman," age 32, and his wife "Alta Ides" [Fixman] age 27 left Antwerp on June 15, 1922 and arrived in New York on June 25th. Their last residence is listed as "Wolomin Russia" which was near Warsaw Poland and their closest relative was Simon's brother-in-law "Szoel Mejler" [Saul Meiler/Malar] in Rowne. They list their birthplace as Staro-Bikhov, Russia (Bykhaw, Belarus today].

It is doubtful that Simon was born in Bykhaw, though we know that some of his father's ancestors were from there. Simon was probably born in Mlynov like all his siblings. It could have been that Simon was hiding the fact he was born in Mlynov that was now part of Poland or perhaps he didn't want to risk exposing the lie that his brother had traveled to the US a year earlier as Symon Shulman.

Bits and pieces of Simon and Edith's story are captured in the short recollection of her life that Edith wrote in broken English at some point later in Baltimore. Edith was born in Berdychiv in 1895. Her birthname was Edith or Ita Fixsman, but everyone called her "Oula" or "Ulla." In 1916, she began studying to be a pharmacist and passed her exams and became an assistant pharmacist in 1919. After the Bolshevik Revolution, chaos reigned in Berdychiv. Some of the pharmacies were taken over and nationalized by the communists. During the civil war that followed, she recalled that "Every 2 or 3 weeks we had a new government with new rubles, new money. We used to get up in the morning and find a new government. Dead people were lying in the streets."

One time the enemy came close and the communists had to leave the city. Edith was reluctant to leave her job and post until "the president of the Union (Simon Shulman) came and I went home. I and Simon loved each other."

The communists began drafting members of the Union who passed physical exams. Edith and Simon decided to get married before they were drafted. The next day they left in freight trains and traveled a long time to Lubin [Poland]. They looked a long time for a place to stay and finally found a nice room. The landlady said it was occupied by a high official, but they didn't believe her, and they settled in. When the official returned, Simon was arrested, and Edith had to talk the officer into releasing him. They eventually found a small dirty room to stay in. They remained in Lubin for a few months and Edith worked in the hospital. Eventually they moved to a bigger city. At some point, Edith recalls, "Simon took me to meet his sister and her family [probably the Meilers in Rowne]. We were there only a couple of days."

After learning that Simon's parents and a number of his siblings were already in the US, they got in touch with them and the family helped the couple make arrangements to leave. Edith got pregnant before they left and their daughter, Tessie, was born 6 weeks after they arrived in the US. A son Melvin was born in 1923 and another son Herman in 1930.

Edith & Simon Shulman
Warsaw, 1922

***

The Shulmans Settle in Baltimore in the 1920s

The Shulmans settled into life in downtown Baltimore. The younger brother, Harry ("Ertz"), and his wife Yetta had a son Bernard in 1922, twelve months after they arrived in the US, and a son Melvin in 1928. In 1930 Harry was manager of a grocery store.

Simon Shulman initially got a position in a music store. His wife Edith recalls this period:

> In Poland, I got pregnant and my daughter was born 6 weeks after we came to the U.S. Her name was Tessie. Life here was very strange to me. I left family in Russia and a good job. We were very poor here. Simon got a job in a music store. All they made him do was clean the instruments....The music store was not doing any good and the man sold it to Simon for 1000 dollars. For a while he did good, until the phonographs came out. Small instruments stopped selling. Simon did not have the money to buy phonographs and the business went to nothing and Simon was forced to close the store and we had nothing.

> We still lived with the in-laws [Tsodik and Pearl]. I had 2 rooms on the second floor. It was full of roaches and bed bugs and even rats. With the help of the family we bought a confectionary store in a very nice new neighborhood. It was

only 1931. The people were getting snowballs [a Baltimore term for snowcones] and it was busy. When Fall came there was no business at all...

Simon Shulman's Confectionery
Pearl Malka Shulman (2nd from right) with
grandchildren (l to r) Ted Fishman, Paula Fishman
(baby), Tessie Shulman (far right)

Courtesy of Ted Fishman

The three Shulman daughters married in the 1920s as well. Sarah Shulman married Paul "Zutelman" in the District of Columbia on January 17, 1922. I asked Ted Fishman when he was still alive why they got married in Washington. Ted reported that their daughter Shirley Leaderman said they eloped. Ted did not know their reasoning and I can't help wondering whether the decision had something to do with their need to hide the identity switch involving Paul's last name. Paul and Sarah's daughter, Betty (married name Edlavitch), was born in 1924, Shirley (married name Leaderman) in 1928 and a son Jack in 1937.

Clara Shulman married Benjamin Fishman her teenage sweetheart from Mlynov. Ben arrived in Baltimore in 1920, a year before the Shulmans, with three other Mlynov families including the family of Aaron Demb (a story told below). Clara and Ben married on April 13, 1924. Their son Theodore "Ted" (my source for many of the family stories) was born in 1927 and their daughter Paula (married name Brodsky) in 1932.

Pepe (Pauline) Shulman married her first cousin Paul H. Schwartz on January 3, 1926. Paul was the youngest son of Yenta (Demb) Schwartz. He too was born in Mlynov but arrived with his family in Baltimore in 1912 when he was still a young boy. It is unclear if they knew each other back in Mlynov when they were kids. In any case, the first cousins fell in love when they got to know each other in Baltimore. Pepe and Paul's daughter Neena was born in December 1926, their son Leon (my father "Moshe Leib") was born in 1928, and their younger daughter Pearl (named for Pearl Malka) was born in 1935.

Figure 48 Clara (Shulman) and Ben Fishman
wedding day

Figure 49 Pepe (Shulman) and Paul Schwartz
wedding day

Courtesy of Ted Fishman

This precious photo below from about 1925 shows the Shulman family during a Passover celebration. Pearl and Tsodik, the matriarch and patriarch, are seated in the center. Standing left to right: Yetta "Etta" Shulman, her son Bernard Shulman [on chair] her husband Harry Shulman, Benjamin Fishman, [his wife] Clara (Shulman) Fishman, Pepe (Shulman) Schwartz, Sara Shulman (holding Betty Shulman), [her husband] Paul (Zutelman) Shulman, [his brother] Frank Settleman. Seated left to right: Pearl Malka (Demb) Shulman, Tsodik Shulman, Simon Shulman holding Melvin Shulman, Oula [Edith] Shulman holding Tessie Shulman.

Shulman Family Passover in Baltimore, Circa 1925
Courtesy of Ted Fishman and Saul Fishman

Shulman Brother-in-Laws
(l to r) Ben Fishman (Clara Shulman's husband), Paul (Zutelman) Shulman (Sarah Shulman's husband), Paul Schwartz (Pepe
Shulman's husband), Harry Shulman, Simon Shulman. Courtesy of Ted and Saul Fishman

A Trip To Atlantic City

Ted Fishman told me a funny story about the Shulman brother-in-laws involving a trip to Atlantic City. The brother-in-laws and their families would vacation together. One day, they were following each other in their cars on the way to Atlantic City. The first car slammed on its brakes to avoid an accident and all the brother-in-laws slammed into one another. All the cars were totaled.

A Yiddish letter written from Tsodik and Pearl to their daughter Clara (in Atlantic City?) during this time gives a flavor of daily life in the late 1920s.

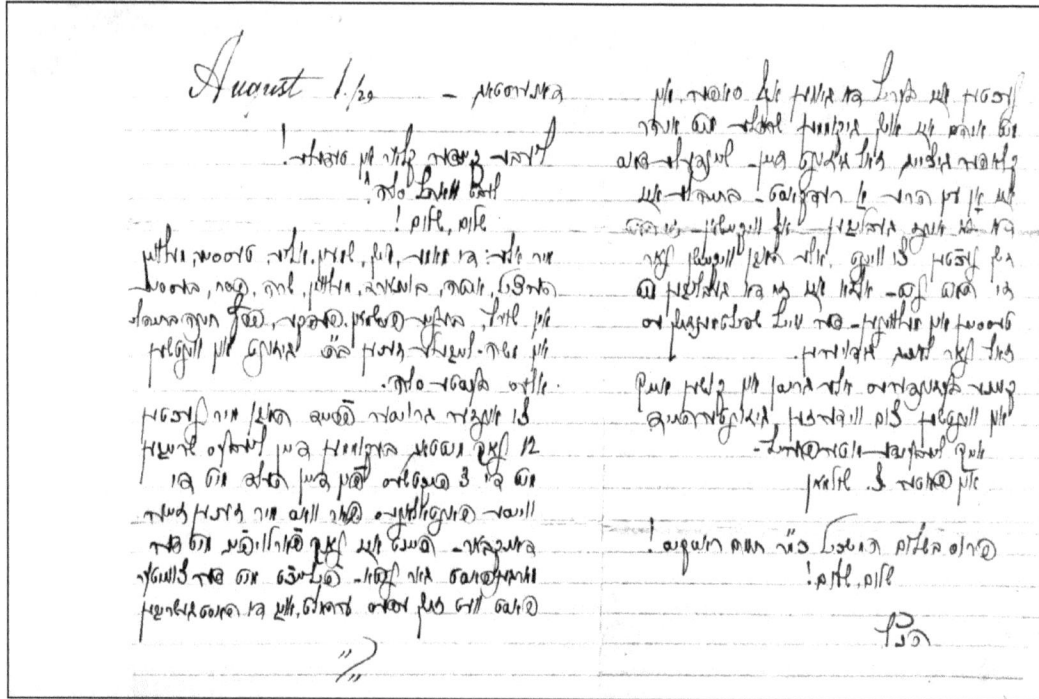

Figure 50 Yiddish Letter from Tsodik and Pearl to daughter Clara

Thursday-August 1, 1929. Dear Children-Clara and Tedelya. A healthy happy life to you. Amen. Shalom Shalom.

We are here–Mother [Pearl Malka] I [Tsodik] Shimon, Olla, Tessy, Melvin, Hertzel [=Harry] Eta, Bernard, Melvin, Sora [Sarah], Peysach, Bessie [Betty], Shirley, Benny Fishman, Pepe-Peritz [Paul Schwartz] Chona, Bassie and Moishe-Leib [Leon Schwartz] are thank God in good health, wishing you the very best, Amen. To our great joy, we received your letter with 3 pictures. You and your hero in the nice uniform [?]. Berel [Clara's husband] was here for supper yesterday also Sarah [Shulman] with the children were here.

Sheindele [Shirley?] is a gifted child out of the ordinary. Sheindel-Boasiley (?) is here for a while for vacation. She compliments? everybody. But her go on vacation.

Now now she plays with [Simon's children] Tessy and Melvin. I don't know how long it will last. We didn't get any mail from you today, it might come on the delivery. Otherwise everyone is well and sending you best wishes-Amen. Give our regards to Chaim Roskes. Shalom and Kol Tov. Your father and Zeidy T. Shulman.

A short letter from Pearl Shulman:

We received a letter from Liza [i.e., their daughter Liza Koszhushner in Russia]. She writes they earn some money by working and they still have a little from what we send them and they send their best wishes. Stay well-Your mother and Bubby-Pearl Shulman.

Pearl passed away at the age of 66 on March 4, 1933. She was the third of the Demb siblings to pass away in Baltimore. She didn't live long enough to know that one of her daughters and her family would perish in the Shoah. Tsodik must have composed the inscription on her tombstone, which spells the acrostic Shulman down the side in Hebrew. The Hebrew is flowery and poetic and the translation is thus an approximate rendering.

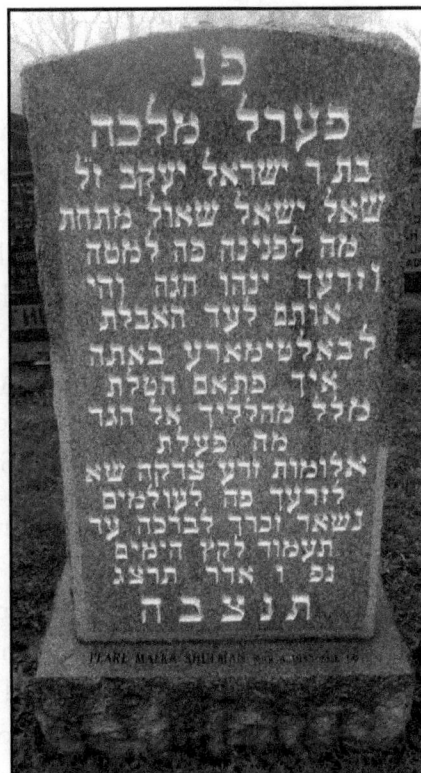

Here lies Pearl Malka

daughter of Israel Jacob, of blessed memory,

SH: if the depths asked why is there such a pearl buried down here

U: and her offspring wailed, and are a witness to mourning

L: To Baltimore you came, how suddenly you were taken

M Words of praise praising your actions.

A: You bestowed sheaves of charity on your descendants here forever

N: Your memory will remain a blessing forever, until you rise up at the end of days.

Passed away 6th of Adar 5693
May her soul be bound up in the bond of life

Pearl Malka's Tombstone in Shomei MIshmeres Cemetery, Rosedale

Pearl Malka Shulman *1933*

Pearl Malka Shulman, aged 66 years, wife of Tsodik Shulman, died Saturday, March 4. The funeral took place from her late residence, 204 N. Chester Street, on Sunday, March 5. Burial was in the Hebrew Rosedale Cemetery. Besides her husband she is survived by two sons, Simon and Hertz Shulman, five daughters, Mrs. Nachum Mejler, Mrs. Lize Koszushner, Mrs. Sarah Shulman, Mrs. Clara Fishman, Mrs. Pauline Schwartz and sixteen grandchildren.

Figure 51 Obituary of Pearl Malka Shulman
Courtesy of Ted Fishman. Original source not identified

***

Memories of Tsodik from grandchildren
Written memories by his grandson (my father) Leon Schwartz (1928-2003)

I do have some memories of all of my grandparents. My Mother's Mother Pearl Shulman died when I was about six so that I have only very faint memories of her. All of her children went to see her at least once a week and really respected and revered her. My Mother was very upset at losing her and developed a chronic problem of heart palpitations around that time that in retrospect seemed to be somehow related to her Mother's death. My Mother's Father Zadek Shulman came to live with us at that time and remained with us for about fourteen years so that I came to know him the best of all of my grandparents. I do not remember any discussion about why he lived with us rather then [sic] the other of his children. Having him around us was important to us from the perspective of an example and because all of our relatives came so often to see him and thus a close family relationship was developed on the Shulman side.

I have many memories of Zadek since he lived with us and for many years we even shared a bedroom. I would talk to him in English and he would respond in Yiddish. He would sit off by himself for many hours reading the Baltimore Sun and the Jewish paper that we received. He was orthodox in his observances and would pray every morning. As long as he was able too [sic], he walked to the Synagogue on Saturdays and holidays. I studied with him for about a half hour a day, learning to read Hebrew fluently. He also prepared me for my Bar Mitzvah. In spite of his beliefs he made no comments as my Father worked in his store on Saturdays and as the family became Americanized and did not observe the Sabbath. I remember him asking me one Saturday when I returned from a ball game "Has de gewinnin" [Did you win?]. There was no reproach only interest. I was home alone with him when I heard a noise upstairs and found him on the floor after a fall. After a call to the Doctor who sent an ambulance to get him, I remember preparing myself to tell my Mother when she returned. This was about 1947 and he lived for a few months longer but never came home again after that.

Oral tradition from his granddaughter Neena Schwartz

Although he was very traditional, he was also very tolerant. One time I came home crying when he was living with us. He asked me what was wrong. I told him that I had eaten "treif" [non-Kosher food] at the home of a friend.

"Did you do so," he asked, "so you wouldn't insult your friend's mother?" When I nodded yes, he said, "then you did the right thing."

***

The Shulmans Who Stayed Behind

When Tsodik and Pearl Malka left Rowne in 1921, they left behind their two oldest daughters who had both married and had children. They would not see them again. The eldest, as noted earlier, was Nehuma who married Saul Meiler (also spelled Miller and Mejler).[82] They had two daughters, Tamara who was born in about 1914. She was the first grandchild of Tsodik and Pearl Malka and she is the little one in the front of the large Shulman family photo above (Figure 40). A second daughter Nina was born a few years later.

We know little about this family after the Shulmans left. We know that Nathan Gruber's wife, Gittel, listed them as closest relatives/friends in Rowno when she left in 1920. And then Simon Shulman and his new wife visited them for a few days in Rowno in 1922 before they left for America. We know that they were still in the area in 1929, when Yenta (Demb) Schwartz and Israel Herman returned to Mlynov for a visit.

These are the last photos we have of the Meiler/Mejler family. In the photo on the right from 1929, Yenta Schwartz is seated center and Israel Herman is seated to the right. Saul Meiler is seated on the left. Yenta's niece Nehuma Meiler (daughter of Pearl Malka) is standing center. Her daughter Tamar is standing left, and daughter Nina is standing right.

---

[82]The family name is spelled various ways: "Miller" in the Demb family scroll, Tsodik's obituary and the manifest of Nathan Gruber's wife, Gitel Gruber, "Mejler" in Pearl Malka's obituary, Simon's passenger manifest, "Mailer" in Harry Shulman's obituary and "Meiler" on a photograph in Ted Fishman's collection. I suspect Saul Meiler may have been a brother or cousin of the man remembered as Yossel Malar who married Ester Gelberg/Goldberg from Mlynov. See the Goldberg family story https://kehilalinks.jewishgen.org/Mlyniv/families.html.

Figure 52 Saul Meiler, Tamar, Nina, Nehuma (l to r)
Courtesy of Karen Passero

Figure 53 1929 Israel Herman (right) and Yenta Schwartz
(seated center) with Meilers
Courtesy of Ted Fishman

When the Germans attacked the Eastern Part of Poland in June 1941, the Meilers were supposed to meet up with Nehuma's sister, Liza and her family, who were living in Novohrad Volinski. They didn't reach there in time and the Koszhushners had to flee without them. My Aunt Pearl believes the Meilers were slaughtered in Babi Yar, but Ted told me no one is sure what happened to them.

Since Nehuma is still listed as alive in Tsodik's obituary in 1947, it appears that the family had not yet learned of or accepted the loss of the Meiler family.

Figure 54 Obituary of Tsodik Shulman
The Baltimore Sun, Mar.13, 1947 p. 21

SHULMAN.—On March 13, 1947, TZO-DICK, beloved husband of the late Pearl Shulman and father of Simon, Harry and Mrs Sarah Shulman. Mrs. Nechuma Miller, Mrs. Liza Kazushner, Mrs. Clara Fishman and Mrs. Pauline Schwartz; also survived by a number of grandchildren and great-grandchildren. 14e
Services at the Jack Lewis Home, 2100-02 Eutaw Place, on Friday, precisely at 12 noon. Interment in Rosedale Cemetery. [Kindly omit flowers.] In mourning at 3813 Calloway avenue

Figure 55 Woven artwork by Nehuma Meiler
Sent to family in Baltimore.
Courtesy of Pearl Schwartz Imber.

First Cousins Meet

Liza (Shulman) Koszhushner was the second eldest Shulman daughter who stayed in Europe when the Shulmans left for America. The Koszhushners at some point migrated further east to Novohrad Volinski. When the Germans attacked the Russian-held part of Poland, the Koszhushners were able to flee East and survive.

The details of their lives under Stalin are not known. But in the 1990s, after the breakup of the Soviet Union, the Baltimore Shulman descendants and the Koszhushner in Russia got in touch with each other. My father Leon Schwartz and my mother Joan made a trip to meet his first cousins in Russia in 1992. From my father's recollections, I learned that the Shulman sisters in Baltimore had been in touch with their sister Liza over the years.

In the course of learning about other Demb family lines, I recently discovered that Liza's husband, Shaya Koszhushner, had a sister named Freida in Novohrad Volinki who married Motel Demb, a son of Rivka and Israel Jacob. Motel, Freida and their children came to Baltimore in the 1920s. As discussed later, a box of photos and documents that was only recently discovered by descendants turned up other photos from this same Koszhushner family (see "Freida's Surname Mystery," p. 163).[83]

---

[83] The descendants of Liza (Shulman) and Shaya Koszhushner are thus related to descendants of Motel Demb and Freida (Koshushner) through both the Demb and the Koszhushner lines.

Figure 56 Shia Koszhusner and Liza (Shulman).
Courtesy of Ted Fishman

Figure 57 Russian Shulman cousins Aug. 1992

The Shulman first cousins in Russia (l to r)
Misha (Mikhail), Nina, Eta/ Etti (Ethel), Fima
(Yefim)

Figure 58 1992 visit of Leon and Joan Schwartz (left) to first cousins in Kiev

***

Visit With Ukrainian First Cousins – by Leon Schwartz

While at Yalta, Olga our Russian tour guide called to make final arrangements to meet our Ukrainian cousins in Kiev. We had asked her to find out whether they could make arrangements to have an interpreter with us since we felt that if we brought an interpreter that it might inhibit the conversation. Olga made the contact and told us that we would be meeting them at the hotel between 5 and 6 on the afternoon of August 21, 1992. She also said there was no need for an interpreter since they indicated they spoke Yiddish and English. They told her they would be picking us up in a car and taking us to their house. I had suggested that we would meet them at the hotel and we would have a dinner for them there.

We wondered how we would know them and exactly who we would be meeting. At about 10 minutes before 5, I was looking out the window and saw three people getting out of a car carrying a big bouquet of flowers and I assumed that they were our cousins. We went down to the lobby where they were seated and had a tearful series of embraces. Waiting for us in the lobby were [first cousins] Nina, Misha, and Fima.

Fima had on a jacket with a number of campaign ribbons on the side of his lapel. Nina had on a dress that we later learned was one that had been sent to her. Outside Boris and Peter, the sons of Misha were waiting for us with their cars. We rode with Peter and Nina in his well cared for, but in his words, old Fiat. We were taken to Misha's apartment which was about 25 minutes away from the hotel.

There we met Clara, who is Misha's wife, and Pearl who is Etta's daughter. We were told that Etta our fourth [first-] cousin was not well enough to come. Later on that evening, Elena the daughter of Pearl also came to the apartment. The apartment had four rooms and was on the second floor of a high rise that was part of a complex of high rises. They were very proud of their view which overlooked a green area and a small stream. The food started to come immediately with dish after dish of meats and vegetables. They really worked hard at being good hosts which was somewhat embarrassing to us since we knew how much food cost them.

They were very interested in the photographs that I had brought with me. They did not have the picture of the Shulman family that we all have and they all studied it carefully to make sure that they knew everyone on the photograph. Nina was delighted that I was leaving it with them. I had photographs of all the family, not all of them recent, but they were appreciated. Nina had pictures of all of us that they had saved over the years. For example, she had my high school year book picture that my Mother had apparently sent to Aunt Lisa. She had a picture of Zadie sitting on a chair on the porch at Callaway avenue that brought tears to my eyes.

Photo of Tsodik Shulman. Courtesy of Ted Fishman.
probably the one sent to cousins in Russia

Communication was difficult so that some of the conversations that I will tell you about may be somewhat misinterpreted, and certainly not at the depth that I would have liked. Nina spoke fluent Yiddish and the main source of information flowed from her to me. I understood her very well; however I could only use words not sentences in responding and asking questions. Fima and Misha's Yiddish seemed to be not quite as good as mine. They understood Nina's Yiddish with some help in Russian but couldn't articulate sentences either. Joan was very helpful with her Russian, in fact she was told that in a few months she would be like one of them. They were so delighted with her that they made her an honorary Shulman. Joan and Elena were also using a Russian/English dictionary to look up words.

Perhaps the most poignant moment of the whole visit came when Nina said to me "I want to visit Zadie Zdick's grave and ask him - why didn't you make my Mother and Father come to America?" She said that her mother wanted to go with the rest of the family but they had a house ("stebe") and her father didn't want to give it up. She said that her Mother missed her family very much over the years. Another comment she made was that she never expected to see an American Shulman.

Apparently Nina and her parents (Shia and Liza) spent the war in the Urals at the city of Sverlovsk and thereby survived. Fima and Misha were both in the service, one at the siege of Leningrad and the other at Stalingrad. Misha showed us a scar on his chest and the bullet that they removed from him. When I asked about what happened to Nahuma and her family I was told that they were killed in 1941. I tried to get more information but either they did not know or I wasn't communicating properly. Nina did say that they were waiting for Nahuma to come before they left, but then they could wait no longer.

I gave each of the three cousins that were there envelopes containing $350.00 and told them who it was from. There was no awkwardness about this and they were very appreciative. Fima said almost immediately that he intended to use the money to visit his son in Israel. When I saw how they lived I wished that I had brought more. However, this was a significant gift for them when you consider the average pension is less then [sic] $2,000 rubles per month and at the existing exchange the gifts were about 60,000 rubles. I also gave Boris, Peter and Pearl each an additional $10 and $5 to Elana. When Peter dropped us off at the hotel, Joan gave him an additional $10.

They very much wanted us to sleep over but we got Peter to drive us back to the hotel. Fima stayed at Misha's apartment and Nina was dropped off at Etta's apartment. The next morning Peter picked us up at 10 after we had breakfast and took us to Etta's apartment. After meeting Etta we understood why she was not there the night before. She really looks old, much older then her then 78 years and couldn't communicate well at all. She appeared to be in some distress during the day and was given a pill for her heart and put to rest during the afternoon. They said that she had not been well since her husband had died a few years before. Pearl and Elena live with her in what seemed to be a 3 room apartment. They had another spread waiting for us, but since we had just eaten we went for a long walk in a park that was very close to their apartment house. They also lived in a large apartment building that was one of a large complex of apartment buildings. Accompanying Joan and me on the walk there was Nina, Fima, Boris, Peter, Pearl and Elena. Clara stayed with Etta and Misha apparently to do some work that morning.

The park was very pleasant and it was a beautiful day. They told us that Khrushchev had been at that park and had given a speech there. This started us talking politics as best we could. They were not all that enthusiastic about Gorbachev, because along with the break up of the USSR and the destruction of the Communist Party has come run away inflation that has really hurt those on pensions...They were completely caught up in the economic chaos and saw no advantages yet from the new freedoms. They were delighted to hear that we were Democrats and intended to vote for Clinton, since the aura around Roosevelt and Kennedy still remains.

They spoke about anti-semitism and how difficult it was for the Jews. Since they all were either employed or had been before pensions I asked about the manifestation of anti-semitism. I did not really get an answer. The probable answer came into focus later as I thought about another conversation we had. I was showing them some of the material I had brought with me, such as the official Astronaut photo of Ellen Shulman, a great article about Neena's scientific accomplishments, and an article about me which indicated my "Director" title. Apparently Directors in the Soviet are important titles so this was passed around for everyone to see. Then Nina said, not in a malicious way, but as a fact- "If you were here you wouldn't be a Director." Anti-semitism doesn't seem to keep you from working but it does seem to affect one's ability to reach his full potential. This was confirmed the next day when we went to Babi Yar where the Ukrainian guide made a very similar comment.

After reciting the Four Questions to Nina to demonstrate one bit of Yiddish that Zadie had taught me, she and Fima said that after the death of their Father they had no observances and that their children had no religious training at all.

There are some observations I want to convey about all of the individuals we met. I will try to do this with little thumbnail sketches.

Nina–Very lively, energetic, maybe the leader in the group, had not been to Kiev in seven years, before retirement was an economist, (I think this means something different in the Ukraine.) 72 years old [~1919/1920]

Misha–Quiet, proud of his family, tv and radio repair work, 77 years old [~1915]

Clara [Misha's wife] -extremely pleasant, warm smile, and sparking eyes.

> Boris [Misha's son]- (some of you have met him) quiet, same occupation as Father, wistful about his visit to the States, wife visiting her family, 45 years old [~1947]
>
> Peter [Misha's son]-exceptionally handsome, same occupation as father and brother, would love to visit the States, wife pregnant and couldn't be there. 39 years old [~1953]
>
> (Neither Boris or Peter had pictures of their wives or children and the fact that neither wife was there made us think perhaps that they were not Jewish and there was some reluctance to have them meet us. It never came out that a number of children in our American families had married non-Jews. It may be as they said, but I couldn't help but wonder afterwards)

Fima–Lively, proud of his daughter and grandson in Kharkov, would like his son in Israel to get to the States, 69 years old. [~1923]

Etta–Appeared old and sick, couldn't contribute to the conversation, 78 years old [~1914]

Pearl [Etta's daughter]–Very likeable, described herself as an economist, took charge of things at her Mother's apartment, 47 years old.

Elena [Pearl's daughter]–Very tall and attractive, going to school for training in computers, 23 years old.

We had another big meal that day with many courses including a watermelon for dessert which was very obviously a real treat. Champaign and vodka were available at both meals with a number of toasts. They wanted to know when we were taking the train the next day to go to Moscow so they could see us off. We didn't know however, since were going to be touring Kiev that day, so we said our goodbyes that afternoon. Nina said "You will be back next year" which allowed us all to act as if this were not a sad parting, but we all cried anyway.

***

My photo with tombstones of my paternal great-grandfathers, Tsodik Shulman and Hyman Schwartz
Shomrei Mishmeres HaKodesh Cemetery, Rosedale, Maryland

US Records Summary for family of Pearl Malka (Demb) and Tsodik Shulman

1921 (June 5) Passenger Manifest	Sailing from Antwerp on May 25, 1921 and arriving in Philadelphia on June 10. List 28 of the manifest: Codyk age 60 with implied birth year as 1861, "Perla" age 56 with implied birth year of 1865, "Pepa" age 16 (implied birth year 1905, "Sura" age 22 with implied birth year of 1899, "Chaja" age 18 with implied birth year of 1903, "Ita" (Harry's new wife) age 21. Last residence and birthplace listed as Rowno, Poland. Nearest relative or friend I. Kartopel in Kowel. Heading to address of "son" [in reality nephew], D. Szulman in Philadelphia. On separate page (List 9) of the same manifest, sons Syman Szulman [= Harry Shulman] and "bro" Naftula Szulman [= Paul Zutelman] are listed. Syman is listed as 28, married, and a bookkeeper. Naftula is listed as 26, a dentist, and single. Their last residence was Bovno [=Rovno] and their closest relative was sister B. Szmulma. Bov. [Rovno] and their destination is their brother David Szulma[n] 612 S. 56th Str. Phildelphia. Their birthplaces: Rovno Poland. A record of aliens held for special inquiry shows that Codyk, Perla, Sura, Chaja and Ita were held as "LPC" [Likely Public Charge]. Pepe is not listed and was in the hospital with measles according to an oral family tradition. A separate record shows Naftula and Syman were both held in customs as "L. P. C." [likely public charge].
1921 (Oct 14) Declaration of Intention	For son Harry Shulman. Listed under the name of his brother, "Shimon Hertz Shulman," age 28, clerk, distinctive mark: scar under left eye, born in "Mlynov-Russia-Poland," born on Dec. 8, 1893, resides at 202 So. Collington Ave, Baltimore. Emigrated to US from Antwerp, Belgium on vessel "Lapland," last foreign residence was Rowno, Russia-Poland, married Yetta born at Rowno Russia Poland, arrived at port of New York Jan 4th 1921.
1922 (June 25) Passenger Manifest	For Shimon/Simon Shulman. Line 12-13. Leaving Antwerp June 15, 1922 on SS Finland arriving in New York June 25, 1922. Szymon Judel Szulman, age 32 with implied birth year of 1890, Laborer Russian, last permanent address Wolomin Russia. Closest relative or friend: Friend Szoel Mejler, Rowne [i.e. his brother-in-law Saul Meiler/Malar married to his older sister Nachuma], headed to Philadelphia, [page 2] to Brother [actually a cousin] David Shulman, Philadelphia PA 612 S.5 [or 55th Street], wife Alta Ides [Ita / Yetta] age 27 with implied birth year of 1895, Russian, last residence: Wolomin Russia. Both listed as born in StaroBychow [Bykhaw, Belarus today].[84] Yetta was pregnant at the time since Tessie was born in August 1922.
1922 (Jan 17) Marriage Record	Sarah Shulman married Paul Zutelman in District of Columbia.

---

[84] Also known as Bichov in Yiddish or Stary Bykhov. A Shulman handwritten family tree shows some of the ancestors living in Stary Bykhov.

1923 (Dec. 28) Declaration of Intention	Simon Shulman age 33, pharmacist, born in Staro-Bikhov,[85] Russia. Date of birth: Nov 19, 1890. Resides at 204 N. Chester Street, Baltimore, last foreign residence was Rowne Poland, wife Edith, born at Staro-Bikhov, Russia
1923 (July 23) Declaration of Intention	For Paul (Settleman) Shulman. I "Naftuli Shulman also known as Paul Zutelman, age 27, grocer, born in Mlynov, Russia, Dec 20, 1895. I now reside at 549 West Preston Street, emigrated from Antwerp, Belgium on Lapland. Last foreign residence was Mlynov, Russia. Wife Sarah, born at Mlynow, Russia, arrived at port of New York on or about Jun 4, 1921. Signed Naftuli Shulman.
1927 (April 26) Petition for Naturalization	Of Yetta (Perelson) Shulman (wife of Harry Shulman) Resides at 1002 N. Durham Street, Baltimore. Born March 6, 1900 in Rovno, Poland. Emigrated to the US from Antwerp, Belgium, on May 26, 1921 and arrived in NY on June 5, 1921 on vessel "Lapland," Husband is Harry, born Dec 21, 1894 at "Linow, Poland." 1 children: Bernard, born Sept. 14, 1922 in Baltimore. Married on May 5, 1921. My husband was naturalized on Nov 1926 in Baltimore.
1927 (Sept. 15) Petition for Naturalization	For Simon Judah Shulman Resides at 204 N. Chester Street, Manager of a music store, born on Nov. 19th, 1890 at Staro-Bikov, Russia. Emigrated Antwerp, Belgium on June 16th 1922, arrived New York June 25 1922 on the vessel "Finland," declared intention on Dec. 28th, 1923, wife Edith, born May 15, 1895 at Staro-Bikov, Russia. Children Tessie Aug. 2, 1922 in Baltimore, Melvin Nov. 1, 1923 in Baltimore. Witnesses [brother-in-law] Paul Schwartz, Grocer 2116 E. Fayette St. and [brother] Harry Shulman, Grocer, 1002 N. Durham St.
1928 (July 6th) Petition for Naturalization	For Tsodik Shulman. Address 204 N. Chester Street, Baltimore. Indicates birthdate April 12, 1863 at Mlynow, Poland. Lists Pearl's birthdate May 12, 1865. Children: Naomi [Nehuma] March 14th 1887, Liza August 20th 1889, Simon November 6, 1890, Harry (Naftula Herz) Dec. 25, 1894; Sarah (Sura) Sept. 5th, 1898; Clara, May 1, 1904; Pauline Sept. 14th 1906.
1929 (May 1) Petition for Naturalization	For Edith (Fixman) Shulman (Simon's wife) Residing at 204 N. Chester St, Baltimore, housewife, born May 15, 1895 at Berdichev, Russia, emigrated from Antwerp, Belgium, June 15, 1922 on the vessel "Finland" My husband Simon born on Nov 19, 1890 at Staro-Bikhov. Children: Tessie born Aug. 2, 1922 at Baltimore, Melvin born Nov 1, 1923 at Baltimore. Witnesses Paul Schwartz (her sister-in-law Pepe's husband], Grocer 901 Bennett Place, [husband] Simon J. Shulman, Merchant 204 N. Chester St.
1929 (May 27) Petition for Naturalization	For Pearl Shulman. Residing at 204 N. Chester St, Baltimore. Lists birthdate May 12, 1865 in Mlynow Poland. Children: Nehuma (March 14, 1887) Resides at Mlynow, Poland. Liza (Aug. 20th) 1889 (Resides at Russia); Simon (Nov. 6, 1890); Harry (Dec. 25, 1894), Sarah (Sept. 5, 1898), Pauline Oct. 12, 1904); Clara May 27th 1902.

[85] See note 43.

1930 (April 1) US Federal Census	Tsodik and Pearl and family of son Simon. Residing at 204 N. Chester St, Baltimore. "Gsodik, Szulman" [census taker put Szulman as his first name and Tsodik as his surname!], head, Owns home, value $3,000 67, age at marriage 23, born Poland, Year of Immigration 1921, Na[turalized], Teacher of Hebrew, wife Pearl, 64 with implied birth year of 1886, age at marriage 20 with implied year of ~1886, born in Poland, year of immigration 1921. Son "Gsodik, Simon" [i.e. mistake for Simon Shulman taking Tsodik as last name] age 39, age at marriage 27, born in Poland, immigration year 1922, Na[turalized], Manager, Music Store, Pauline [=Itta] age 35, age at marriage 25, Born in Russia, immigration year 1922, Na[turalized], their children Tessie age 7 born in Maryland and Melvin, age 6 born in Maryland.
1930 (April 18) US Federal Census	For Harry Shulman, son of Tsodik and Pearl Residing at 618 Arlington Ave. Head, renting home $70 value, married, age 34 with implied birth year of 1896, age at marriage 25, arrived in 1921, Na[turalized], manager grocer store; Yetta, wife, age 29, age at marriage 20, arrived 1921, Na[turalized]; [children] Bernard age 7, born in Maryland, Melvin son age 2. Father-in-law Meir Pzelson [Yetta's father, Meir Perelson] age 63, age 1929, al[ien]
1930 (April 10-11th) US Federal Census	For Sarah Shulman and husband Paul (Zutelman) Shulman. Residing at 1853 Lorman. Paul Shulman, head, Renting, value $45.00 age 34, age at marriage 24, Year of immigration 1922 [incorrect], al[ien], proprietor of retail grocery; Sarah Shulman, wife, age 34 with implied year of birth 1896, age at marriage 24, Year of immigration 1922 [incorrect], al[ien]; [Children]: Bessie age 5 born in Maryland (later Betty Edlavitch), Shirley, daughter, born in Maryland [later Shirley Leaderman], Frank Settleman, brother-in-law [Paul's brother], born in Poland, Year of immigration 1923, Na[turalized], clerk in retail grocery.
1930 (April 11) US Federal Census	For Clara (Shulman) Fishman and her husband Benjamin Fishman Residing at 900 Payson St. Benjamin Fishman, Head, Renting, value $63, has Radio, age 27, age of marriage 22, immigration year 1920, Na[turalized], Proprietor, Grocery Store; Clara, wife, age 25 with implied birth year 1905, age at marriage 20; son Theodore 2 11/12
1930 US Federal Census	For Pepe Pauline (Shuman) and husband Paul H. Schwartz [son of Yetta Demb]. Residing at 901 Bennet Place. Paul H., head, O[wns], home value $7700, age 27, age at marriage 23, born in Russia, arrived in 1912, Na[turalized], Merchants, Own Business; Pauline [Pepe], age 23 with implied birth year of 1907, age at marriage 19, born in Russia, Immigration year 1922 [incorrect], Naturalization pending; [children] Neena, age 3 and 7 months, born in Maryland; Leon, age 1 ½ born in Maryland.
1930 (June 12) Petition for Naturalization	For Paul (Zutelman/Settleman) Shulman. Residing at 1853 Lorman St. Balto, Md. Merchant. Born in Mlynow, Poland [probably Mervits, not Mlynov] Dec. 20, 1895. Declared Intention July 23, 1923. Wife Sarah, married on Jan 17, 1922 in Wash. D.C., She was born in Mlynow, Poland. Entered the US on June 11, 1921. [Children]: Bessie [Betty Edlavitch] birthdate Feb 26, 1924 in Baltimore and Shirley, Oct. 30, 1927 in Baltimore. Last foreign residence was Rawne, Poland. I emigrated to US from Anwerp Belgium to NY under the name "Naftula Zulman" on June 11, 1921 on the vessel Lapland. He signed his name Paul Shulman and scratched out his surname of Settleman.

	Witnesses [his brother-in-laws] Paul Schwartz Merchant 901 Bennett Place and Benjamin Fishman, Merchant 900 N. Payson St.
1939 (Jan. 6) Petition For Naturalization	[typed] For Pauline Schwartz [i.e., Pepe Shulman, wife of Paul H. Schwartz], No. 17082, resides at 3813 Callaway Ave., Baltimore Md, born in Kovno, Poland on Oct. 19, 1905. Declaration of Intention omitted pursuant to provision of Act of Sept. 22, 1922. Name of husband Paul Howard, married on Jan. 3, 1926 at Baltimore, Maryland, born at Mlynow, Russia on March 6, 1903, entered US at Baltimore on Nov. 22, 1912. I have 3 children: Neena, Dec. 10, 1926, Leon; April 26, 1928, Pearl; February 24, 1935 all born at Baltimore. My husband was naturalized in U.S. District Court at Baltimore, Md, on May 17, 1926 and Certificate No. 2275753 issued to him." My last foreign residence Kovno, Poland, emigrated from Antwerp, Belgium to New York, New York under the name Pepa Szulman on June 5, 1921 on vessel S. S. "Lapland." Witnesses Ephraim Alliker, Merchant, 1240 Scott Street, Balt., and Isaac Fershtut, Merchant, 407 Delphine Street.
1940 (April 12) US Federal Census	for Paul H. Schwartz and Pepa (Shulman) with Pepe's father Tsodik in the household Residing at 3813 Callow Ave, Baltimore. Paul is age 37, buyer for Wholesale Grocery, resided in same location in 1935, Pauline age 36, Neena age 13 born in Maryland, Leon age 11 born in Maryland, Pearl age 5 born in Maryland. (Pearl was named for Tsodik's late wife Pearl). "Lavdek" [=Tsodik listed living with family]age 80, with implied birth year of 1860. widowed.
1940 (April 5) US Federal Census	For Sarah and Paul (Settleman) Shulman Residing at 3401 Liberty Heights Ave, Paul head, age 42, Na[turalized] resided at same place in 1935, Grocer own store, Sarah age 40, [Children] Betty, daughter age 16 born in Maryland, Shirley, daughter age 12, born in Maryland, Jack age 3 born in Maryland.
1940 (April 4) US Federal Census	For Simon Shulman and family Residing at 2653 Aisquith St. Simon head, age 49, owns home, home value $6,000, Na[turalized] same house in 1935, store keeper, own Business, wife Edith 44, Na[turalized], [Children] Tessie age 17 born in Maryland, Melvin age 16 born in Maryland, Herman age 10 born in Maryland
1942 (April 26) WWII Draft Registration	April 26, 1942 WWII Draft Registration, Simon Judah Shulman, 2653 Aisquith Street, Baltimore, age 51. Place of Birth Province of Volyn, wife Mrs Edith Shulman. Owner Confectionery 2653 Aisquith St.

***

CHAPTER 6

THE FAMILY OF YENTA DEMB AND CHAIM SCHWARTZ

Yenta Demb (1870–Oct. 21, 1962) is my other Demb great-grandmother. She was the mother of my paternal grandfather, Paul H. Schwartz. In Baltimore she was known as Yetta Schwartz in some of the records, but family remembers her as Yenta, which was her original name. In photos she usually has a frown on her face and granddaughters remember her as a bitter woman. She had a few good reasons to be bitter, as I was to learn.

Yenta Demb was listed as the second eldest daughter in the family tree scroll. However, in her memoir Clara Fram recalls that her Aunt *Pearl* was the "second daughter." It thus seems probable that Yenta was the third daughter of Rivka and Israel Jacob, which seems borne out by US records which consistently imply her birth year is 1870. Yenta was likely fourth in the birth order, probably older than her brother, Motel Demb (later Max Demming), whose records inconsistently list his birth in 1869, 1870 and 1871.

From photos, Yenta was not nearly as attractive as her older sisters, Pesse and Pearl, who both were beautiful and resembled each other. Yenta married a man named Chaim Schwartz (later known as Hyman Schwartz) who was also from Mlynov and the oldest of five brothers, four of whom also came to Baltimore.[86] I was named for Chaim Schwartz and thankfully the name "Hyman" was no longer in vogue.

Chaim is listed consistently as six years older than Yenta in the US records. They were probably married by at least 1881 when their oldest son, Benjamin, was born, according to most of his records. He was followed by two other sons. Norton is listed as born in 1892 (according to his 1930 census), 1893 (according to his 1912 passenger manifest, his Declaration and Petition) and 1897 which seems like an outlier (according to his 1920 census).

Paul H. Schwartz, my grandfather, was the youngest. He is listed as born in 1894 (in his passenger manifest) but it was more likely 1903 as listed in the 1920 and 1930 census and his Declaration. It seems likely the passenger manifest was making the boys older than they were, perhaps to help the family with their immigration.

---

[86] The Schwartz brothers who came to Baltimore were Israel, Michael (Michel/Heschie), Morris (Moses) and Chaim. The memory of a fifth brother who stayed in Mlynov whose name is unknown was reported to me by Eugene "Gene" Schwartz, son of Israel Schwartz. There are photos of Schwartzes in the Mlynov Memorial book and names in the martyr list as well as a photo of Yetta with a Schwartz niece back in Mlynov (as discussed below).

Chaim died in 1946 and there are not many family memories recorded of him, in contrast to Yenta who died in 1962 and is remembered as a busybody by everyone who remembered her.

***

From the written memories of grandsons

"Zade Hyam was a quiet man who I have since been told, was very learned, probably more so than Zade Zadek. Hyam had the ability of drawing with both hands at the same time creating a mirror image of his designs. You can imagine how that fascinated a kid.

"My first memory of Hyam was in his store on Monument Street offering me a big slice of salami. How I used to enjoy a visit to his little deli. Yenta was a "yenta", a real busybody. My Mother did not get along with her Mother-in-law and Aunt. When she came to visit, you could feel the tension mount. She would have a comment about everything and everyone. I do not know how my Aunt Kate (Norton's wife) put up with her for as long as she did [since Yenta lived with them]. Hyam died about the same time as my other Zade, both in their eighties. Yenta lived into her nineties and died while at Levindale, the Jewish Home for the Aged."

From Leon Schwartz

*Figure 59 Carving on snuffbox
by Chaim Schwartz
Courtesy of Yoni Schwartz*

Marvin Schwartz, now 96, recalls Chaim and Yenta living with his family when he was a boy when they were at 2606 Park Heights Terrace. In the 1940 census, Chaim and Yenta are listed and Marvin was 13. Marvin tells me that Chaim and Yenta never spoke directly to one another. Chaim used to come downstairs and sit in a chair that was next to a small, black table with a telephone. He would never move the chair to get closer to the light from the window. Instead, he would always lean forward with books in hands extended to reach the light. Marvin recalls that Chaim and his father, Norton, both wanted the other to sit at the head of the table at meals and during Passover. Chaim wanted his son at the head of the table because it was Norton's house. Norton wanted his father, Chaim, his senior to sit at the head of the table. Since they couldn't agree, 13-year-old Marvin ended up sitting at the head of the table.

Figure 60 Yenta (Demb) and Chaim Schwartz

***

A Story About Yenta's Unhappy Marriage

As I dug into the family history, a number of stories emerged that might explain Yenta's difficult personality. One story apparently circulated in the family indicating that Yenta was not in love with Chaim Schwartz, the man she married and the man for whom I am named.

The story appears in an appendix that was added to the memoir of Clara Fram at some unknown date after 1982. It was written by Alma Finkelstein, the oldest daughter of Clara Fram's sister, Rose. Alma was born in Baltimore in 1924. After reading her Aunt Clara's memoir she was inspired to write down the stories she heard about the family. Her appendix was short. But one of the few stories she recorded concerned Yenta Schwartz. We can guess Alma heard this story from her mother Rose who may have heard it from her mother Bessie, Yenta's oldest sister. Here's Alma:

> As I think of it–I'd better get it down on paper–certainly not with the style or even the spelling that Aunt Clara [Fram] produced in her autobiography - but here goes: Our grandmother (Baubie Bessy) [Bessie Hurwitz] had 3 sisters and 1 brother that I'm sure of - Aaron (Fetta Aaron he was) [= Aaron Demb] and the sisters were Perel (Shulman I think), Molly Roskes, and Yenta Schwartz.[87]

---

[87] Alma obviously did not know about the other siblings.

Molly and Yenta were close in age and were both engaged to be married. Yenta was older - so she was first. She was pirouetting in front of the mirror during a dress fitting at the tailor shop-arms extended-when the tailor's apprentice-was a boy from an undistinguished family and not even a scholar-grabbed her hand-put a ring on her finger-and said the Hebrew words that are traditionally said by the groom under the Chuppa.[88] All of this in front of witnesses-which was the essential setting [to legally formalize a marriage]. They were therefore married in the eyes of the whole town-religiously-in every way. Her parents [Rivka and Israel Jacob] refused to allow this union-and a divorce was arranged almost immediately-but poor Yenta was now considered a marked woman-a divorcee-even though she was untouched-she was 'blemished'. Her [former] fiancée's family refused to allow their son to marry a divorcee-so she was given to a widower who needed a wife and was quite a bit older than she [this would be Chaim Schwartz].

This widower's brother was engaged to a sister [of Yenta's named] Molly and it was quite a love match but because his brother was marrying his love's sister-2 brothers couldn't marry 2 sisters-TRADITION-so that wedding was called off and poor Molly was given in marriage to Shimon Roskes-who she hated from the very first. So all because of a love-sick tailor's apprentice-the loves and lives of 2 young girls and 2 young men were ended and ruined.

Everyone [sic] of these characters ended up in Baltimore-and there was an organization called the "Mlinova Verein" that met several times a year to socialize and to help any of their landsmen who needed it. It was said that Mema Molly and her ex-fiancé used to sit together-off away from the group-and talk-and just be together. -And this was long after they were old -I am told.

The story has the definite feel of folklore about it, though, as I said, it probably did originate with Rose who was born in Mlynov or even Rose's mother, Bessie (Pesse Demb), who was Yenta's eldest sister. As far as I can tell, there is in fact no prohibition in Jewish law against two sisters marrying two brothers, though it may have been frowned on by custom.[89]

I found a letter my father wrote in 2002 after he read Alma's story about his grandmother Yenta. The letter was addressed to his cousin Ted thanking him for sending him the copy of the memoir. He wrote, "Alma's story about my grandmother and Mme. Molla [Aunt Mollie] was incredible to me and some things didn't hang together, but [my sister] Neena tells me that Aunt

---

[88] Alma is referring to the Hebrew words of betrothal "hare at medusshet li...".

[89] In fact, a hilarious chapter of Mishnah (Yebamot 3) assumes that, in fact, it was permissible for two men to marry two sisters. In these texts, the rabbis discuss what happens to the Levirate duty (Deuteronomy 25:51-6) that a man marry the widow of his brother, if his brother died childless. They discuss a case of four brothers, where two of them were married to two sisters. Suppose one brother dies, they speculate. Must a man marry his deceased brother's widow if she is the sister of his existing wife? The text thus assumes that it is permissible for two brothers to marry two sisters.

Sarah [Sarah Shulman] told a similar story to [her daughter] Shirley." Perhaps the story had some truth to it and explains why their grandson Marvin never remembers Yenta and Chaim speaking to one another when they lived with his family.

Later, during the project to translate the Mlynov Memorial Book, I was surprised to read an essay about a ladies tailor who lived on the main street of Mlynov. Residents remembered the gramophone which he owned and the records he played from his window at the end of Sabbath.[90] The presence of the lady's tailor in Mlynov hardly proves the truth of Alma's story. But it is a tantalizing connection. Could the story have some truth to it?

***

The Migration of Benjamin Schwartz

By 1910, Yenta and Chaim sent their oldest son, Benjamin, to Baltimore ahead of the rest of the family. He sent for them when he saved enough money to help bring them to America.

Benjamin left Bremen, Germany on June 9, 1910 on the SS Rhein and arrived in Baltimore on June 23rd. He was headed to his "uncle Yokel Fax [Getzel Fax] at 836 E. Pratt Street." Getzel was not actually Benjamin's uncle, but three of Benjamin's paternal uncles[91] and two of his mother's sisters[92] had already arrived in Baltimore and several of them had gotten their start at the Fax residence.

The official's handwriting on Benjamin's manifest was almost illegible, but the destination of 836 E. Pratt Street was a giveaway that this was another Mlynover heading to Baltimore.

---

[90] See Baruch Meren, "Khaykl Shnayder's Gramophone." In *Mlynov Memorial Book*, pp. 181-183.

[91] His uncle Moses (Morris) Schwarz arrived on the SS Nieuw Amsteram in Baltimore May 22, 1907. He was headed to a brother (probably Israel Schwartz) who was already at the Fax residence at 836 E. Pratt Street. Morris Schwartz's wife, Ester, accompanied by his brother Michael (Heschie) Schwarz arrived on the SS Brandenburg Nov. 14, 1907. They were headed to Morris who was at the Fax home at 836 E. Pratt Street.

I used to think that Benjamin's uncle, Israel Schwartz, arrived for the first time in Baltimore on March 31, 1911 when he appears on a manifest. I now suspect he was the brother who was already at the Fax residence in 1907 when Moses (Morris) Schwartz arrived. Israel appears on a 1911 manifest arriving in Baltimore on the SS Chemnitz with two other men, Nathan Fischman and Usher [Harry] Tatelbaum. But in the columns labeled nationality, the customs official wrote "mourning" and last residence "USA." Israel Schwartz had apparently already been in the US and returned to Mlynov because someone had died. In this 1911 manifest he was returning to the US from that trip home.

[92] Benjamin's maternal uncles, David Hurwitz (husband of Pesse Demb) and Samuel Roskes (husband of Mollie Demb) arrived in 1901 and stayed with the Faxes. Both had recently moved out to other addresses as their families arrived.

Figure 61 Benjamin Schwartz (right) with unidentified probably back in Mlynov

The manifest of the SS Rhein June 9, 1910

Benjamen Schwarz age 19 tailor

Right-columns—nearly illegible closest relative father, Chaim Schwarz Mlynov, Volyn

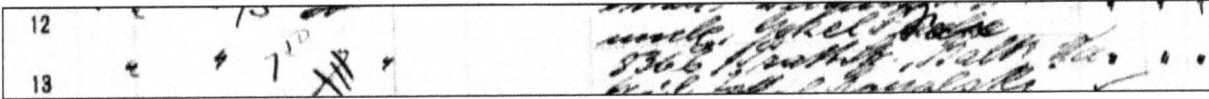

Page 2–destination, headed to uncle Yokel Fax 836 E. Pratt Street, Balto

***

The Migration of Chaim and Yenta

Yenta and Chaim and their two youngest sons, Norton and Paul, followed their eldest son Benjamin to Baltimore in 1912. They left Bremen November 10th on the SS Neckar and arrived in Philadelphia on November 22nd. They may have stayed on the ship all the way to Baltimore which was its final destination.

In the manifest, Chaim is age 48, a "dealer," his closest relative in Mlynov listed is his mother Lea Swarts. Since Chaim's mother is listed as his bclosest relative, his father Peretz must have died earlier.[93] "Jenta" [Yenta] is age 42, Nuchim [Nathan] age 17, Poritz [Peretz /Paul] age 18. Paul's age was certainly wrong as he was probably 8 or 9 when they arrived based on photos and records, which give his birthyear as 1903. Their birthplace is listed as "Mlynow." They were heading to their son, Benjamin Schwartz, who was at 111 N. Gay St.

As discussed earlier, the Schwartz family was traveling with other Mlynov immigrants. Yenta's nephew Nathan Gruber was also on the ship, as well as Chaim's sister-in-law, Sarah (Fishman) Schwartz (who married Israel Schwartz), and Sarah's nephew Morris Fishman.

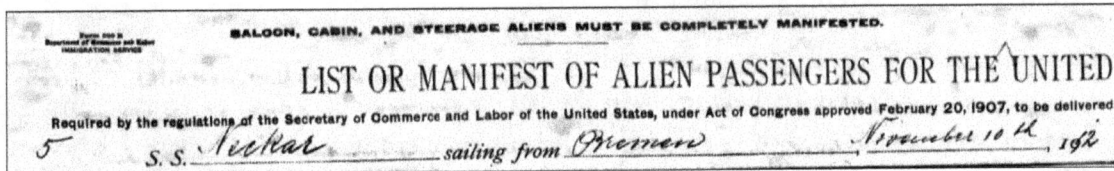

Manifest of SS Neckar Nov. 10, 1912

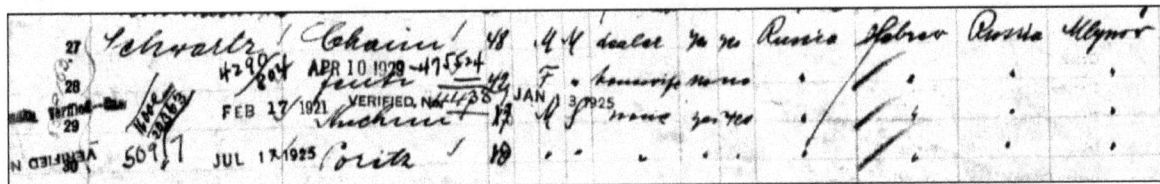

Manifest of Chaim, Jenta, Nuchim and Poritz

---

[93] It is uncertain when Peretz died. The fact that three of the grandsons are named for him suggests he may have died as early as 1894 when the eldest of the Paul Schwartzes was born.

Page 2 showing destination is son Schwartz Benj 111 Gay St. North

Figure 62 1912 Paul H. Schwartz in Baltimore

A precious photo of Paul in 1912 (above) shows him with a book in his hand and knickers, standing next to a cellar cover, not long after they arrived.

In a family photo from Baltimore probably from about 1914, Yenta and Chaim are seated with youngest son Paul (my grandfather) between them. Standing left is older son Norton and on the right is eldest son Benjamin with his new wife, Annie Fishman (Chane Fischmann), who was also from Mlynov and arrived in Baltimore in April 1911.

Benjamin probably already knew Annie from Mlynov. She was the daughter of Malka and Nathan Hyman Fishman from Mlynov.[94] Annie was supposed to be on the SS Main with her father who arrived in Baltimore on March 31, 1911. But her name is scratched out and she must have remained behind for some reason. She arrived in Baltimore a few weeks later on April 11, 1911. Both of them were headed to the home of Getzel and Ida Fax at 836 E. Pratt St.

---

[94] Annie's father, Nathan Hyman Fishman, was a brother of Berel Dov Fishman, the father of Moishe and Meyer Fishman and Sarah (Fishman) Schwartz.

Figure 63 The family of Yetta (Demb) and Chaim Schwartz circa 1914 in Baltimore
(seated l to r) Yenta, Paul H., and Chaim Schwartz,
(standing l to r) Norton, Annie (Fishman), Benjamin Schwartz. Courtesy Howard Schwartz

Benjamin and Annie Fishman married in 1914. Their marriage license date appeared in *The Baltimore Sun* in early September 1914 just weeks after WWI broke out and just after Baltimore celebrated the centennial of the Star-Spangled Banner. Whether these events moved the young couple to announce their engagement is unknown. Benjamin was 22 and Annie 19. By this point Benjamin is listed living at 104 Albemarle Street, the flat of his mother's sister, Aunt Mollie (Demb) Roskes, where the rest of his family was also living that year. That address became the second launch pad for Demb and Mlynov immigrants, as discussed later.

Marriage Licenses 1914 (Sept. 14) *The Baltimore Sun*, p. 4	ROSENHEIM—NEW.—Sylvan Rosenheim, 39; Clara New, 31. Applicant, Augusto C. Blumager, 563 Calvert Building. SCHWARTZ — FISCHMAN.—Benjamin Schwartz, 22, 104 Albemarle street; Annie Fischman, 19. WENEKU—WILSON.—John Weneku, 24; Jessie Wilson, 25, both of New York. WINKS — KRELLER. — John Winks, 51; Marie Kreller, 41, widow, 714 South Albemarle street.

Ben and Annie had a daughter Lillian (married name "Lily Lutins") in 1917 and a second daughter Selma (married name Selma Hyman) in 1922.

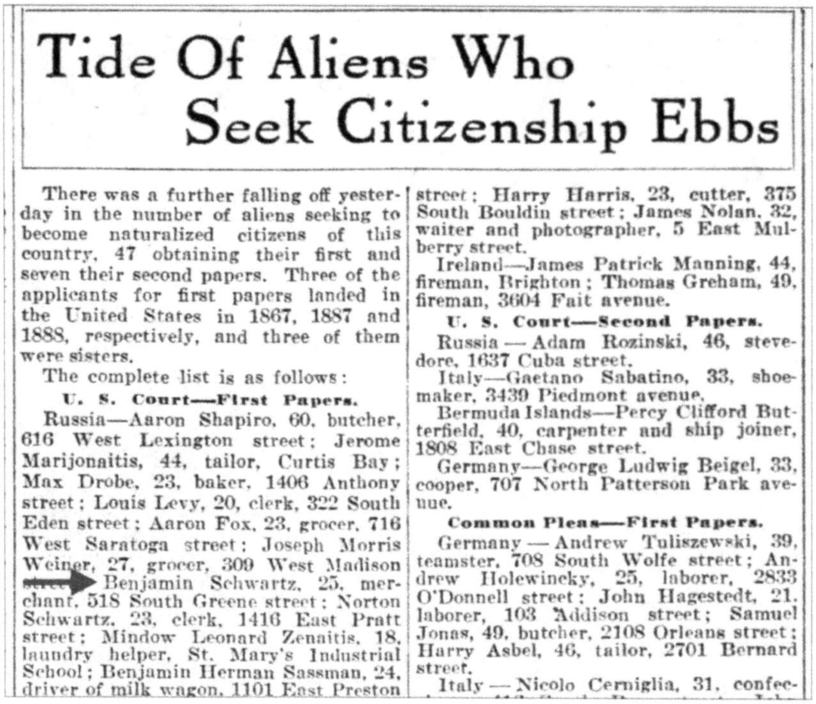

Tide Of Aliens Who Seek Citizenship Ebbs

There was a further falling off yesterday in the number of aliens seeking to become naturalized citizens of this country, 47 obtaining their first and seven their second papers. Three of the applicants for first papers landed in the United States in 1867, 1887 and 1888, respectively, and three of them were sisters.

The complete list is as follows:

U. S. Court—First Papers.

Russia—Aaron Shapiro, 60, butcher, 616 West Lexington street; Jerome Marijonaitis, 44, tailor, Curtis Bay; Max Drobe, 23, baker, 1406 Anthony street; Louis Levy, 20, clerk, 322 South Eden street; Aaron Fox, 23, grocer, 716 West Saratoga street; Joseph Morris Weiner, 27, grocer, 309 West Madison street; Benjamin Schwartz, 25, merchant, 518 South Greene street; Norton Schwartz, 23, clerk, 1416 East Pratt street; Mindow Leonard Zennitis, 18, laundry helper, St. Mary's Industrial School; Benjamin Herman Sassman, 24, driver of milk wagon, 1101 East Preston street; Harry Harris, 23, cutter, 375 South Bouldin street; James Nolan, 32, waiter and photographer, 5 East Mulberry street.

Ireland—James Patrick Manning, 44, fireman, Brighton; Thomas Greham, 49, fireman, 3604 Fait avenue.

U. S. Court—Second Papers.

Russia — Adam Rozinski, 46, stevedore, 1637 Cuba street.

Italy—Gaetano Sabatino, 33, shoemaker, 3439 Piedmont avenue.

Bermuda Islands—Percy Clifford Butterfield, 40, carpenter and ship joiner, 1808 East Chase street.

Germany—George Ludwig Beigel, 33, cooper, 707 North Patterson Park avenue.

Common Pleas—First Papers.

Germany — Andrew Tuliszewski, 39, teamster, 708 South Wolfe street; Andrew Holewincky, 25, laborer, 2833 O'Donnell street; John Hagestedt, 21, laborer, 103 Addison street; Samuel Jonas, 49, butcher, 2108 Orleans street; Harry Asbel, 46, tailor, 2701 Bernard street.

Italy — Nicolo Cerniglia, 31, confec-

Figure 64 Tide of Aliens Who Seek Citizenship
The Baltimore Sun, April 21, 1917, p. 6

When WWI began in 1914, immigrants who were not yet naturalized feared that they might be treated as an enemy and moved into segregated areas or even worse deported. Many immigrants rushed to start the naturalization process as covered in *The Baltimore Sun*. Among those listed in the rush were the brothers Benjamin and Norton Schwartz. Paul, being younger, did not seek his naturalization at this time.

In his 1920 Petition for Naturalization, Benjamin is listed as a grocer across town at 574 Presstman Street but he starts dabbling in real estate during this period as well. His parents, "Hyman" (Chaim) age 57 and "Yetta", age 50, are living still in East Baltimore at 206 South Collington Ave. Hyman is a proprietor of a bakery. Norton and Paul are still living with the family. Norton, now age 26, is a bookkeeper in a bargain company and Paul, age 17, is a clerk in a Dept. store.

1920 Census for Hyman, Yenta, Norton and Paul at 206 Collington Ave.

Norton's son Marvin (now 96) tells me a funny story about Norton's first job at Jacob Epstein's Bargain house and how he ended up shifting to the grocery business. Norton answered an ad for a clerk in the business and got the job. Apparently on his first day of work, he entered the office and saw some hooks on the wall where men hung their jackets. He took off his jacket and hung his there as well. He was then told that these hooks were just for management; he was instructed to put his jacket in another spot designated for workers. So Norton took his jacket off the hook, left the office and never came back. That was the end of his job at the bargain house.

By 1921, Norton filled out his Petition for Naturalization and is now listed as a grocer. He received his marriage license to marry Kate Spector on July 3, 1925. Their son, Marvin, was born in 1926, Nesanel ("Sonnel") in 1928, Milton in 1930, and Mayer in 1937.

Hyman must have been doing relatively well at this time since he was assessed $260 in 1924 for improving his property with a two-story building. A year earlier, in 1923, Norton and Paul apparently went out on their own and started "Schwartz Bros," a joint grocery business and used their home address that year. In 1924, they apparently moved their venture well up in the Northeast at 3500 Old York Road. This was not an area of Jewish concentration and may explain why the "Schwartz Bros" business appears at the address of their parents back in East Baltimore the following year, though Norton and Kate are still running a grocery on Old York Road there in 1929 and 1930.

1924, Tax Assessment *The Baltimore Sun,* Nov. 24, p. 19	T.—2116 E. FAYETTE, 16x100 feet. Improved by two-story building. Assessed to Hyman Schwartz.................$260.85
1923 City Directory "Schwartz Bros"	" Norton (Schwartz Bros) 2116 e Fayette " Paul (Schwartz & Rubin) 223 w Mulberry " Paul (Schwartz Bros) 2116 e Fayette
1924 City Directory "Schwartz Bros"	" Bros (Norton and Paul H) gros 3500 Old York rd
1925 Marriage License The Baltimore Sun, July 3, p. 18	SCHWARTZ — SPECTOR. — Norton, 31, 2116 East Fayette street; Kate, 23.

Paul married his first cousin Pauline (Pepe) Shulman on January 3, 1926.[95] Their daughter Neena B. Schwartz was born in December 1926, their son Leon (my father "Moshe Leib") in 1928 and their daughter Pearl (married name Imber) in 1935.

---

[95] The date appears on Pepe's Petition for Naturalization in 1939.

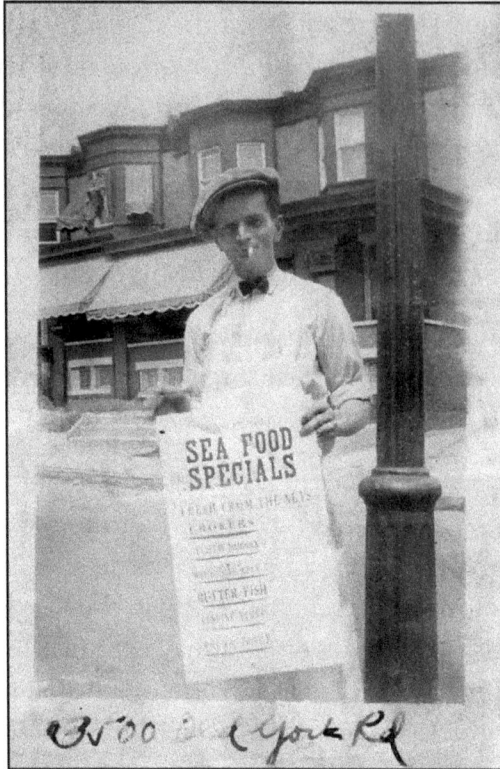

Figure 65 Paul H. Schwartz (my grandfather) advertising for a grocery

***

Yenta Goes Back to Mlynov

In 1929, Yenta went back to Mlynov along with Israel Herman, the husband of Yenta's niece, Mollie (Gruber) Herman. For such an important event, it is surprising how few oral traditions there are about this trip.

When I asked Yenta's granddaughter, my Aunt Pearl, about this trip she laughed and said, "Yenta would go into her son Benjamin's cash register in the grocery and just take what she wanted. That's how she paid for the trip." I don't know whether this is true or not or just another one of the tales about how intrusive Yenta was. In any case, several photos of Yenta back in Mlynov during this period have come to light. In one of the photos, discussed earlier, Yenta and Israel Herman are with the family of her niece, Nehuma (Shulman) Meiler.

In another photo, Yenta is seated center with five other women. My Aunt Neena, who had the photo in a box, had no idea who the other women were with her grandmother.

"She went back to Mlynov in the 1930s," Neena told me when I found it.

A year or so later, I found a copy of the same photo in the front of a book about the survival of Liba Tesler, who fled from the Mlynov ghetto only days before its liquidation.[96] Liba is standing

---

[96] David Sokolsky, *Monument: One Woman's Courageous Escape From The Holocaust.*

in the center behind Yenta. I tracked down the author, David Sokolsky and learned that Liba was his step-grandmother in Baltimore. Liba miraculously survived the Holocaust and came to Baltimore where she married. The young women in the photo seated on either side of Yenta were Liba's sisters, Hinda (seated left), Golda (seated right). Both of them perished in the Shoah. David didn't know who Yenta was until I told him.

Figure 66 Yenta Schwartz (seated center) with Liba Tesler (standing center) Courtesy of Neena Schwartz

We both concluded that Yenta must have been related to the younger women in the photo. That there was such a relationship is suggested by a conversation subsequently with Sheila Mandelberg, whom I met in Baltimore in 2017. Sheila's mother, born Sarah Marder in Mlynov, was Liba's first cousin. Sarah was one of the children in the group of three families that left Mlynov for Baltimore in 1920 (discussed later).[97] After Liba survived the Shoah, Sarah's family helped Liba make her way to Baltimore.

The first thing Sheila said to me when I met her was, "You and I are related. I was at your Aunt Pearl's fifth birthday party."

Neither Sheila nor my Aunt Pearl could explain the relationship. But I subsequently discovered a decent DNA match with Sheila and her son seeming to confirm the biological

---

[97] Sheila's mother, Sarah, arrived in Baltimore in 1920 with the group of Mlynov families who traveled with the wife of Aaron Demb, discussed below. Sarah Marder became Sarah Mutter after marrying in Baltimore.

connection. I assume, therefore, that when Yenta went back to Mlynov, she was in a photo with Liba and her sisters because they were relatives, though no one understands the relationship anymore.[98]

Figure 67 Yenta standing with niece Rivka (Schwartz) Grintsveig

Photo postcard with Yiddish inscription on back: "For Cousin Peretz and Cousin Fefe, From me, Rivke Schwartz"

There was one additional woman in that 1929 photo of women that I have since been able to identify. The woman in the back left corner of the group looked familiar. As Ted Fishman once said about her, "she looks like a Schwartz." I discovered another photo of her when a packet of photos arrived from my father's first cousin, Marvin Schwartz. Marvin dug them out of his attic and had gotten them from another first cousin, Eugene Schwartz.[99]

"I don't know who any of these people are," he wrote to me. "Maybe you can do something with them."

Among them was a photo postcard with the very same woman standing with Yenta. It must have been taken on the same occasion. On the back was some Yiddish. The postcard was addressed to Cousin Peretz[100] and cousin Fefe and it was signed Rivka Schwartz.

---

[98] Liba's grandfather, Avrum Kotel from Ostrog, took the surname Tesler and came to Mlynov to escape conscription. He was set up with a local woman named Hannah. They had a son Jacob who also married a Mlynov girl named Blima Woskobojnic. See David Sokolsky, *Monument*, p. 18.

[99] Marvin Schwartz was son of Norton Schwartz. Eugene Schwartz was son of Israel Schwartz.

[100] Probably Eugene's father, Paul Schwartz, son of Israel Schwartz and Sarah (Fishman). Fefe is probably Paul's sister, Irene.

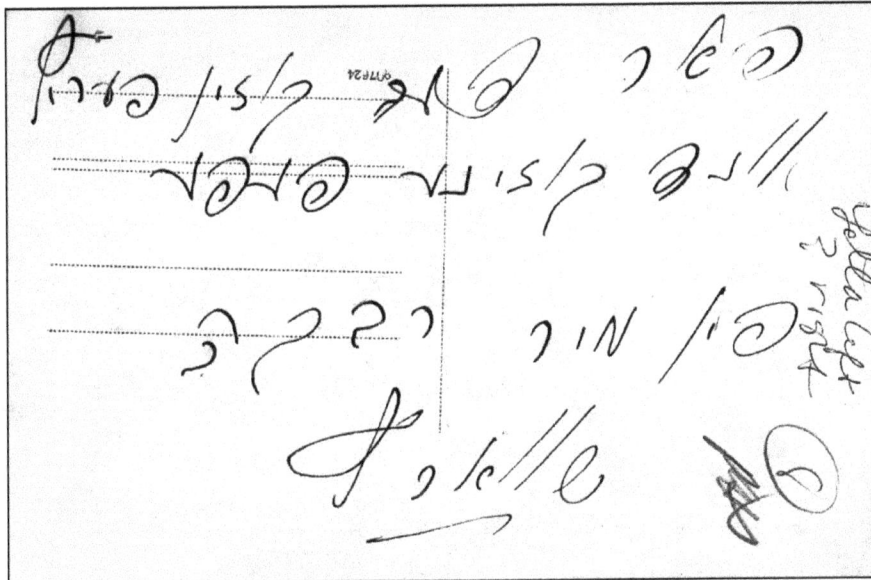

Another photo in the same packet showed this same Rivka with her husband and was signed Rivka Gruntzveig. Another showed her with two children and the young family of her sister. I later found the name Rivka "Grintzveig" among the list of Mlynov martyrs. Like Liba's sisters in the photo, she too had perished in the Shoah.

I believe, therefore, that Yenta was in the photo with one of her Schwartz nieces, probably the daughter of her husband's brother, the Schwartz brother who stayed in Mlynov and whose name we don't know. Of the relatives in the photo, Yenta would only see Liba again.

Yenta's granddaughter, Neena (my Dad's sister), told me that her grandmother had gone back to Mlynov in the 1930s. I later found Yenta's passenger manifest returning from Mlynov in 1929.

"Jenta Szwartz," age 59, departed Cherbourg, France on the SS Aquitania and arrived in New York on Sept. 27, 1929. She was traveling back to the US with Israel Herman, her niece Mollie's husband. He was on a different list of the manifest along with US Citizens. Since Yenta was not yet a citizen, she was grouped with other "Alien Passengers in Possession of Permit to Re-Enter the United States." Her permit number was 474032-475524 issued in Washington to reenter the country. It had been issued on April 22, 1929. The trip had probably been that summer of 1929.

Perhaps the most revealing bit of information on Yenta's manifest was her closest relative back in the place she visited: "father-Srul Dejb" in Mlynov. Israel Jacob Demb was still alive in September 1929. If only we had a photo of Yenta with him! It was probably the last time that Yenta saw him alive and it must have been very difficult leaving him. We don't know if her mother Rivka was still alive at that point in time or why Yenta chose that date to visit Mlynov. Was she back there for a funeral of her mother, Rivka?

Manifest of SS Aquitania, sailing from Cherbourg Sept. 21, 1929

10	FRIDMAN ✓	~Malka	59	V	F	M	H'wife	yes	Polish	yes	Polish	Jewish
11	SZWARTZ ✓	Jenta	59	✓	F	M	H.Wife	yes	Polish Hebrew	yes	Polish	Hebrew
12	BOGIAN ✓	Oszar	48	V	M	M	Baker	Yes	Polish	Yes	Polish	Jewish

Manifest for "Jenta Szwartz" 1929 returning from trip to Mlynov

| Polish | Hebrew | Poland | Mlynow | Reenter Permit No.474032 — 475524 issued at Washington 22/4/29 | U.S.A. | Baltimore ✓ |
| Polish | Jewish | Poland | Mlcowiecka | Reenter Permit No.486654 — 488812 issued at Washington 14/5/26 | U.S.A. | Brooklyn ✓ |

Jenta Szwartz had a permit to reenter the US issued April 22, 1929

| 11 | father-Srul Dejb Nlynov pow Dubno Poland | Poland | Md. | Baltimore | yes | self | ... | ... | Balti-more | Return Home address-2116 E.Fayette str.Baltimore Md. |
| | Wife Odys Bocian | | | | | | | | | |

Her closest relative was "father-Srul Dejb" in Mlynov Poland.

Yenta was on her way back to the States in September 1929, the same month the Great Crash began; Black Tuesday took place a month later and the tragedy of the Depression became evident. As a result of the crash, Yenta's son, Benjamin, lost a lot of money in real estate and had to refocus on his grocery business to make ends meet. That decision would ultimately seal his fate.

***

A Humorous Grocery Store Robbery

In 1935, a few years after Yenta returned from Mlynov, a story appeared in *The Baltimore Sun* involving Yenta's husband, Hyman Schwartz, now about 68 years old, and still a proprietor of a grocery store. "Aged Man Captures Negro Store Thief," the title of the article read. Apparently, Hyman grabbed the man who allegedly stolen $1.79 from his cash register. Despite blows being reigned on him, Hyman held onto the thief for twenty minutes until the police arrested the man. The story in some ways foreshadowed and perhaps even modeled a later tragedy that was just around the corner with Hyman's son Benjamin.

The Baltimore Sun,
March 29, 1935, p. 26

Aged Man Captures Negro Store Thief

Hyman Schwartz Battles Man Who Is Alleged To Have Taken $1.79

Hyman Schwartz, aged proprietor of a store in the 2000 block East Fayette street, yesterday morning fought with a Negro who is alleged to have taken $1.79 out of the cash register in the store.

Oblivious to blows delivered by his assailant, Schwartz managed to hold him captive for twenty minutes until police arrived. At Northeastern district police station the Negro gave his name as Stanford Davis, 200 block South Dallas street.

Davis will be arraigned on a larceny charge today before Magistrate Edwin Windle.

The sad undercurrent of this humorous story was the increasing tension between the Jewish grocers in downtown Baltimore and the African-Americans who had made their way to Baltimore as part of the Great Migration north. Both communities fled oppression and were seeking economic opportunity. In the long run there was far more prejudice in America against race than against religion. By submerging into "white" culture, Jews in Baltimore were able to escape poverty and become part of America's white middle class. These tensions also became evident in a family tragedy that was to unfold just two years later.

***

The Murder of Ben Schwartz

Two years after Hyman Schwartz wrestled the robber of his grocery to the ground, his son Benjamin was robbed at gun point by three "Negroes." Perhaps Ben was inspired to resist by the earlier success of his 68-year-old father. We'll never know for sure what happened. But the results were tragic.

On October 8, 1937, near midnight, as Benjamin was preparing to close, his wife, Annie, heard a scream and a shot rang out. As she came running to the front of the store from the back living quarters, Benjamin fell at her feet. Their two daughters, Lillian and Selma, were upstairs at the time of the shooting and rushed to her aid when they heard her scream.

An article the next day said Anna had witnessed the murder. Benjamin had just finished counting the money when one of the men demanded his money and then fired without warning, as Anna stood looking over his shoulder. Benjamin staggered back into her arms and she began screaming. A man named Harry Thron happened to be driving past the store a few seconds after the shooting and heard Annie's screams. He drove Benjamin to University Hospital where physicians said he had been shot through the left eye, the bullet penetrating his brain. The "bandits" did not get any money which was found in Benjamin's pockets in the hospital.

A short while after the robbery, a Negro was arrested in a nearby tavern but was released after questioning. That evening police found a tavern proprietor, a man named Joseph Kazla, in the next block who had been robbed recently and threatened again the day before by a trio believed to be the same "colored men" who murdered Benjamin. They had stolen $20 from him at gunpoint a few weeks earlier and he said he could identify the men.

A grocer named James A. Walsh, whose store was directly across the street from Benjamin's, gave the most accurate description of the "three Negroes." He had seen the three men on the corner for about 20 minutes before the shooting. He had closed his store and was standing on the sidewalk outside when the men went into Schwartz's store and reappeared on the run a few minutes later.

Benjamin's niece, Neena, who was just 11 at the time, remembered waking up in the middle of the night when her father, Benjamin's younger brother, Paul, got the call. She remembers hearing her parents talking in hushed tones and knowing something terrible had happened.

That same night, six "Negroes" including two women were picked up in a "general round up" and grilled all night by chief of detectives, whose name, believe it or not, was Capt. John A. Cooney. Four of the six were subsequently released. Cooney assigned some of his best men to the case. The autopsy suggested that Benjamin was killed by a .38-caliber pistol.

By the next evening, the headlines said that "Police mobilize 19 in Schwartz Murder Hunt."[101] It was the largest number dedicated to such an effort since a famous case in 1922 called the Norris Case. Two of the original six men arrested were still in custody and known to have records as police "searched pool parlors, saloons, and other hangouts in various parts of the city to find new suspects." The Commissioner Lawson told the men that "he wanted them to crack this case and to keep at it until they got somewhere."

---

[101] A series of articles appeared in October and November 1937 in *The Baltimore Sun* and *The Evening Sun* about the murder and the investigation.

BARRE STREET GROCER SLAIN BY ROBBERS

Benjamin Schwartz Shot In Head By Negroes, Who Escape

Falls At Feet Of Wife. Assailants Fail To Obtain Loot

The Baltimore Sun, p. 2
Oct. 08, 1937

POLICE MOBILIZE 19 IN SCHWARTZ MURDER HUNT

Crack Investigators Out To Find Robbers Who Killed Grocer

Largest Number Put On Job Since Norris Case In 1922

The Evening Sun, p. 18
Oct. 09, 1937

On November 4, nearly a month after the murder, a "Negro" named Mayfield Smith, was held on an unrelated charge related to 10 pocketbook snatchings, from the period June 11th to June 23rd, which netted $70. Smith had been arrested before in 1934 when a gang of "colored boys" were said to be responsible for a series of pocketbook snatchings. After his arrest, it was determined he was also wanted on an assault charge for biting a man when an earlier arrest was attempted.

The next day a "colored woman" "unexpectedly" identified Mayfield Smith as one of the three bandits who shot Benjamin Schwartz. The woman picked him out of a lineup. She saw him run from the store at Barre and Warner streets and jump into a cab the night of the murder. The woman told police that from the way he ran from the store with two others, she knew he had done something wrong. It wasn't until later she knew it was a case of murder. Her name was not mentioned in the papers that day.

On Saturday, November 6, an inquest into the fatal shooting was scheduled for 8:30 Monday night. The papers reported that the "19-year-old colored youth" was twice identified as being one of the bandits. The second witness, not named in the article, was a man standing nearby at the time of the murder, who "got a good look at the bandits and was sure the Negro was one of them." Mayfield Smith was held on $7,500 bail and transferred to the Baltimore City Jail. The same day an article reported that Benjamin's widow, Annie, could not identify the man in the lineup.

On November 9th, Mayfield Smith was formally charged in an inquest that lasted three hours. The witnesses were now named in the paper. J. J. Walsh, the grocer across the street, said he recognized Smith as one of the bandits who ran from the store, "while a third stood in the doorway and shot Schwartz." Sarah Brown, "Negro" of the 600 Continental block, identified him as "one of the three men who ran past her house, two blocks from the grocery a minute or two after the shooting." John Horried, another "Negro, of the 600 block Conway street," said he visited the store a few minutes before the killing and picked out Smith as "one of three Negroes he saw standing on the street corner."

Police "also produced several Negroes from East Baltimore, who testified Smith had visited them and boasted of killing a man in West Balitmore [sic]."

Mayfield Smith was arrested and put in prison. His name appears in prison in the 1940 Federal Census. He must have been released from prison not longer afterwards because he was rearrested in September 1941 for purse snatching again. In 1946, Mayfield Smith, now 28-years-old, was held on four new charges of purse snatchings and given 5 more years in prison. Smith presented a plea of mistaken identity.

**

In this era of Black Lives Matters, there is good reason to wonder whether Mayfield Smith was involved in the murder of Ben Schwartz. The interaction of the Black and Jewish communities is not often talked about in Jewish families, at least it wasn't in mine. My father, like many in the Jewish community, held the view that we Jews pulled ourselves up by our bootstraps and earned everything we achieved. But there is a deeper story lurking here.

I spent quite a bit of time trying to understand who Mayfield Smith was and how his path had intersected with my great uncle's. In the end, I don't really know if he was involved in the murder, and it doesn't really matter anyway. In some sense, Mayfield and my great-uncle Ben were stereotypes or metaphors for their respective communities, foist on them by their circumstances.

Mayfield Smith was born in Baltimore in 1918. He was the grandson of sharecroppers who had been freed from slavery; his father Golden Smith was from Georgia, and his mother, Rose Brown, from Virginia. They came to Baltimore as part of the Great Migration north to take advantage of the promised jobs and opportunities that Northern States were advertising to African Americans following WWI.

Baltimore had the largest mixed population of African Americans and Jews in the country.[102] Both men, Benjamin and Mayfield, landed in Baltimore as their families and communities were seeking to escape oppression and find better opportunities. Each was a stereotypical member of his community—Ben Schwartz, the grocer, Mayfield Smith the neer-do-well. Ben's murder was ultimately a symptom of the deepening divide and tension between black and white, racism and antisemitism, assimilation and suppression. The underbelly of American life was writ large in their stories.

The murder of Ben Schwartz was a tragedy for both men and their families. Ben's family was torn apart by the loss. My grandfather previously lent his brother Ben some money for real estate deals and the money was never repaid. The unpaid debt created a rift in the family and the two sides of the family drifted apart. I never knew about Ben's descendants until I started this family history

---

[102] Antero Pietila, *Not in My Neighborhood: How Bigotry Shaped a Great American City.* 2010.

project. How wonderful to heal that breach and connect with his descendants, even hosting one of them in my home.[103]

The murder was a tragedy for Mayfield Smith as well. He spent most of his life in prison. As far as I can tell he finally got out and eventually married a woman named Evelyn but they apparently had no children. I tried reaching out to a few people who appeared to be Mayfield's cousins, but for understandable reasons there was some hesitation to engage with a white Jewish guy who wanted to connect over his great Uncle's murder.

***

Ben Schwartz died in 1937. His father Hyman Schwartz died April 18, 1946. By then, Yenta had lost her first-born son, her husband, and perhaps knew the fate of the family she had visited in Mlynov in 1929. Yenta lived on to torture her children and grandchildren, though one can certainly understand why she might have had a hard time letting go of her bitterness. Yenta died on Oct. 21, 1962. I was six years old, but I don't ever remember meeting her or even knowing that she had passed.

SCHWARTZ.--On October 21, 1962, YETTA (nee Demb), beloved wife of the late Hyman Schwartz, mother of Norton and Paul H. Schwartz, sister of Mr. Aaron Demb. Also survived by 9 grandchildren and 12 great grandchildren. 23
Services at the Jack Lewis Funeral Home, 2100-02 Eutaw Place, on Monday at 1 P.M. Interment United Hebrew Cemetery Corp. Shomrei Mishmeres Congregation, Rosedale. [Kindly omit flowers]. In mourning at 2606 Park Heights Terrace.

The tombstone, which is in the Shomrei Mishmeres Hakodesh cemetery in Rosedale reads "Yetta" in English, but the Hebrew says "Yenta." Her tombstone is separated from her husband Hyman, whose tombstone stands next to his brother-in-law's, Tsodik Shulman, my other great-grandfather. This is the only cemetery in the county as far as I know that separated men and women in death just as they did in the synagogue.

---

[103] I had the opportunity to meet Benjamin's granddaughter Rona (Hyman) Kappelman for the first time and host her and her husband at our home. She was Benjamin's granddaughter, a daughter of Selma (Schwartz) Hyman.

A Summary of Records for the family of Yenta (Demb) and Chaim Schwartz

1910 Passenger Manifest	Benjamin Schwark, tailor, age 19 (implied birth year of 1881) left Bremen on June 9th, 1910 on the SS Rhein arrived in Baltimore June 23, his father Chaim Schwartz is closest relative back in Mlynow and his destination is "836 E. Pratt uncle Yokel Fax"
1912 Passenger Manifest	Leaving Bremen on Nov 10, 1912 on the SS Neckar arriving in Philadelphia on Nov 22, 1912. Chaim Schwartz age 48 with implied year of 1864, a dealer, last residence Mlynov. His mother Swarts Lea is his closest relative; his wife Jenta [Yenta] age 42 with implied birth year of 1870; [his sons], Nuchim age 19 with implied birth year of 1893 and Poritz (Paul H. Schwartz) age 18 with implied birth year of 1894. Destination: son Benjamin at 111 Gary St.-North
1917 (April 20) Declaration of Intention	For Norton Schwartz, No. 4186, age 23, clerk, born in Mlynov, Russia on Dec. 8, 1893, resides at 1416 E Pratt Street, emigrated from Bremen Germany on the vessel "Neckar", arrived at port of Philadelphia on the 28th day of Nov. 1913 [incorrect], last residence was Mlynov, not married
1917 (April 20) Declaration of Intention	Benjamin Schwartz, age 25, merchant, white, fair complexion, 5' 6", 125, brown hair, brown eyes, born in Mlynov, Russia on Sept 22, 1891. Resides at 518 S Greene Street. emigrated from Bremen, Germany on vessel "Rhein," last residence Mlynov Russia, married Annie, she was born in Mlynov Russia and now resides with me. Arrived port of Baltimore on or about June 22, 1910.
1917 (June 5) WWI Draft Registration	Benjamin Schwartz, 519 S. Green Baltimore. Date of birth Step 22, 1891. born in Mlynov, naturalization "Declarant." present trade: Store Keeper, married, supports a wife, claims exemption "physical"
1917 (June 5) WWI Draft Registration	For Norton Schwartz, residing at 1416 E. Pratt St. Balto Md, date of birth Dec. 18, 1893 naturalization status: Declared Intention. Born Mlinov Volin Russia, employed Hechts Reliable Store on S. Broadway, supports: none, single, seeks exemption for "poor health"
1920 (Dec. 30) Petition for Naturalization	Benjamin Schwartz, 574 Presstman Street, Baltimore. Grocer, born Sept 22, 1891 in Mlynov, Russia. Wife's name is Annie. She was born on Feb. 1894 in Mlynov. [Child] Lilly born Oct. 9th 1917. Witnesses Samuel Roskes, Grocer, and Israel Schwartz, Grocer. 2127 E. Pratt St. and 1152 E Lombard St.
1920 (Jan. 8) US Federal Census	For Yenta, Hyman and family. Residing at 206 South Collington Avenue, Baltimore. Hyman age 57 with implied birth year of 1863. Owner with mortgage. proprietor of a bakery. "Yettia," age 50 with implied birth year of 1870. Norton age 26 with implied birth year of 1897, Paul age 17 with implied birth year of 1903. Norton's [naturalization] is PA [pending], the rest are still AI(aliens).
1921 (May 3) Petition for Naturalization	For Norton Schwartz, residing 2116 E. Fayette St. Baltimore, Md, Grocer, born Dec. 8th 1893, emigrated from Bremen, Germany on or about 15 day of November 1912 and arrived Philadelphia PA on November 22, 1912 on vessel "Neckar", no children, filed May 3, 1921. Witnesses: [Uncle] Sam Roskes, Grocer, 2127 E. Pratt St. [Uncle] Israel Schwartz, Grocer 1152 E. Lombard St. [next page]: Order of Court Denying Petition by Chief Naturalization Examiner on Sept 26, 1921 "the petitioner has claimed exemption under the selective draft

	act after he had declared his intention to become a citizen of the United Stated and said petition is hereby dismissed.
1923 (July 6) Declaration of Intention	For "Paul Schwartz, also known as Paul Howard Schwartz," No. 15838, age 20, clerk, color white, complexion fair, 5'8", 120 pounds, hair color brown, eyes hazel, born in Mlynow, Russia on March 6, 1903, resides at 2116 E. Fayette Street, Baltimore, emigrated from Bremen Germany on vessel "Neckar" last residence was Mlynow, Russia, not married, arrived at the port of Philadelphia on or about the "? day" November 1911
1925 (July 3) Notice of Marriage License	For Norton Schwartz and Kate Spector: Norton, 31, 2116 E. Fayette Street; Kate 23. Baltimore Sun, p. 18.
1925 (Aug. 11) Petition For Naturalization	For Paul Schwartz, No. 8237. Residence 2116 E. Fayette St, Baltimore, Maryland, occupation: Merchant, born on March 6, 1903 at Mlynow, Russia, emigrated from Bremen Germany on or about 29th of October 1912 and arrived Philadelphia Nov. 22nd on vessel "Neckar". Declared intention on July 6, 1923, I am not married. Witnesses: [brother] Benjamin Schwartz, Real Estate, 1616 Moreland Ave, Balto, Md and [Uncle] Israel Schwartz, Merchant, 1162 E. Lombard Street, Balto Md.
1926 (May 17) Naturalization Record	For Norton Schwartz, age 32, Petition 7966, issued by District Court at Baltimore. Grocer, Date of order of admission, May 17, 1926. Declaration of Intention No. 13825, issued by the Clerk of District Court of Baltimore Maryland on Nov. 24, 1921.
1930 (April 5) US Census	For Hyman Swartz, Yenta and Benjamin Residing at 2116 Fayette Street Hyman Swartz Homeowner, Home value $8,000, age 68 (implied birth year 1862), age at marriage 38 (implied year 1892), proprietor of Grocery Store; wife Etta (Yetta) age 60 (implied birth year 1870), age at first marriage 30 implied marriage year 1900, and son Benjamin, age 29 (with implied birth year of 1901), age at marriage 15, real estate agent. Benjamin is Na[turalized], his parents are not [Benjamin's wife and daughter not listed for unknown reasons]
1930 US Federal Census	For Pepe Pauline (Shuman) and husband Paul H. Schwartz [son of Yetta Demb]. Living at 901 Bennet Place. Paul H., head, O[wns], home value $7700, age 27 with implied birth year of 1903, age at marriage 23, born in Russia, arrived in 1912, Na[turalized], Merchants, Own Business; Pauline [Pepe], age 23 with implied birth year of 1907, age at marriage 19, born in Russia, Immigration year 1922 [incorrect], Naturalization pending; [children] Neena, age 3 and 7 months, born in Maryland; Leon, age 1 ½ born in Maryland.
1930 (April 5) US Federal Census	For Norton Schwartz and family. Residing at 2606 Park Heights Terrace, Norton Schwartz, Head O[wns home] home value: $8,000, age 38 with implied birth year of 1892, age at marriage 33 born in Poland immigration year 1908 [incorrect] Na[turalized], Proprietor Grocery Store, Kate wife, 29, age at marriage 24, born in Poland, Children: Marvin N, son, 3 6/12, born in Maryland, Samuel A., son, 1 4/12, born in Maryland, father-in-law, Joseph D. Spector, 56, marriage at 21, born in Poland, immigration year 1900, Al[lien]; mother-in-law, Mary, age 55 age of marriage 20, born in Poland, immigration year 1904 Al[ien]
1939 (Jan. 6) Petition For Naturalization	[typed] For Pauline Schwartz [i.e., Pepe Shulman, wife of Paul H. Schwartz], No. 17082, resides at 3813 Callaway Ave., Baltimore Md, born in Kovno, Poland on Oct. 19, 1905. Declaration of Intention omitted pursuant to provision of Act of Sept. 22, 1922. Name of

	husband Paul Howard, married on Jan. 3, 1926 at Baltimore, Maryland, born at Mlynow, Russia on March 6, 1903, entered US at Baltimore on Nov. 22, 1912. I have 3 children: Neena, Dec. 10, 1926, Leon; April 26, 1928, Pearl; February 24, 1935 all born at Baltimore. My husband was naturalized in U.S. District Court at Baltimore, Md, on May 17, 1926 and Certificate No. 2275753 issued to him." My last foreign residence Kovno, Poland, emigrated from Antwerp, Belgium to New York, New York under the name Pepa Szulman on June 5, 1921 on vessel S. S. "Lapland." Witnesses Ephraim Alliker, Merchant, 1240 Scott Street, Balt., and Isaac Fershtut, Merchant, 407 Delphine Street.
1940 (April 13) US Federal Census	For Paul Schwartz and Pepe (Shulman) and Pepe's father Tsodik Residing at 3813 Calloway Avenue. Home value: 7500, Paul, head, age 37, born in Russia, lived in same place in 1935; Pauline (Pep) wife age 36, born in Russia, Neena, daughter, age 13, born in Maryland; Leon, son, age 11, born in Maryland; Pearl, daughter, age 5, born in Maryland; Lsodik [Tsodik] fath-in-law, age 80, widowed, born in Russia, lived in same place in 1935.
1940 (Aug. 12) US Federal Census	For Norton's family with Yetta still living with the family. Residing at 2606 Park Heights Terrace, O[wns home] home value $5,000, Norton Schwartz, head, 46, lived in same place in 1935, Occupation: grocer, retail grocery; Kate wife, age 40; Marvin, son age 13 born in Maryland, Samuel son, age 11 born in Maryland; Milton, son age 7, born in Maryland; Mayer, son age 3 born in Maryland; Hyman father age 77 born in Russia, lived in same place in 1935; Yetta, age 70, born in Russia, lived in same place in 1935.
1950	For Norton's family and his mother Yetta Residing at 2606 Park Heights Terrace, Norton Schwartz, head, 56, Occupation: clerk, retail grocery; Kate wife, age 50, proprietor retail grocery store, Sonnel, son age 21, clerk retail grocery store; Milton, son age 19, clerk retail grocery store; Mayer, son age 13; Yetta, mother age 85

***

CHAPTER 7

THE FAMILY OF MOTEL DEMB (AKA MAX DEMMING)

Motel (also called Mordko) Demb (~1870/71–January 17, 1928[104]) became Max Demming in America. He was the second son of Rivka and Israel Jacob Demb. The family tree scroll lists him 4th in the birth order (after Pesse, Yenta, and Simha), though the US records suggest he was probably 5th.

We don't know much about his life before he arrived in the US in 1924. He was almost certainly born in Mlynov, though his passenger manifest from 1924 says he was born in Novograd. This was probably a simplification to get through customs, since he had been living there before the family migrated and at least two and probably all three of his children were born there.

"Malinow" is in fact listed as his birthplace in a 1924 Antwerp Police Immigration Index as he, his wife Freida, and youngest daughter Marion passed through Antwerp before sailing for America. Similarly, his 1926 Declaration of Intention lists "Mlynow, Poland" as his birthplace, though of course Mlynov was part of Russia when he was born but became part of Poland following WWI. Motel's birth year is given inconsistently as 1869 (according to the 1924 Antwerp Police record), 1870 (in his Declaration of Intention) and 1871 (according to his 1924 passenger manifest).

Motel changed his surname to Demming in the US and there are two oral traditions about why this change occurred.

"The story I heard," his great-grandson Ira Deming told me, "was that when they came over from Russia and went through immigration they were asked their name and in a very heavy Russian accent they said Demb which sounded like "Dumb" and the officials changed it to "Demming." There is no evidence in the immigration records, however, that the name was changed then.

The second version of the story I heard in an old recording of the Demb reunion from August 1992. Martin Deming, a grandson of Motel, recounted "the story that came down" to him:

> My grandfather was very religious and learned when he came to this country and
> things were difficult and he was teaching at Talmud Torah in South Baltimore.
> He got very upset that people took his name in vain, 'God-demb this' and 'God-
> demb that.' So he changed his name.

The earliest record in which Max appears as "Demming" is his Declaration of Intention from January 1926. By this point, he was in Baltimore for two years. He described himself as "Motel Demb

---

[104]Listed under "Max Denning" in Jack Lewis Funeral Home Records: http://jewishmuseummd.org/wp-content/uploads/2013/06/Jack-Lewis-records-index.pdf. Retrieved June 2023.

also known as Max Demming." He and his wife "Freda" [also Freida] appear in the Baltimore City Directory that year under the listing "Demming Mark (Freada) tehr [teacher] 2119 e. Baltimore St." Records seem to concur that Max in fact changed his name to Demming when he was a teacher and before his son, Julius, snuck into the US from Buenos Aires in June 1926 under the name Julio Deming, a story told below.

Records indicate that Max and Freida's daughter, Sonia (married name Sylvia Penn), who arrived in Springfield, Massachusetts in 1921, also used the surname Demming by 1922 before she got married. The name "Sylvia Demming" appears in an Index to Marriages in Springfield in 1922 as well as marriage records recently sent to me by Sylvia's grandson, Glen Mollerick. Apparently Sylvia initiated the name change before her father Motel arrived. Her reasons for the name change are not known or remembered.

NAME		TOWN	YEAR	VOL	PAGE
Demitropoulos	Vasilios A	Lowell	1921	29	238
Demiyere	Rose	Lawrence	1921	27	409
Demling	Anna C	Boston	1922	2	111
Demlinger	Morris	"	1922	1	145
Demma	Christopher John	Framingham	1922	20	262
"	Guiseppina	"	1924	20	242
		Hudson	1924	25	167
Demne	Helen Mae	Springfield	1923	58	408
Demming	Sylvia	"	1922	54	54
Demmons	Lucy M	Dracut	1921	14	340

INDEX TO MARRIAGES IN MASSACHUSETTS 1921-1925

Figure 68 Sylvia "Demming" 1922 Marriage Record

It is not entirely clear when Motel (later called "Max") initially left his birthplace Mlynov for Novohrad Volinksi where his children were born. He appears to have married by 1897-1900 when his eldest daughter Sonia Demb (married name Sylvia Penn) was born. Sylvia's records indicate she was born in "Zwichel" [Ziahvel being another name for Novohrad Volinski). A social security record lists her birthdate as August 9, 1897, though the censuses imply she may have been born a year or so later. In any case, it appears Motel was in Novohrad by 1900 or a few years before.

Motel and Freida's daughter, Marion/Marian, was also born in Novohrad in 1914 (according to the Antwerp record and her social security record) suggesting that Motel and family remained in Novohrad for that whole period. Their son Julius was born in 1908 (according to most of his records). We can guess that he too was born in Novohrad but he had to sneak into the US via Buenos Aires and therefore his records list Argentina as his birthplace. It is of interest to note that Motel Demb's older brother, Simha Gruber, and Simha's two sons, Nathan and Samuel, were also in Novohrad sometime around 1911-1913 before they left for America.

Figure 69 Family Photo of Motel Demb

Circa 1912, Motel Demb with wife Freida (seated), daughter Sonia (standing), and Julius (seated). Courtesy of Barry Laken.

Figure 70 Sylvia and Julius in Novohrad Volinski ~ 1914–1917
Courtesy of Glen Mollerick

***

Freida's Surname Mystery

There is a decent amount of confusion about the surname of Motel's wife, Freida (also called Freda). The family tree scroll lists her birth surname as "Herman." From the recording of the 1992

Demb family reunion, I also heard her grandson, Martin Deming, say her birth surname was "Herman" and that she was the sister of "Joseph Herman the husband of Mollie Gruber." Others spoke out in disagreement, though they might have been disagreeing about Martin's mistake calling Mollie's husband *Joseph* (the name of her son) rather than Israel, her husband.[105] To complicate matters, a social security record lists Freida's original surname as Gruber, oddly the original surname of Israel Herman's wife, Mollie.

Records from Motel and Freida's immigration give Freida a different surname at birth. In the 1924 Belgium Antwerp Police Immigration Index, "Nordko Demb is married to Freida Korusnia" and their 1924 passenger manifest lists their closest relative in Novohrad as Motel's "brother-in-law Schaja Kosushner" (discussion of manifest below).

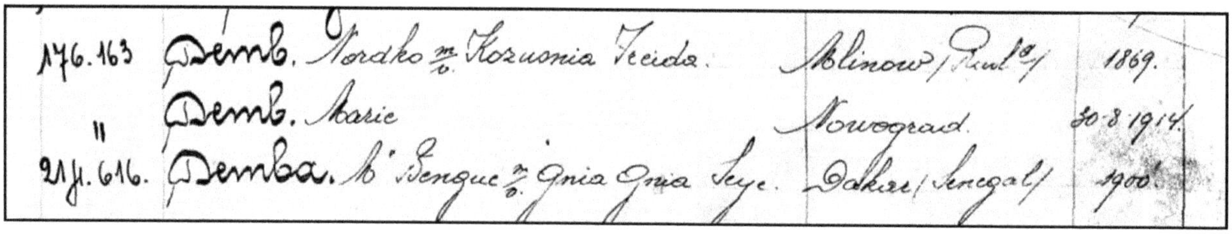

176.163	Demb. Nordko m/v Korusnia Freida.	Alinow / Russie	1869.
"	Demb. Marie	Nowograd.	30-8-1914.
214.616.	Demba. M'Bengue m/v Gnia Gnia Seye.	Dakar / Senegal	1900.

Figure 71 Antwerp Police Index of Immigrants in 1924
Freida's birth surname given as Korusnia

Schaja Kosushner, I initially guessed, referred to the man remembered in the Shulman family as Shaya/ Shia Koszhushner (see his photo and discussion above in "First Cousins Meet," on page 125). Shia married Liza (Shulman), Motel Demb's niece. She was a daughter of Motel's sister, Pearl Malka (Demb) and her husband Tsodik Shulman.[106]

Motel and Freida's two immigration records thus suggest that Freida's surname at birth was Koszhushner and she was a sister of Shia Koszushner.

This identification of Freida's brother, initially a hypothesis, was just recently confirmed by a batch of photos that arrived this week as I was trying to complete this book. They were sent to me by Glen Mollerick, a great-grandson of Motel and Frieda. The photos were in the collection of Motel and

---

[105] Joseph Herman was a son of Mollie (Gruber) and Israel Herman. Martin may have been confused and meant that his grandmother was a sister of Mollie's husband "Israel Herman."

[106] Oral traditions in the Shulman family recall that this Koszhushner family moved to Novohrad Volinski at some point too. This family escaped the German invasion by fleeing East and survived the War in Russia. US Shulman descendants met these first cousins (children of Shia Kozshushner and Liza [Shulman]) for the first time in Russia in 1992.

Freida's daughter, Sylvia Penn. The photos were passed down to Sylvia's daughter (Marlene) and then to Glen's sister. "They sat unopened in a box for thirty years," Glen tells me. He found them after his sister passed away. The box was a treasure trove of documents and photos.

One of the photos in the collection was of the Shulman family back in Mlynov identical to the one circulating among Shulman descendants in Baltimore (see Figure 40 The Shulman Family ~ 1913). This copy of the photo had Sylvia's handwriting on it. Above the head of Shaya Koszushner, Sylvia wrote "Uncle Shaya," confirming that Motel's wife, Freida, was a sister of Shaya Koszhushner, the man who married Motel's niece, Liza Shulman. Motel, in other words, married the sister of his niece's husband.

Similarly, a photo postcard that appears to be from 1922 shows Julius (left), his mother Freida (center), and a Koszushner cousin. The back reads: "Julius, Baba [grandma] Cousin Zeidel Kozhushner." On the next line it reads, "Uncle Zalman's son who was in the U. S. A. and returned to serve in the army." The postcard is stamped with the studio's name and address: "Zaklad Fotograficzny Sz Galpernia, Rowne"

Figure 72 Julius, Baba [grandma], Cousin Zeidel [Kozhushner]
Courtesy of Glen Mollerick

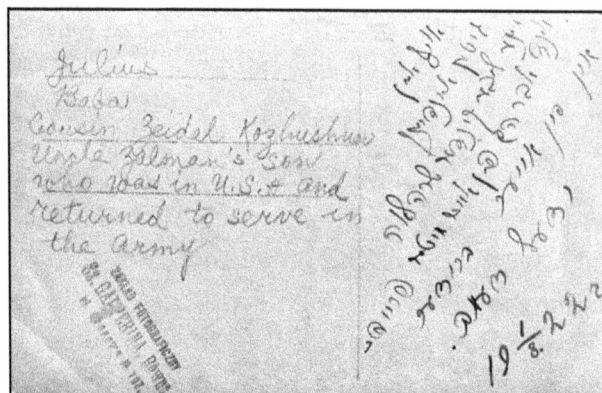

Another photo from the same collection (see below) shows a large family photo around the dinner table, possibly during Passover, in circa 1923–1925. Sylvia sits in the middle (labelled "me" in Sylvia's handwriting) with her new husband Abraham Penn. On the wall behind everyone is a large photo of an elderly religious man. In handwriting, Sylvia wrote next to his photo: "Grandpa Kozhushner," confirming again the relationship with the Koszhushner family. It seems possible that a number of the cousins in the photo were Kozhushner relatives and they were standing in front of a photo of their ancestor.

It is possible that the conflicting traditions and confusion about Freida's surname (Herman, Gruber, Koszushner) may be partly explained by another story circulating in the family. Barry Laken, a son of Motel and Freida's youngest daughter, Marian, told me he heard the following story from Glen Mollerick. Glen was told that his great-grandfather, Motel, had married one woman who died and then he married her sister. According to the story:

> Motel's first wife died shortly after the birth of Sylvia. His wife was Freida's older sister. We believe that Freida was promised as the replacement wife for her deceased older sister once she got her first period. This may have been the common custom at that time. Supposedly she was frightened about being married to an older bearded man. Nonetheless, they were married and [the eldest child] Sylvia was raised as her child. Subsequently, Julius and Marion were born [children of Freida].

Was this a true story? Glen believes that Freida told Sylvia's son, Mitchell Penn, this story and he relayed it to his sister Marlene (Glen's mother). Barry Laken writes,

> Unfortunately, none of that generation is still with us to confirm or deny the story. In support of the story, we believe that Freida's and Sylvia's dates of birth were fairly close, and that there was a time lapse before the closer arrival dates of Julius and Marion. Additionally, Sylvia's facial appearance was far different than the common shared appearance between Julius and Marion. As children, some of us may have noticed this, but never pursued any explanation.

Records don't give an indication one way or another whether this story is true, though Freida was about 10 years younger than Motel.

***

The Immigration of Sonia Demb

Motel's eldest daughter Sonia (married name Sylvia Penn) was the first to leave for America. There is a record of her leaving Southampton, England on February 15, 1921 on the SS Aquitania and arriving in New York on Feb. 22nd. She is listed as 23 years old with an implied birth year of 1898 and her last residence and birthplace as "Zwichel" [= Novohrad Volinsky]. Her closest relative listed is her father Mordko Demb in "Swichel."

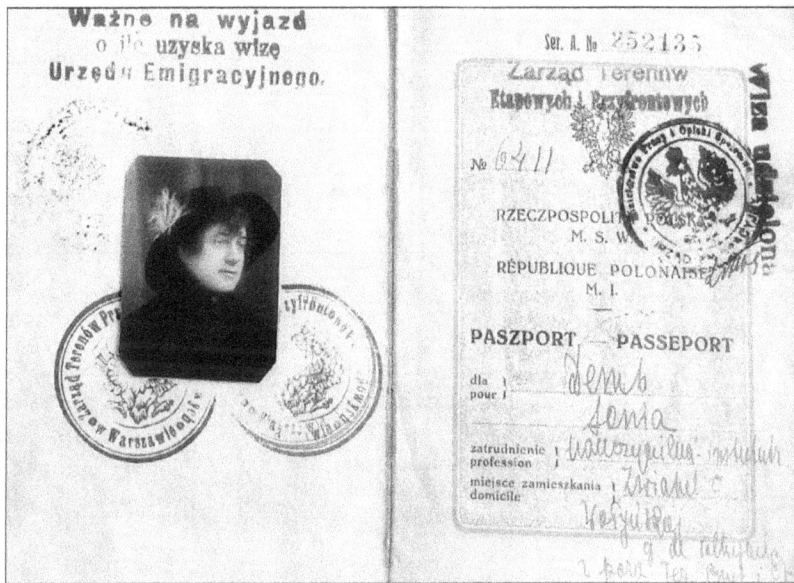

Figure 73 Passport of Sonia Demb

Manifest of SS Aquitania, sailing from Southampton

Sonia Demb's passenger manifest on the SS Aquitania

Right-hand columns of Sonia's manifest: closest relative is Father Mordko Demb in Swichel

Page 2 of Sonia's manifest – headed to Uncle Jacob Goldstein 133 [Orleans] Str, Springfield

It is of note that Sonia was not headed to Baltimore where so many other Demb relatives were already living, and where her parents would settle a few years later. Instead, she was headed to her uncle, Jacob Goldstein, in Springfield, Massachusetts, at what looks like 133 [Street name illegible]. Research turned up the Jacob Goldstein in question at 133 Orleans Street in Springfield, Massachusetts when Sonia arrived.

For unknown reasons, the Goldstein family soon adopted the surname Cummins and moved to Baltimore where they established the Cummins Hardware by 1928.[107] The labels "Uncle Jake Goldstein" and "Auntie Sluba" (Sadie) are associated with the two people standing behind Sylvia in the large family photo that was in the collection of photos Glen sent me from circa 1923–1925 (see below). It is not known how Sylvia was related to her Uncle Jacob and Aunt Sadie Goldstein / Cummins, but it seems possible that her aunt Sadie, was a sister of Motel's wife Freida. An obituary for Sadie Cummins in 1944 lists Motel's wife, Freida Deming, as a sister.[108] Other surnames from this obituary appear in the family photo as well.

> **CUMMINS.**—On October 17, 1944, SADIE, beloved wife of Jacob Cummins, of 4021 Barrington road, mother of Mrs. Ethel Kaufman, Mrs. Betty Barez, of Springfield, Mass.; Nathan and Harry Cummins, and sister of Mr. Sam Sussman, of Haverhill, Mass., and Mrs. Frieda Deming.

By 1922, Sylvia married Abraham B. Penn, who was 8 years her senior. The name on his passport from Odessa was Avrum Ber Mikelev Paneyakh, according to a letter found among the documents sent to me. He arrived from Russia in 1912. In the 1920s, he was working for a steamship agency dealing with "foreign remittance and general insurance." Their son Mitchell was born in 1924 and a daughter Marlene (married name Marlene Mollerick) was born in 1931.

***

Sylvia's Harrowing Journey

I wondered for many years why Sylvia left for America before her parents and why she went to Springfield rather than Baltimore. The answer showed up in the treasure trove of photos and documents sent to me recently by Glen Mollerick. Included was an old clipping from *The Springfield Union* newspaper published on February 15, 1922, which is worth transcribing in full. The article included a photo of Sylvia teaching English to new immigrants and told the story of her harrowing journey in exquisite detail. We don't often get such a detailed look at the experience of a new immigrant.

---

[107] A Jacob Goldstein is found in the Springfield City Directory at 133 Orleans in 1921–1923. His daughters, Ida (later Ida Kaufman) and Bessie Goldstein (later Betty Barez), appear at the same addresses in the directory. The Goldstein family is not at that address in the 1920 Springfield Census and appears to be the family at 57 Abbe Ave in 1920. If so, Jacob's wife's name is Sadie, and his children are Ida E, Bessie, Nathan D, Harry Goldstein. Their names disappear from Springfield after that. I was able to confirm that they became the Cummins family in Baltimore. There is a Petition of a "Nuchem Goldstein" from Novograd Volinsk in Baltimore who is "also known as Nathan Daniel Cummins." On Nuchem Goldstein's 1911 passenger manifest he is traveling with his mother and two sisters. Their last residence was Novoghad and his destination is his father Jacob Goldstein at 4 Ferry Str in Springfield, Mass. I later confirmed that Ira Deming (a grandson of Julius Deming) remembers cousins in Baltimore by the name of Cummins. I have no idea why this family changed their names to Cummins and two descendants of the Cummins family I spoke to didn't know.

[108] This record still raises other puzzles. Sadie's brother in this obituary is identified as Samuel Sussman, which would imply that Sussman is the family's surname, though Freida Deming appears to have had the surname Kozhushner. Perhaps DNA tests can later resolve some of these puzzles.

The article appeared a year to the day after Sylvia left Southampton, England for New York. The article recounts the difficult series of events that separated Sylvia and her brother from her parents and the way in which she ended up in America. The article also shows Sylvia was already using the surname Demming within a year of her arrival.

On the blackboard behind her, Sylvia is pointing to a marching song, "Marching Thru Georgia" written by Henry Clay Work at the end of the American Civil War, which became popular by Union soldiers and internationally.

Figure 74 1922 Article About Sylvia Demming

Miss Sylvia Demming, Russian Refugee, Conducting Her Americanization Class. Escaped from Bolsheviks, Is Now Teacher in Springfield
The Springfield Union, Feb. 15, 1922

Story of Miss Sylvia Demming, Russian Girl, Assistant in Americanization Classes, Is Replete Thrills and Hardships.

Just about a year ago Jacob Goldstein of Orleans Street received a letter from Kelce, Poland. It was written by his young niece and on the surface it told simply of how she had left her native [Russia some?] months before and had wandered from city to city in Poland, fleeing from the advance of Bolshevik forces. Communication with her parents had been entirely cut off and so she was writing to her relatives in America. She did not ask for help.

But her uncle, rightly guessing that she had suffered hardships that were not chronicled in the letter, cabled at once to Kelce a message which read "Wait for money. Don't worry." But not a word of the message could his niece decipher. Finally a friend was found who knew the Russian equivalent of "money" and also knew that "don't" was a negative. "It means they won't send you any money," she said. But this did not sound a reasonable message to put in a cablegram, and so Kelce was canvassed for a student of English, and before nightfall friends of Sylvia Demming were rejoicing with her in her great good fortune. After months of uncertainty, loneliness and terror she was to leave the miseries of Europe behind and start life in the New World.

Now Teaches Others.

Even now as Miss Demming talks of her experiences, they are so vivid that her fluent English, so recently acquired, fails her in the excitement of remembrance.

"I shall never forget one bit of it," she says, "as long as I live, I know so well how I felt when I first came to Springfield and how I understood nothing of what was being said around me. That is why it is easy for me to know what it is that my pupils do not understand and why it is all so hard for them and so confusing."

For Miss Demming, the young Russian immigrant of less than a year ago, is now a regularly employed teacher of English to the foreign-born pupils of the Americanization class at the High School of Commerce.

In June 1920, MIss Demming was living with her parents in the town of Novograd Wolynsk, Ukraine, a city with about a population of about 25,000. She had finished the high school and was taking a special course of preparation to enter the college for men in Kiev, suddenly word came that the Bolsheviks [word illegible] were about to take the town and that the Polish army, then in possession, would be forced to evacuate.

At 10 o'clock that night, Miss Demming, her brother and another girl left Novograd Wolynsk on foot, and by the next day were 30 miles from home. Here they stayed for three months until the Polish army recaptured their home when they returned. But again, the Bolsheviks advanced, the Poles retreated, and this time she and the other girl were taken into a wagon by two Polish officers' wives and they rode with the ammunition train of the Polish army to the city of Rovno, Poland.

This was just the beginning of their wanderings. The Bolsheviks continued to advance, the Poles to retreat. They were befriended by a medical officer in the Polish army and traveled to Kovel on the medical truck, piled high with boxes and supplies. So rough was the going, over mountain roads, that their guardian was thrown from the truck, fell down a steep hillside and broke his arm. In Kovel they found some acquaintances who were afraid at first to take them in, and they spent part of a night in tears on the doorstep. Neither had any money but Miss Demming had 20 pounds of sugar. The Poles, it seems, have salt but no sugar and the Russians sugar but no salt. So the sugar was sold and they traveled on, finally meeting another physician who came from their home town. He was able to find a position for Miss Demming's friend with a military hospital. The girl lived at the hospital and gave her salary to Miss Demming who found lodging in a hotel. After three days, the hospital was ordered to Brest Litovsk and from there to Kelce.

Understands America

Here there were many Russian refugees, and for three months Miss Demming was taken in by a family of three who lived crowded into two rooms.

During all these months of wandering, Miss Demming had heard nothing from her parents. The strain was growing unbearable when she decided to write to America. And then the cable came.

"I am so glad," she says, "that I came to Springfield instead of going to some of my other relatives in cities where they do not have schools for immigrants. I understand America now as I never should have if I had had to go to work at once. When I first came I did not believe there were any really good people left in the world, but now I know better. I see that American stands for brotherhood and really wants to help her new citizens and I teach this to my pupils as Miss Hodgson taught it to me. But I have been very lucky, that is all. I happened to come to the right place at once and everyone has helped me. Many, many newly arrived immigrants never have America explained to them and it is not surprising that they do not understand her. I think America is the finest country in the world."

Figure 75 Sonia Demb now Sylvia Penn ~ 1923–25 with Cummins and other cousins

1) Sonia/Sylvia (Demb) Penn
2) Sylvia's husband Abraham Penn
3) Sylvia's uncle and aunt, Jacob and Sonia ("Sluba") Goldstein / Cummins
4) Photo of "Grandpa Kozhushner"
5) Esther (surname?)
6) Ben (surname?)
7) Jacob's daughter Betty (Goldstein/Cummins) Barez
8) Uncle Marcus (surname?)
9) Stephanie (surname?)
10) Ida (Goldstein/Cummins) Kaufman, Jacob and Sonia's daughter
11) Lillian and Dave (surname?)
12) Uncle and Aunt Sam Sussman and Fannie
13) Friend Emma
14) Izzie Kaplan
15) Shapiro

***

The Migration of Motel, Freida and Marion

Motel, his wife Freida and their youngest daughter, Marion, left for America three years after Sylvia. Motel was the last of the original Demb siblings to migrate to the US. As noted earlier, the family appears in records of Antwerp police among immigrants passing through the city. Marion's son, Mark Laken, remembers his mother talking about seeing the beautiful gardens and tulips on their migration. This memory seems consistent with their travel from Poland to Antwerp, Belgium. Perhaps they also passed through the Netherlands.

Figure 76 1922 Max, Marion, and Freida Demming
handwriting of Sylvia Penn. Courtesy of Glen Mollerick.

Sylvia and her husband, Abraham, typed up an Affidavit of Support for her parents and sister who were already at the time in the port of Antwerp. A copy was in the box that Glen sent me. The Affidavit was signed in front of a notary on June 24, 1924 and submitted to the Commonwealth of Massachusetts. The letter explains that Sylvia and Abraham are law-abiding citizens and that Abraham is gainfully employed. The document promises to support Sylvia's parents and sister and prevent them from becoming a public charge.

Motel, Freida and Marian left Antwerp on October 25, 1924, on the SS Pittsburg and arrived in New York on November 5th. "Mordko" was 53, Freida was 43, and Marian was 9, according to the manifest. Their son Julius could not leave with them because of tightening US quotas. Instead, he headed to Buenos Aires to try to get into the US, as we shall see.

Manifest of SS Pittsburgh sailing from Antwerp Oct 25, 1924.

Passenger Manifest of Mordko, Freida and Marian Demb

As noted above, Motel's closest relative in Novohrad before they left was "BR. I. L. [brother-in-law] Schaja Kosushner," apparently Freida's brother and the man who married Motel's niece Liza Shulman (daughter of Motel's sister Pearl Malka). Shia and Liza eventually fled with their children ahead of the Nazi invasion in 1941 and survived in Russia as discussed in the Shulman narrative.

We can see from the manifest that Mordko, Freida and Marion were headed to Springfield, Mass. to the home of Abraham Penn, Sylvia's husband.

Page 2 of the manifest showing the destination of the family to "Sohn.I.L. [son-in-law] Abraham Penn

Motel, Frieda and Marion were held in detention for special inquiry when they landed in New York and given the status "LPC"—Likely Public Charge. Immigration standards had tightened after WWI, and custom officials were turning away individuals whom they suspected were poor and would have to live off the state or turn to criminal activities to survive. In their passenger manifest, "admitted" is stamped next to their names indicating that they were approved to enter after their special inquiry. Perhaps they had a copy of the Affidavit of Support Sylvia and Abraham had written on their behalf.

Special inquiry detention record showing "LPC"

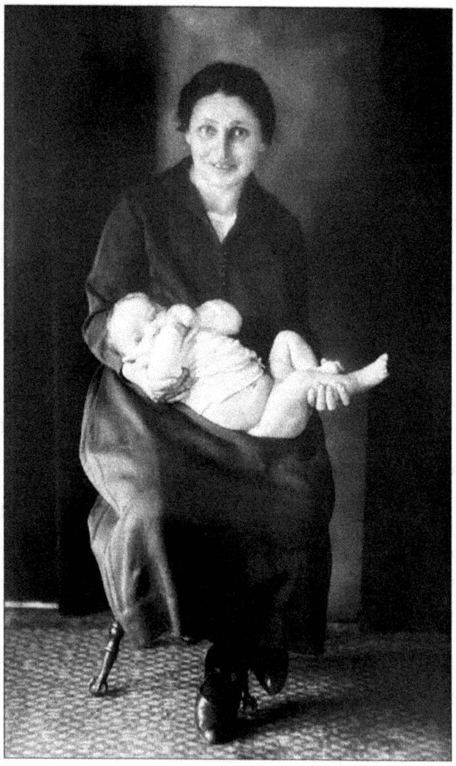

Figure 77 1925 Freida with grandson Mitchell Penn

Two months after arrival in Springfield
Courtesy of Glen Mollerick

***

The Journey of Julius Deming

The newspaper clipping narrating Sylvia's experience indicates she and her brother Julius were separated from their parents at the time. It appears they returned home after a Bolshevik retreat and then had to flee again during another advance of the Bolsheviks. Perhaps this time they were separated, accounting for why Julius did not leave for America with his sister.

By the time his parents Motel and Freida left, Julius could not leave with the rest of his family due to the increasingly xenophobic attitudes that were tightening US immigration quotas. Males who reached the age of adulthood were subject to quotas and could not easily get visas into the US. Since Julius was a Jewish male in Eastern Europe over age 18, he could not be included in the quota and leave with his family. But if he pretended to be a native in the Western Hemisphere, he could more easily get into the US and possibly bypass the quota system. Julius managed to follow his family to the US after a stay in Buenos Aires.

The 1924 Immigration Act

The immigration Act of 1924 in conjunction with the Immigration Act of 1917 was part and parcel of an anti-immigrant reaction following WWI and an attempt to reduce the flow of immigration to the US. The 1924 Immigration act placed the first permanent limitation on immigration and established the "national origins quota system." Together the two acts governed American immigration policy until they were replaced by the Immigration and Nationality Act of 1952.

This first provision of the 1924 act set quotas on certain nationalities at "two percent of the number of foreign-born persons of such nationality resident in the continental United States in 1890." This constituted a drastic reduction in the number of immigrants from Eastern European countries. Certain individuals were allowed in as "non-quota" immigrants, meaning that they were *not* counted in the quota and had a lower barrier for entry. Non-quota immigrants included unmarried children under 18 years of age, or the wife of a citizen. Natives of Western Hemisphere countries with their families were also excluded from the quota.

The act defined "Western Hemisphere countries" as follows: An immigrant who was born in the Dominion of Canada, Newfoundland, the Republic of Mexico, the Republic of Cuba, the Republic of Haiti, the Dominican Republic, the Canal Zone, or an *independent country of Central or South America*, and his wife, and his unmarried children under 18 years of age, if accompanying or following to join him...

U.S. DEPARTMENT OF LABOR
Immigration Service

List ___ 15

LIST OR MANIFEST OF ALIEN PASSENGERS FOR THE UNITED

ALL ALIENS arriving at a port of continental United States from a foreign port or a port of the insular possessions of the United States, and all aliens arriving at a port of said insular possessions from a foreign port, a port of continental United States. This (white) sheet is for the listing of

S. S. WESTERN WORLD   Passengers sailing from BUENOS AIRES, ARGENTINA   JUNE 3RD.   , 19 26

No. on List	Head-Tax Status	Family Name	Given Name	Age Yrs.	Age Mos.	Sex	Married or single	Calling or occupation	Able to Read	Read what language	Write	Nationality	Race or people	Country	City or town	Name and complete address of nearest relative or friend in country whence alien came	State	City or Town
1		ROSSI	JULIO	26		M	S	UPHOLSTERER	YES	SPANISH	YES	ARGENT.	LAT.AMER.	ARGENT.	B.AIRES	FA- NICOLAS ARENGREN 1135,B.AIRES	N.Y.	NEW YORK
2		CLASS	PAUL	28		M	M	MECHAN	YES	GERMAN	YES	GERMAN	GERMAN	ARGENT.	B.AIRES	FD- ERNESTO STIRN COSTA RICA 4729-B.AIRES	N.Y.	NEW YORK
3		CLASS	KLARA	26		F	M	WIFE HOUSE	YES	GERMAN	YES	GERMAN	GERMAN	ARGENT.	B.AIRES	SAME AS ABOVE FD- J.MONROE	N.Y.	NEW YORK
4	TRANSIT	MC DONALD	JOHN	54		M	M	FARMER	YES	ENGLISH	YES	BRITISH	ENGLISH	ARGENT.	B.AIRES	FRICORIFICO ARMOUR,B.AIRES	CAN.	ALBERTA
5	TRANSIT	MC DONALD	ANGELA	30		F	M	HOUSE WIFE	YES	SPANISH	YES	BRITISH	SPANISH	ARGENT.	B.AIRES	SAME AS ABOVE FD- JUAN CANICOBAR	CAN.	ALBERTA
6		GANSS	HEINRICH	28		M	M	MECHAN.	YES	GERMAN	YES	GERMAN	GERMAN	ARGENT.	B.AIRES	GRAL.HORNOS 610,B.AIRES FD- ADOLFO TRAEGER	N.J.	NEWARK
7		GERMAN	EUGEN	35		M	S	ENGNR.	YES	GERMAN	YES	GERMAN	GERMAN	ARGENT.	B.AIRES	CORDOBA 1724,B.AIRES FD- KORNER & CO.	N.J.	NEWARK
8		LABZIG	PAUL	26		M	S	BARBER	YES	ENGLISH	YES	BRITISH	ENGLISH	ARGENT.	B.AIRES	25 DE MAYO 433,B.AIRES SISTER- CATALINA SITTNER	N.Y.	NEW YORK
9		BITTNER	ALEJANDRO	20		M	S	STUDENT	YES	SPANISH	YES	ARGENTINE	ARGENTINE	ARGENT.	B.AIRES	PINO 3801,BELGRANO ARG. MO- MARIA JOABNE DOURAO	MICH	BERRIEN SPRINGS
10		DA SILVA	JOSE MANOEL	37		M	S	LABORER	YES	PORTUGUESE	YES	BRAZIL	LAT.-AMER.	BRAZIL	PARA	PARA ,BRAZIL. FD- MAX MASEL	N.J.	NEWARK
11		DEMING	JULIO	18		M	S	MECHANIC	YES		YES	DUTCH	DUTCH	ARGENTINE	B.AIRES	OMBU 555,B.AIRES FD- OSCAR MALBOSE	MASS	SPRINGFIELD

Line 11 of SS Western World Passenger Manifest shows Julio Deming line 11 Dutch leaving Buenos Aires

List 15

The entries on this sheet must be typewritten or printed.

STATES IMMIGRATION OFFICER AT PORT OF ARRIVAL

States, or a port of another insular possession, in whatsoever class they travel, MUST be fully listed and the master or commanding officer of each vessel carrying such passengers must upon arrival deliver lists thereof to the immigration officer.

STEERAGE PASSENGERS ONLY

Arriving at Port of **NEW YORK, N.Y.** , JUNE 22ND, 19 26

No. on List.	14	15 Whether having a ticket to such final destination.	16 By whom was passage paid?	17 Whether in possession of $50, and if less, how much?	18 Whether ever before in the United States, and if so, when and where? (Yes or no / Year, period of time / Where?)	19 Whether going to join a relative or friend, and if so, what relative or friend, and his name and complete address.	20 Purpose of coming to United States	21 Whether a polygamist	22 23 Whether an Anarchist	24 25	26 Whether a person who believes in or advocates the overthrow by force or violence of the Govt.	27 Condition of health, mental and physical	28 Deformed or crippled. Nature, length of time, and cause.	29 Height (Feet/Inches)	30 Complexion	31 Color of — Hair	Eyes	32 Marks of identification	33 Place of birth — Country.	City or town.
1	YES	SELF		YES NO ---		FD— THOMAS D. VALENTINE 29 BROADWAY, N.Y.C.	YES 2 YRS.	NO	NO NO	NO	NO	GOOD	NO	5 6	LT	BLK	GR	NONE	ARGENTINE	B.AIRES
2	YES	SELF		YES NO ---		BRO-IN-LAW: ALFRED RIEGER 62 W.96 ST., N.Y.C.	PERM.	NO	YES NO	NO	NO	GOOD	NO	5 6	LT	BR	BR	NONE	GERMANY	WAIBLINGEN
3	YES	HUSBAND		YES NO ---		SAME AS ABOVE	PERM.	NO	YES NO	NO	NO	GOOD	NO	5 6	LT	BLD	BL	NONE	GERMANY	WAIBLINGEN
4	NO	SELF		YES WES 1924 N.Y.		NONE — IN TRANSIT ***	NO	NO	NO NO	NO	NO	GOOD	NO	6 0	LT	BLD	BL	NONE	CANADA	MANITOBA
5	NO	HUSBAND		YES NO ---		SAME AS ABOVE	NO	NO	NO NO	NO	NO	GOOD	NO	5 4	LT	BLK	BR	NONE	SPAIN	BARCELONA
6	YES	SELF		YES NO ---		BRO— GEORGE GANSS 692E-20TH.ST.-NEWARK, N.J.	NO	NO	NO NO	NO	NO	GOOD	NO	5 7	LT	BLD	BL	NONE	GERMANY	STUTTGART
7	YES	SELF		YES NO ---		FD— G. GANSS 692E-20TH.ST.-NEWARK N.J.	PERMAN. YES	NO	NO NO	NO	NO	GOOD	NO	5 10	FR	BLK	BR	NONE	GERMANY	BIETIGHEIM
8	YES	SELF		YES NO ---		FD— CHAS.A.GARDINER 1989 AMSTERDAM AVE. N.Y.C. EMMANUEL MISSIONARY COLLEGE	PERMAN. YES	NO	NO NO	NO	NO	GOOD	NO	5 7	FR	BLD	BR	NONE	GERMANY	GONSWEN
9	NO	SELF		YES NO ---		BERRIEN SPRINGS, MICH. FD— JOAO MARQUES DE MOURA 30-FERRY ST.-NEWARK, N.J.	PERMAN. YES	NO	NO NO	NO	NO	GOOD	NO	5 7	FR	BLD	BL	NONE	BRAZIL	PARA
10	YES	SELF		YES NO ---		FD— ABRAHAM B.PEM 702 NEWTON ST.-SPRINGFIELD, MASS	PERMAN YES	NO	NO NO	NO	NO	GOOD	NO	5 6	FR	DK	BR	NONE	ARGENTINE	E.RIOS
	NO	SELF		YES NO ---		FD— OSCAR ROLLER	NO							5 6	FR	BR	GR	NONE	ARGENTINE	

Line 11 shows Julius line 11 headed to Abraham B. Pem in Springfield, Mass

Julius did not talk much about his journey to America. "He had been through a lot," Julius's nephew Mark Laken told me, "and he would never talk about it." But one night after some schnapps on the first night of the Seder, Julius told the following story:

When he left home, he and friend walked sixty to eighty miles, all at night, hiding out in forest and trees during day. After many days and nights, they got to the Polish border, found an open doorway, in a multi-tier building. His friend slept on one of the stoops, and he went to the next highest landing. When he woke up the next morning, his shoes and coat were missing and his friend was dead with his throat slit. His friend must have awakened in the middle of the night and startled the thieves.

We don't know anything about Julius's passage to Buenos Aires. His arrival in the US, however, is documented. He sailed from Buenos Aires on June 3, 1926, on the SS Western World and arrived in New York on June 22, 1926. "Julio Deming" traveled under a partially false identity. It is not clear whether Julius spelled "Deming" with one "m" as part of his subterfuge or simply didn't know how his family in the US was spelling it. In any case, his descendants spell their name with one "m," thus linking Demb, Demming, and Deming.

The manifest indicates his nationality was Dutch, his age 18, his last residence Buenos Aires, and his friend there Max Masel. His race originally said "Dutch," but someone handwrote "Hebrew" over it, perhaps later in the US after he started his naturalization process, though this is not certain. His language originally was typed "Argyntyne" but someone later handwrote over it, though the writing is illegible. On page 2 of this manifest, his destination listed is his brother-in-law, "Abraham Pem" [i.e. Penn] in Springfield, Mass and his birth place is E. Rios, which may refer to "Entre Rios," a province in Argentina that is just north of Buenos Aires.

**

The Discovery of Julius's Photo in Buenos Aires

When I first discovered Julius's manifest, I had no idea he was in Buenos Aires with a group of Mlynov boys who were also trying to get into the US. I eventually learned about a photo of him in Buenos Aires standing with these young men from Mlynov. Although Julius probably grew up in Novohrad, he may have known these young men from visits back to Mlynov with his father. Julius turned out to be the one labeled Etool (seated right) in the photo.

I serendipitously learned about this photo which was in the collection of Audrey (Goldseker) Polt, whose father Samuel Goldseker was born in Mlynov and came to Baltimore in the 1920s as a young man. I was first introduced to Audrey in email by one of my Demb third cousins, Carol Engelman (in the Pesse Demb line), whom I met in 2017 when I made my first family history trip back to Baltimore. Carol happened to live across the street from Audrey and wondered if I was interested in talking to her.

"You might like talking to my neighbor Audrey," Carole emailed, not long after my visit. "She is a photo album maker, and her father was from Mlynov too."

"Sure," I said, "why not?" I had heard the Goldseker family name previously from my cousin Ted Fishman and knew that they were Mlynov relatives of his and had become a prominent Baltimore family. Morris Goldseker, who was also born in Mlynov had bequeathed the Goldseker Foundation, one of the largest foundations in Maryland.

Argentina ~ 1924
Top Row, Lt to Rt: Dad (Samuel Goldseker), Woodluck, Unknown
Bottom Row: Muttle Meizlish, Woodluck's brother, Etool

Figure 78 Boys in Buenos Aires. Courtesy of Audrey Goldseker Polt

One day I was talking to Audrey about her father's story when I learned he came to Baltimore via Buenos Aires.

"That's interesting," I said. "I have a distant cousin, Julius Deming, who came to Baltimore from Buenos Aires too."

While we were talking, I pulled up Julius's manifest and then asked Audrey to open her father's. Lo and behold, they left Buenos Aires for the US only a few months apart. Julius left in June 1926 and Audrey's father, Sam Goldseker, left in early August that same summer. They must have been there at the same time. Even more surprising, they both listed the same friend back in Buenos Aires. Julius listed "Max Masel" and Audrey's father listed, "Mr. Masel."

"They must have been roommates," Audrey exclaimed. "My father told me he stayed with a few young men in Buenos Aires. In fact, I have photos of the young men with him in Buenos Aires."

One photo showed a group of young friends. Audrey's father told her the names of the young men as he remembered them, but he used Yiddish nicknames and didn't know or remember their surnames. Audrey's handwriting under the photo recorded the names of the boys as her father remembered them. The one he called "Etool" (seated on the right) turned out to be Julius Deming. Over time, I identified several other Mlynov young men in the photo. Like Julius, several of them falsified their records when they entered the US.[109]

***

After the Migration

By January 17, 1928,[110] Max Demming passed away, just a few short years after his immigration. He was buried in the Mt. Carmel Cemetery in Baltimore. His widow appears as "Freda" Demming (widowed) in the 1929 Baltimore City Directory.

1929 Baltimore City Directory	Demmie Lillie h2033 Guilford av Demming Albert waiter r422 w Hoffman " Clyde driver h1744 Jackson " Freda (wid Max) h2041 e Balto " Wm (Margt) chauf h1744 Jackson

Julius married a woman named Ida Weiner on October 18, 1930 in Brooklyn. Ida was from Novohrad Volinski just as Julius was, though there is no evidence that they knew each other before Julius arrived in New York, though it is possible.

As I researched Ida's background, I learned she was 17 and called "Nechama Marejda" in 1921 when she arrived in the US on the SS Samland with her mother and two siblings. Her father Israel Weiner (originally Asriel Marade) arrived earlier in Boston in 1913 before the War and was separated from his wife and children until 1921 when they could join him. They landed in Philadelphia only six months after Julius's older sister Sylvia made her way stateside. When they arrived, the "Marade" family headed to Ida's father, Israel, who was still living in Boston at the time. Boston was his destination in 1913 when he arrived to join his brother "Meyer Weyner." The name Weyner was adopted first by Israel's brother in the US for unknown reasons. By 1925, Ida's family moved to New York and settled into Brooklyn where they appear on a 1925 census under the name Weiner. Ida was listed as employed in "dresses" and still an "alien" at the time.

There is no oral story of how Julius and Ida met each other in New York. But Julius was reportedly involved in the needle trades for a time and perhaps they met in the industry. In any case, it must have felt risky for Ida to take up with this dashing young man who snuck into the US and

[109] See https://kehilalinks.jewishgen.org/Mlyniv/mlinov_in_WWI.html#BuenosAires for my discussion of the "Mlynov Boys in Buenos Aires."
[110] Max's date of death appears as "Max Denning" in the Jack Lewis Funeral Home Records Index published by the Jewish Museum of Maryland, http://jewishmuseummd.org/wp-content/uploads/2013/06/Jack-Lewis-records-index.pdf. Retrieved May 21, 2023.

had to continue to hide his birthplace. By 1932 they too were in Baltimore where their son Martin was born.

Figure 79 Julius and Ida, 1930 Brooklyn
Courtesy of Glen Mollerick

A second story that Julius shared with his grandson Mark over schnapps may explain why he left New York so quickly. Mark recounts the story to me:

> At some point after his arrival, Julius got involved in the needle trade. Julius's needle business had a building with many women working on needles. One day a guy visited him and told Julius he needed to buy insurance because "you never know when these buildings will burn down."
>
> Julius told the visitor that his partner was not present and that he should come back later. A week or two later the visitor came back this time with another man. They insisted he had to buy insurance. Julius told them that his partner was on the roof.
>
> "Okay," they said, "let's go see him." So they went up the elevator and "somehow or other the two guys got pushed down the elevator shaft." Julius got away jumping from roof to roof. He never went back to New York.

In his 1940 census and 1941 Petition for Naturalization, Julius is still keeping up the pretense of having been born in Argentina. He finally was naturalized in 1944.

	40	R	25 No	DEMING, JuLLuis		HEAD		M	W	32	M	No	8	ARGENTINO	
				, IDA	Ⓧ	WiFE		F	W	35	M	No	7	Russia	
				, MARTIN E		SON		M	W	7	S	Yes	1	MARYLAND	

1940 Census for Julluis Deming showing his birthplace was still "Argentino"

By 1940, Julius's widowed mother, "Freda" is living with her daughter Marion and son-in-law. Marion's son, Mark, remembers growing up with Freda. She had a green card but never became a citizen and she never remarried. Mark recalls that Freda:

> lived many years with my family. My father owned a bar or tavern in the most urban parts of Baltimore city. He worked strange hours. He had already left for work when I came home from school. I saw him on Tuesdays, his day off, and we would go out to dinner on Tuesdays.
>
> My mother was a bar owner's widow. She played cards, bingo, etc., and from my early memories I remember being raised by Freda. She would get me off to school, and she would be there when I returned. She was a very religious woman.
>
> I remember one story. I was a teenager, and had started smoking, and I asked her, 'Are you allowed to smoke on the holiday?"
>
> "I don't know," she said, "Go ask the rabbi." I went over to the rabbi's house and it was already the minor holiday. When I showed up to his residence, he was already smoking a cigarette.
>
> "How can I help you," he asked. "My question," I explained, "was whether you can smoke a cigarette on the minor holiday, but you already answered."
>
> He said, "Since you asked, the answer is 'no.'"
>
> "This is how I learned the meaning of hypocrite," Mark concluded.

Figure 80 1950s Wedding of Mitchell Penn

seated (l to r) Freida Demb, son-in-law Abraham Penn, daughter Sylvia (Demb) Penn; standing (l to r) Marlene Penn (married name Mollerick), Mitchell Penn and his wife Eta. Courtesy of Barry Laken.

Figure 81 Family of Marion (Demb) Laken

Marion with husband Joshua and sons, Mark and Barry, 1953. Courtesy of Mark Laken

US Records of Sonia and Motel Demb (Max Deming) and children

1921 (Feb. 22) Passenger Manifest	Leaving on Feb. 15, 1921 from Southhampton, England on SS Aquitania, arriving in New York on Feb. 22, 1921. Sonia Demb, age 23, implied birth year, 1898, last residence and birthplace Zwichel [=Novohrad Volinski], Wolyn [District], Poland, closest relative father Mordko Demb in Swichel, heading to Springfield, Mass to uncle Jacob Goldstein 133 [illegible but prob. Orleans] Str. Springfield, Mass
[1924] Belgium, Antwerp Police Immigration Index	Demb, Nordko [i.e., Mordko / Motel] married to Freida Korusnia, [he was] born in Malinow, Russia[?] 1869. Daughter Marie Demb, born in Nowograd, 30-8-1914.
1924 (Nov. 5) Passenger Manifest	Traveling on SS Pittsburg from Antwerp, Belgium leaving Oct. 25, 1924 and arriving Nov 5th 1924 in New York. Mordko Demb, age 53 with implied birth year of 1871, merchant, closest relative: Br. I. L. [brother-in-law] Schaja Kosuschner* [i.e., brother of his wife, who married Motel's niece Nehuma Shulman], Novograd Russia, last permanent address Antwerp, Belgium, heading to Springfield, MASS, to his Sohn. I. L [son-in-law] Abraham Penn [who married his daughter, Sylvia (Sonia). Traveling with wife Freida, age 43 (implied birth year 1881), closest relative is [Schaja Kosuschner] "brother," with daughter Marian,

	age 9 with implied birth year of 1913, closest relative her uncle. A record also shows they were held in customs for special inquiry as "LPC" [likely public charge]. Note: Schaja Kosuschner is very likely the same man who married Liza Shulman in Mlynov, daughter of Pearl Malka (Demb) and Tsodik Shulman.
1926 (Jan. 19) Declaration of Intention	Motel Demb also known as Max Demming, 56 years with implied birth year of 1870, occupation Hebrew teacher, born in Mlynow Poland on March 15, 1870. Now residing 2127 E. Pratt Street, Baltimore. Wife Freida born at Novogradvolinsk, Russia.
1926 (June 22) Passenger Manifest	For Julio Deming (Julius Demb) Leaving from Buenos Aires, Argentina on June 3, 1926 on the SS Western World arriving in New York on June 22, 1926. Julio Deming 18 [implied birth year 1908] mechanic, [posing as] Dutch, [language] ~~Dutch~~ Hebrew, Argentine, B. Aires [Buenos Aires] closest friend Max Masel, OMBU 533, B. Aires heading to Mass, Springfield Visa issues in Buenos Aires, June 1, 1926.
1930 (April 2) US Federal Census	For Sylvia Penn (Sonia Demb) and husband Abraham, residing at 99 Jefferson Ave, Springfield, MA, Abraham Penn, Head, R[enting] age 38, age at marriage 31, immigration year 1912, occupation: Steamship Agency, Sylvia, age 30, age at marriage 23, year of immigration, 1921. Mitchell Penn, son age 5, born in Massachusetts, boarder Abraham Rispler from Austria
1936 (Sept. 14) Naturalization Record Index	Marion Demming, residing at 2114 E. Baltimore St., Baltimore, age 23 (with implied birth year of 1913, Date of order of admission: September 14, 1936.
1940 (April 4) US Fed. Census	Freda Demming, age 58, mother-in-law, widowed, living with daughter Marion, age 25, and her husband, Joshua Laken, 1621 Gwynns Falls Parkway Baltimore. Listed as widowed. Joshua, age 24, was born in Maryland, is a tavern keeper
1940 (April 16) US Federal Census	For Sylvia and Abraham Penn, residing at 144 Prospect Street, Springfield, Ma; Abraham Penn, head, age 41, Na[turalized], Salesman, Insurance Co; Sylvia wife, age 41 with implied birth year of 1899, Na[turalized], [Children]: Mitchell, son, age 15, birthplace Massachusetts, Marlene, daughter, age 2, birthplace Massachusetts, lodger William R Rispeler
1940 (April 4) US Federal Census	For "Julluis" Deming, age 32 [implied birth year 1908], Garrison Ave 2854, born in Argentino, still an alien, painter, married to Ida [Weiner] age 35, born in Russia, alien; son Martin E, age 7, born in Maryland.
1941 (June 21) Petition For Naturalization	For Julius Deming. Occupation painter, residence 2614 Quantico Ave, Balto, Md. Age 35, born on March 2, 1908 in Pareno Argentina, male, white dark complexion, blue eyes, 5'5" 158 lbs, present nationality Argentino, wife Ida, married on Oct 18, 1930 at Brooklyn, New York. She was born at Novograd, Russia July 23, 1904 and entered the US at Philadelphia on July 1, 1921. one child: Martin, born June 4, 1932 in Baltimore. Last foreign residence, Buenos Aires, Argentina, lawful entry at New York under the name Julio Deming, on June 22, 1926 on the SS Western World.
1950 US Federal Census	Freda Demming, mother-in-law, age 67, widowed, living with [son-in-law and daughter] Joshua Laken, age 35, on 4004 Boarman Ave, Proprieter of tavern, wife, Marion (Demb) age 35, son Mark age 9, and Barry, age 5, both born in Maryland.

1950 US Federal Census	Abraham B Penn, head, residing at 86 Knollwood Street, Springfield, Mass, age 59, birthplace Russia, Proprietor Insurance, Sylvia D, wife, age 51, birthplace Russia, Mitchell E, son, age 25, "armed forces," Marlene, daughter, age 18, Medical Assistant for Doctor
1950 US Federal Census	Julius Deming, head, residing at 2604 Quantico Ave, age 42, birthplace Argentina, painter, Ida, wife, age 44, born Russia, Martin, son, age 17, born in Md.

***

CHAPTER 8

MOLLYA (DEMB) AND SAMUEL ROSKES

Mollya Demb (~1872–Jan. 9, 1962) was the fourth daughter of Rivka and Israel Jacob Demb and the sixth child according to the family history scroll. US records appear consistent with this order. Mollie was the first of Rivka and Israel Jacob's children to arrive in America, though her manifest has not been located despite extensive searching. Later in life, when she was a widow, she made aliyah to Israel and was buried there.

Mollie was born in Mlynov and migrated to Baltimore in ~1908 to join her husband. Her married name in Baltimore was Mollie Roskes. She was born in 1876 according to the 1910 census, but she is listed as born in 1872 according to the 1920 census, and 1871 according to the 1930 census. Pick a date.

Figure 82 Samuel and Mollie Roskes
Courtesy of Saul Roskes

Mollie married Samuel Roskes from Lutsk, a town that was 21 miles NW of Mlynov. It was not uncommon for a Mlynov girl to marry a man from Lutsk, as evident by the beautiful recollection of just such a wedding that took place in Mlynov, recalled through the childhood eyes of Silka Borodacz (later known as Sylvia Barditch Goldberg).[111] Mollie and Samuel Roskes married by about

---

[111] Sylvia Barditch, later an editor of the Mlynov Memorial book, was born in Lutsk in 1902, but her mother, Basa, was born in Mlynov and married a man from Lutsk and went to live in her husband's hometown where Sylvia was born. As

1897 according to the 1910 census and moved to his hometown of Lutzk. A story circulating among Demb descendants in Baltimore discussed above,[112] suggests that Mollie was really in love with one of the Schwartz brothers, but was not allowed to marry him when her sister, Yenta, was arranged to be married to the eldest Schwartz brother, Chaim.

Samuel and Mollie's son, David Shimon Roskes, was born in Lutsk in April 1898 according to several later records. In America he appears in some records as David Stanley Roskes. Mollie was about 22 years old at the time. David may not have been the first child that Samuel and Mollie had together. The 1910 US Federal census indicates that Mollie had 4 children but only 1 (David) was living at the time. We don't know how or why the other three children died.

***

Samuel Roskes's Migration in 1901

Mollie's husband Samuel left for Baltimore in January 1901 not long after their son David was born. "Schame Roskis" departed Bremen on the SS Dresden on January 19, 1901 and arrived in New York on February 3rd. His manifest lists him as 27, born in Luck with $5 in his pocket. The handwriting in the righthand column is faint but you can see he is headed to his brother-in-law "Pitzele" Fax [Getzel Fax] at 818 E. Pratt Street.

Getzel Fax, as discussed earlier, was the brother-in-law of Mollie's sister, Pesse, not Samuel's own brother-in-law. In other words, Getzel was a brother-in-law of Samuel's sister-in-law. But the immigrants often obfuscated the exact relationships this way to ease migration and perhaps their Yiddish terminology was more elastic than its English equivalents. Samuel's last residence is listed as Luck (Polish for Lutsk). We don't know if Mollie and son David went back to Mlynov from Lutsk in the period before she rejoined Samuel in 1908 but we can guess that she did.

Samuel was the first Demb husband to arrive permanently in Baltimore. He was joined in the Fax household in Baltimore by David Rivetz/Hurwitz (the husband of Pesse, his wife's sister). As discussed earlier in the story of Pesse's family, David was commuting between Mlynov and Baltimore in the 1890s and living with his brother-in-law and sister, Getzel and Ida Fax. Now both Demb husbands (Samuel and David) were living permanently with the Faxes at 818 E. Pratt Street.

Norddeutscher Lloyd, Bremen, Steamship pany.

LIST OR MANIFEST OF ALIEN IMMIGRANTS FOR THE COMMISSIONER OF IMMIGRA..ON.

Required by the regulations of the Secretary of the Treasury of the United States, under Act of Congress approved March 3, 1893, to be delivered to the Commissioner of Immigration by the Commanding officer of any vessel having such passengers on board upon arrival at a port in the United States.

S.S. *Dresden* sailing from Bremen ____ 189   Arriving at Port of New York ____ 189   64

Manifest of the SS Dresden sailing from Bremen Jan 19, 1901

---

a young girl, Sylvia used to visit Mlynov to see her grandparents. On one such visit, Sylvia participated in "A Wedding in Mlynov," pp. 24-25, between a woman from Mlynov and a man from Lutsk.

[112] See my discussion earlier "A Story About Yenta's Unhappy Marriage," on page 139.

No. on List.	NAME IN FULL.	Age		Sex.	Married or Single.	Calling or Occupation.	Able to		Nationality.	Last Residence.	Seaport for landing in the United States.	Final destination in the United States. (State, City or Town.)	Whether having a ticket to such final destination.	By whom was passage paid.
		Yrs.	Mos.				Read.	Write.						
1	Hitna Fsma	43		f		none			Hungary	Szerege	New York	Balt	yes	self
2	Ealio Eorubet	4				"			"	"	"	"	"	"
3	Roskis Schame	2?				laborer			Russia	Luck	"		"	"

Passenger manifest for Schlame Roskis (line 3) from Luck

					brother, Balt			Jox 818 E Pratt St				

Right-hand columns of Samuel's manifest headed to "brother in law Pitzel Fax [Getzel Fax] 818 E Pratt Str"

Samuel lived with the Faxes until about 1905 and was there during the Great Baltimore Fire of 1904, which destroyed much of the city. As discussed earlier above (p. 34ff), the descendants of Getzel Fax report that he was on the roof with water trying to protect their building during the fire and perhaps Samuel and David Rivetz were up on the roof with him.

It appears that Samuel Roskes may have moved out of the Fax home by 1905 when he appears as a tailor at 910 E. Pratt Street which was just a few buildings away from the Fax residence.

1905 Baltimore City Directory	Roskelly Wm G, bldr, 1419 w Pratt Roskes Saml, tailor, 910 e Pratt Roskey Jas, lab, 605 s Wolfe
1909 Baltimore City Directory	Rosinsky Abe, turner, 22 s Exeter Rosinski Frank, lab, h 527 s Ann Rositzky Wm F, ins, h 220 s Chapel Roskas Saml, tailor, 104 Albemarle

Samuel's wife Mollie and son David arrived in Baltimore sometime in 1908, according to the memoir of Mollie's niece, Clara Fram. Clara recalls that when she arrived in 1909, "There was no room [in the flat her father rented] for my 23-year-old sister Minnie, so it was arranged that she would sleep at Aunt Mollie's around the corner, until her wedding which was to take place in a couple of weeks. Aunt Mollie was mother's younger sister who had preceded her to Baltimore by one year."

Unfortunately, Mollie and David's manifest has so far not been located. Mollie's 1910 census misleadingly says she and David arrived in 1900 but her 1920 census indicates she arrived in 1908 and her 1930 census lists 1907, consistent with Clara Fram's memory. As noted above, Mollie was the first of the Demb children to land in America. Her son David was the second grandson of Rivkah and Israel Demb to arrive in America (Yitzhak Rivetz was the first).

After 1906, Samuel Roskes doesn't appear again in the Baltimore City Directory until 1909 (a year after Mollie arrived). This time he is at 104 Albemarle Street just around the corner from where the Faxes lived. Albemarle intersects E. Pratt Street right at the corner of the Star-Spangled Banner Flag house. The Roskes were living just down the street from the historic shot tower, built in 1828 and the largest building in the US at the time it was built.

***

104 Albemarle–Launching Pad #2

The Roskes home at 104 Albemarle Street became the second major launching pad for the Demb and other Mlynov immigrants. By 1914 there were 15 different Demb and Mlynov immigrants living at this address and several more stayed there before that year.

As more Demb and Mlynov immigrants arrived, they spilled into the adjoining addresses of 102 and 106 Albemarle as well. I suspect these were all flats in a single building, but I'm not sure. In any case, one might think of 102–106 Albemarle Street and 836 E. Pratt Street, which was just around the corner, as "Little Mlynov." In fact, 106 Albemarle St. was the address where the congregation Shomrei Mishmeres was meeting before it purchased the Lloyd Street synagogue. The Roskes family remained at 104 Albemarle until 1920 when they appear at 102 Albemarle.[113] It appears from records they continued to own the building until much later, even after they moved to a new address.

---

[113] The 104 Albemarle address is used in their 1910 Census, the 1914 Petition for Naturalization, the 1918 WWI Draft Registration. The 1920 Census switches to 102 Albemarle and the 104 address disappears and is probably submerged into the 102 address.

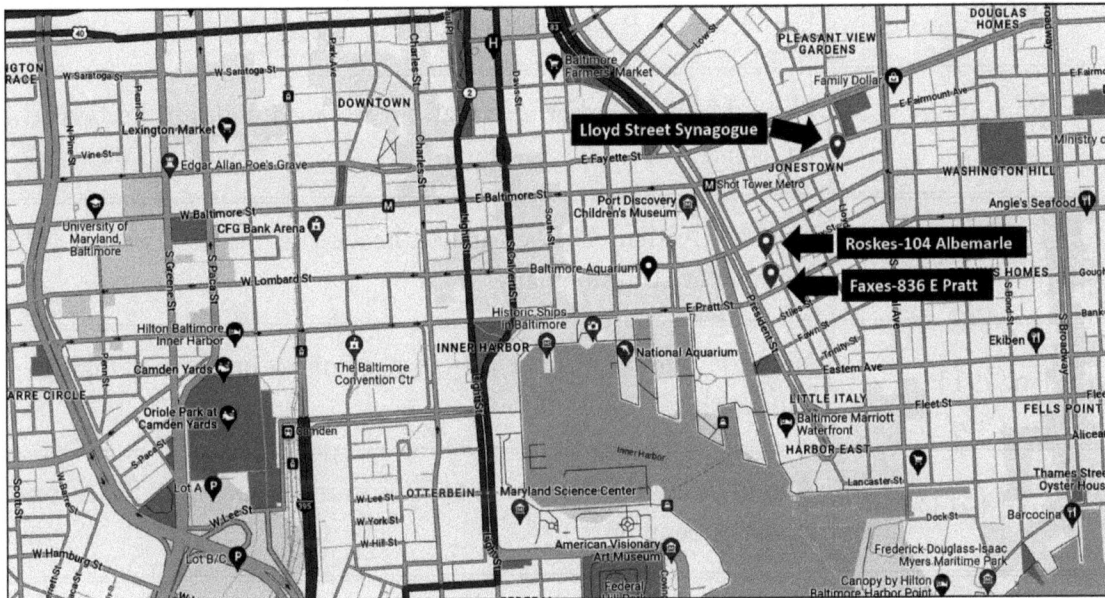

Baltimore harbor showing location of 104 Albemarle

In the 1910 census, Samuel, Mollie and David are residing at 104 Albemarle. Samuel is listed as a pants maker in a clothing factory. We know that Mollie also worked for a time in the pants industry from the memoir of Clara Fram:

> My mother soon realized that her husband never was, and never would be, a money maker in America; and so she began to listen to her younger sister, my Aunt Mollie, whose life in Baltimore was no rosier. Aunt Mollie was a "pants-finisher" by hand, working at home on stacks of men's pants sent to her by the shop where her husband was one of the pants operators. And so Mother also became a "pants-finisher" at home. She probably earned about two or three dollars a week.

***

Mlynov Arrivals at 104 Albemarle Street

Immigrants from the Demb family and other Mlynov relatives and friends began landing at the Roskes flat at 104 Albemarle.

Nov. 1911	Israel Herman (husband of Mollie Roskes's niece Mollie Gruber) is headed to 104 Albemarle St.

Mar. 1911	Israel Schwartz (brother of Chaim Schwartz) headed to brother-in-law[114] Samuel Roskes at 104 Albemarle St.
Aug. 1912	Niece Mollie (Gruber) Herman arrives with children headed to 104 Albemarle St.
Nov. 1912	Nephew Nathan Gruber arrives headed to his brother-in-law Israel Herman at 106 Albemarle St.
Jan. 1913	Nephew Samuel Gruber arrives heading to brother Nathan at 104 Albemarle
Aug. 1913	Abram [Joseph] Lerner from Mlynov headed to nephew Israel Herman at 106 Albemarle St.
Oct. 1913	Samuel Gruber's wife Bessie arrives headed to her husband at 104 Albemarle St.
Dec. 1913	Itzig Israel Lerner (Isadore Lerner) headed to father Avram Lerner 106 Albemarle St.
Mar. 1914	Brother Aaron Demb arrives heading to his sister's at 104 Albemarle St. He remains at this address for several years.
1914	Nephew Benjamin Schwartz is living at 104 Albemarle St. when he gets engaged to Annie Fischmann
1914	Sister Yenta, and her husband Hyman Schwartz, living at 104 Albemarle St.
Nov. 1919	Nephew Nathan Gruber's Declaration of Intention residing at 102 Albemarle St.

Mollie Roskes must have been pregnant as all these new arrivals landed at their doorstep. Their second son, Herman (Hyman) Roskes was born in 1913. There was a 15-year difference in age between Herman and his older brother David. Herman's birthdate is sometimes given as July 4, 1913, but a descendant, Eric Roskes, told me he shifted his birthday to July 4th because he liked the

---

[114] Israel Schwartz and Samuel Roskes were not actually brothers-in-law. Israel's brother, Chaim, was a brother-in-law of Samuel's wife, Mollie.

significance. He was actually born on August 16, 1913 according to his father Samuel's Petition for Naturalization. What better proof that Americanization was well under way than a boy moving his birthday to the birthday of the Country?

In Samuel's 1914 Petition for Naturalization, they are still listed at 104 Albemarle Street and he is listed as a dairyman. Mollie is listed in the Baltimore City directory in dairy in 1915.

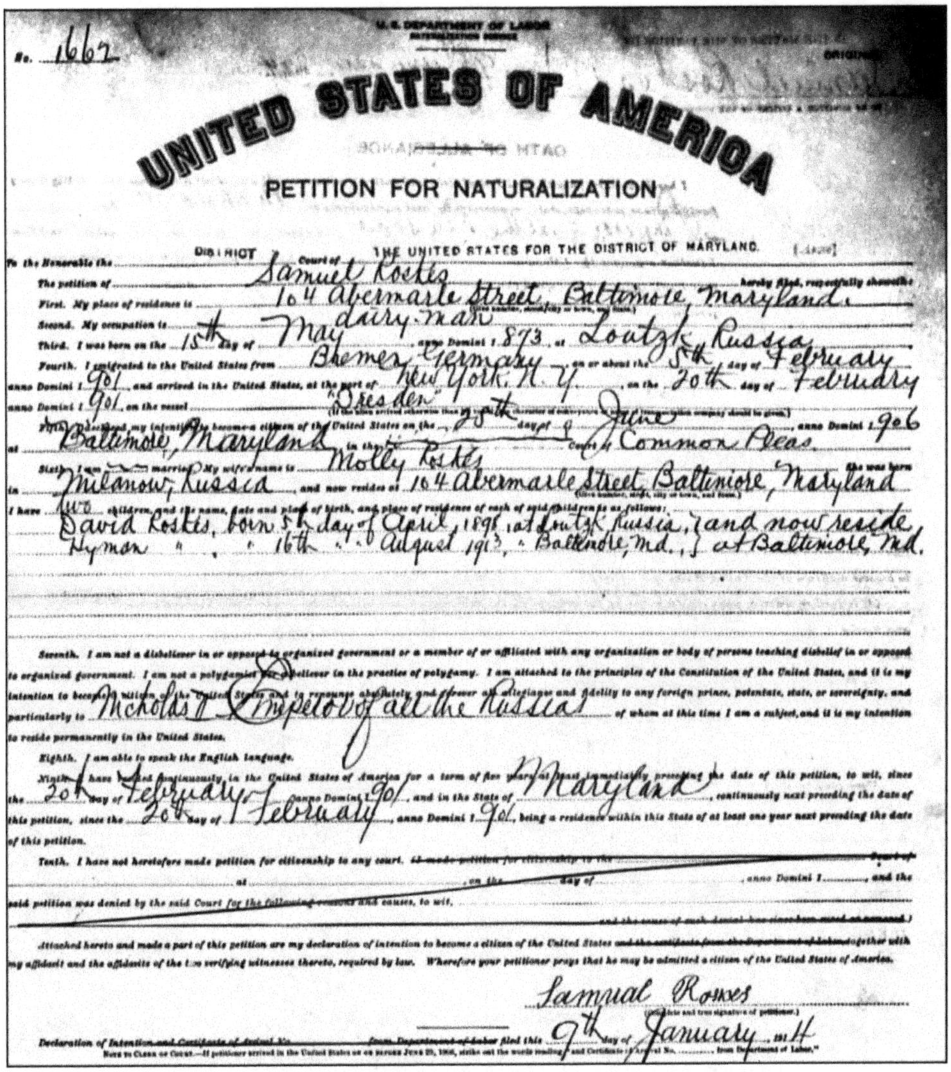
No. 1662

U.S. DEPARTMENT OF LABOR

UNITED STATES OF AMERICA

PETITION FOR NATURALIZATION

To the Honorable the District Court of the United States for the District of Maryland.

The petition of Samuel Roskes hereby filed, respectfully showeth:

First. My place of residence is 104 Albemarle Street, Baltimore, Maryland.

Second. My occupation is dairy man

Third. I was born on the 15th day of May anno Domini 1873, at Loutzk, Russia

Fourth. I emigrated to the United States from Bremen, Germany on or about the 5th day of February anno Domini 1901, and arrived in the United States, at the port of New York, N.Y. on the 20th day of February anno Domini 1901, on the vessel "Dresden"

Fifth. I declared my intention to become a citizen of the United States on the 23th day of June anno Domini 1906 at Baltimore, Maryland, in the Court of Common Pleas.

Sixth. I am married. My wife's name is Molly Roskes she was born in Milanow, Russia and now resides at 104 Albemarle Street, Baltimore, Maryland

I have two children, and the name, date and place of birth, and place of residence of each of said children is as follows: David Roskes, born 5th day of April, 1898, at Loutzk Russia, and now reside Hyman " " 16th " " August 1913, " Baltimore, Md. at Baltimore, Md.

Seventh. I am not a disbeliever in or opposed to organized government or a member of or affiliated with any organization or body of persons teaching disbelief in or opposed to organized government. I am not a polygamist nor a believer in the practice of polygamy. I am attached to the principles of the Constitution of the United States, and it is my intention to become a citizen of the United States and to renounce absolutely and forever all allegiance and fidelity to any foreign prince, potentate, state, or sovereignty, and particularly to Nicholas II Emperor of all the Russias of whom at this time I am a subject, and it is my intention to reside permanently in the United States.

Eighth. I am able to speak the English language.

Ninth. I have resided continuously in the United States of America for a term of five years at least immediately preceding the date of this petition, to wit, since the 20th day of February anno Domini 1901, and in the State of Maryland, continuously next preceding the date of this petition, since the 20th day of February, anno Domini 1901, being a residence within this State of at least one year next preceding the date of this petition.

Tenth. I have not heretofore made petition for citizenship to any court.

Attached hereto and made a part of this petition are my declaration of intention to become a citizen of the United States and the affidavit and the affidavits of the two verifying witnesses thereto, required by law. Wherefore your petitioner prays that he may be admitted a citizen of the United States of America.

Samual Roskes

Declaration of Intention filed this 9th day of January 1914

Figure 83 Samuel Roskes's 1914 Petition

By 1918, when Samuel filled out his Draft registration, he is self-employed in a grocery store at the same address. The grocery business was an ideal way for the Mlynov immigrants to move out of the garment industry, which was dominated by sweatshops. There are stories, in fact, of other Mlynov immigrants who returned home during this period because they detested life in the garment industry. The grocery store occupied the front and the family could live in the back or upstairs.

Family members including children could help manage the store freeing up husbands to also get involved in real estate as many did. Samuel remains a proprietor of a grocery in his 1920 and 1930 census.

Apparently Samuel and Mollie's son, David, enlisted in the army on October 1, 1918. This was just weeks after both he and his father Samuel filled out their Draft registration cards in September 12, 1918. This was the third draft regisitration targeted for men ages 18 through 45 who had not already been registered. David wrote that his birthday was September 15, 1898 and that he was a "Draughtman" at a "Park Plant" for a firm called Bartlett Hayward. He was already launched on a career that would make him, according to his obituary, "a Baltimore city employee for nearly 25 years and a building superintendent in the bureau of building inspection for the last 10 years of his life." He would eventually be in charge of "a staff of more than 150 people and was responsible for the operation and maintenance of City Hall, the Municipal Building, the Court House, Pier 2, Pratt Street, the Peoples Court Building and part of Police Headquarters."[115]

The War was already beginning to wind down by the time David enlisted that October 1, 1918. Armistice Day was November 1, 1918 and David was honorably discharged by December 10, 1918. It is not clear if he ever ended up in Europe.

Draft registration cards of Samuel and son David Stanley Roskes

---

[115] *The Baltimore Sun*, Dec. 29, 1964, p. 10.

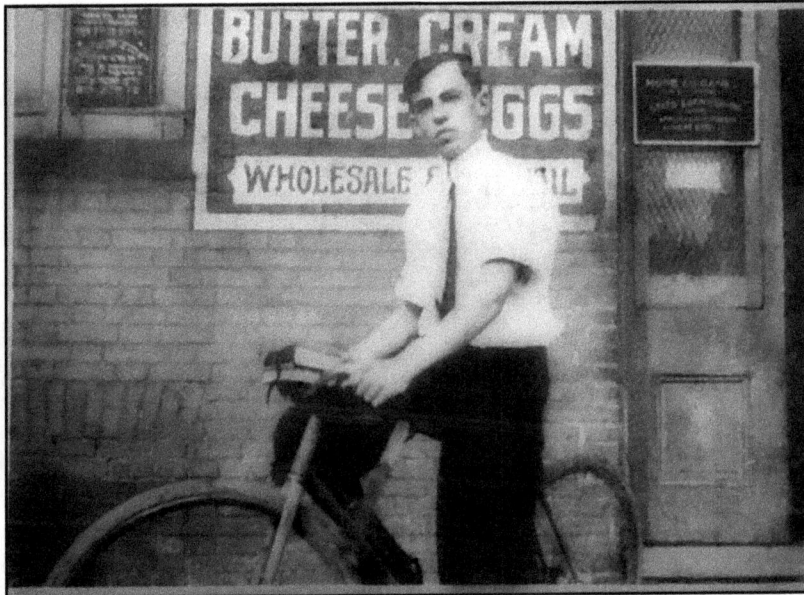

*Figure 84 David "Stanley" Roskes with books in Baltimore.
Courtesy of Ted Fishman*

In the 1920 Census, Samuel and Mollie appear for the first time at 102 Albemarle Street instead of 104 Albemarle. They appear with the surname spelled Oskis. The address 104 Albemarle no longer is listed at all on the Census and it seems that the two units (102 and 104) have been consolidated under a single address. There must have been some fluidity in the two addresses already by this point in time. Mollie's brother, Aaron Demb, for example, was living at 102 Albemarle when he filled out his 1918 Draft registration card and he lists Samuel Roskes as his close relative also at 102 Albemarle.

As discussed earlier, the address 102 Albemarle was raided during the Red Scare when Mollie's nephew, Nathan Gruber, was living there and possibly her brother Aaron Demb (see above p. 76 and following). Whether the raid triggered the consolidation of 102 and 104 addresses or was involved in an intentional misspelling of the Roskes surname is unknown but tantalizing.

Perhaps the raid also accounted for the Roskes's move to 2127 E. Pratt Street sometime by 1920. Samuel uses that address when he signs as a witness for the Naturalization Petition for Benjamin Schwartz (his wife's nephew). The Roskes still held onto the address at 102 Albemarle and they appear to still have it in the 1940s when it is eventually sold.

By 1921, Samuel and Mollie's son David earned his engineering degrees from Johns Hopkins. Soon thereafter, David married a woman named Dorothy (or Dora) Cluster and their first child Estelle was born in 1922.

HOLD-UP FOLLOWS POLICE CONFERENCE

Two Youths Escape With Loot From East Pratt Street Grocery Store.

GAITHER ADDS PROTECTION

Revises Schedule Of Patrolmen To Check Boldness Of Bandits.

An hour after the adjournment of a conference of police inspectors and captains with Charles D. Gaither, Police Commissioner, at which steps were taken to curb the series of holdups that have occurred during the last 10 days, two youths last night held up the grocery of Samuel Roskes, 2137 East Pratt street.

Four dollars was taken from the cash register. The youths escaped on foot. Only a short time before Roskes had taken more than $100 from the register and put it in a strong box in the rear of the house.

According to Roskes, he and his son David were putting in a pane of glass in the front window when the men entered the store. One of the men asked for a can of tobacco. Roskes turned to the tobacco shelf and inquired the brand. Receiving no response, he turned around. One of the men had two pistols and the other covered him with a third pistol. They ordered him to throw up his hands, while one of the bandits moved toward the cash register.

Got Lone Dollar Bill.

The bandit found a $1 bill and over $3 in change. As the men turned toward the door one of them remarked:

"It's a darn shame to take it, the poor fellows are broke."

Both men, according to Roskes, were about 18 or 19 years old and wore caps. One had on a brown overcoat, while the other wore a pepper colored coat.

"The situation is serious," Mr. Gaither told the police executives at the police conference. "Thus far the loss of money has been negligible and there has been no shooting, but the highwaymen go armed and eventually they will kill someone.

"Young men from Baltimore and not from out of town seem to be mixed up in these affairs. They seem to have singled out Jewish stores for robbery. They go armed with pistols of .38 and .44 caliber."

1923 Grocery Robbery of Roskes Grocery
The Baltimore Sun, Feb 16, 1923, p. 20

David was helping his father Samuel replace a pane of glass in their front grocery window the day it was robbed at gunpoint in February 1923. *The Baltimore Sun* ironically pointed out that the robbery occurred only an hour after police inspectors and captains met to discuss the series of hold-ups during the previous 10 days which had singled out Jewish stores. Arrests were eventually made on March 1, 1923.

By 1930, David and family is renting a unit in Philadelphia at 5827 Beaumont Ave. and David is listed as an electric engineer. The next generation was beginning their climb up through education. David and Dora's daughter Estelle (married name Greenberg) is listed as 8 years old. A daughter Marilyn (married name Kerpelman) was born in 1934.

Figure 85 ~ 1932 Estelle Roskes Bday Party with some Demb Cousins.
Courtesy of Ted Fishman.

1. Tessie (married name Kremer) holding Herman Shulman
2. Neena Schwartz
3. Bernard Shulman
4. Estelle Roskes
5. Marilyn Roskes
6. Alma Finkelstein
7. Gilbert Finkelstein
8. Melvin Shulman
9. Leon Schwartz (my father)
10. Ted Fishman

Mollie and Samuel's second son, Herman, married Mildred Rose Alliker on June 1, 1936 in the District of Columbia. Mildred's mother, Hinde (Settleman) Alliker was from Mervits, the nearby sister town of Mlynov, and she was related to (possibly a half sibling) of the Pesach Suttleman/Zutelman who married into the Shulman line. Herman and Mildred's son, Saul Roskes, was born in 1938 and a second son Geral ("Jerry") was born in 1943. Saul Roskes is still beloved as a Baltimore pediatrician, and he has been the doctor for the children of many Demb descendants.

*Figure 86 Herman Roskes,
bar mitzvah invitation, ˜1926*

*This photo is also displayed as part of the Lloyd Street
Synagogue exhibit.*

Samuel Roskes passed away on March 13, 1938. He was buried in the Chernigover Congregation New Cemetery in Rosedale, Baltimore.

Here lies

Shmuel son of Moshe

Passed 10ᵗʰ of Adar 5698

Samuel Roskes

Died Mar. 13, 1938

Age 67

FATHER

Figure 87 Tombstone of Samuel Roskes

***

Mollie's Aliyah to Israel

Mollie does not appear in the 1940 censuses of her sons, and her 1940 census has not been located. Family oral traditions reported to me by two Demb descendants in other lines say that Mollie was unhappy that her son or sons would not take her into her home the way other Demb children had taken their aging fathers and mothers into their homes. Another version of the story attributes the tension to Mollie and her daughter-in-laws.

I suspect that the decision to make aliyah was more complicated than that and that something about the new State of Israel and the new project of the Jewish community also spoke to her. If only she had left behind a journal or letters about her decision. In any case, Mollie's decision to make aliyah to Israel in 1949, not long after Israel announced statehood, was truly remarkable.

A record shows her leaving indefinitely for Israel on August 10th, 1949. It was just over a year after David Ben-Gurion proclaimed the State of Israel on May 14, 1948.

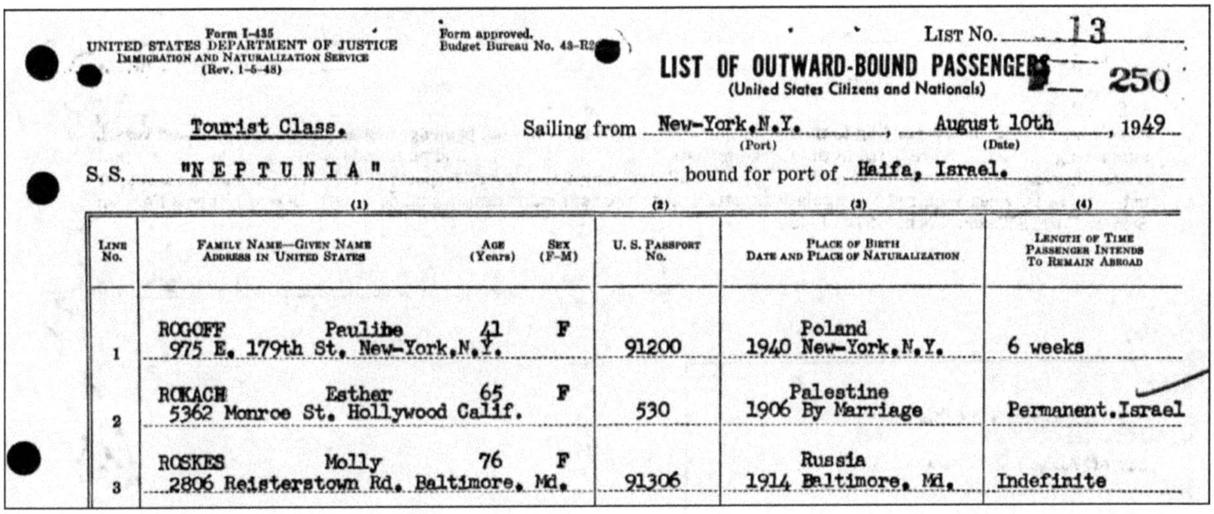
Form I-435
UNITED STATES DEPARTMENT OF JUSTICE
IMMIGRATION AND NATURALIZATION SERVICE
(Rev. 1-5-48)
Form approved.
Budget Bureau No. 43-R2
LIST NO. 13
LIST OF OUTWARD-BOUND PASSENGERS
(United States Citizens and Nationals)
250
Tourist Class. Sailing from New-York, N.Y. (Port), August 10th (Date), 1949
S.S. "N E P T U N I A" bound for port of Haifa, Israel.

Line No.	(1) Family Name—Given Name / Address in United States	Age (Years)	Sex (F-M)	(2) U.S. Passport No.	(3) Place of Birth / Date and Place of Naturalization	(4) Length of Time Passenger Intends to Remain Abroad
1	ROGOFF Peulibe 975 E. 179th St. New-York, N.Y.	41	F	91200	Poland 1940 New-York, N.Y.	6 weeks
2	ROKACH Esther 5362 Monroe St. Hollywood Calif.	65	F	530	Palestine 1906 By Marriage	Permanent. Israel
3	ROSKES Molly 2806 Reisterstown Rd. Baltimore, Md.	76	F	91306	Russia 1914 Baltimore, Md.	Indefinite

Figure 88 Mollie Roskes Passenger Manifest to Israel Aug. 10, 1949

A photo of Mollie in Israel shows her with other Mlynov-born individuals at Moshav Balfouria during a Passover visit of Ben Fishman from Baltimore. Ben was married to Mollie's niece, Clara (Shulman). He must have been on a trip to Israel see his father Moshe Fishman who made aliyah from Mlynov in 1921 and settled on Moshav Balfournia. Also present was other Mlynov born friends, Samuel Mandelkern and his wife Malcah Lamdan.[116] The photo was taken before January 1962 when Mollie passed away.

---

[116] Malcah Lamdan was the sister of the now famous poet Yitzhak Lamdan who wrote the poem "Masada." She was a teacher in Mlynov before making aliyah in about 1923 with her husband Shmuel Mandelkern (or Mandelkoren). Shmuel wrote an essay for the Mlynov Memorial book, pp. 108–135, on self-defense efforts in Mlynov following WWI.

Figure 89 Mollie Roskes (standing center) in Moshav Balfouria.

(r to l) Mlynov-born Shmuel Mandelkern, Benjamin Fishman, Mollie Roskes,
Moshe Fishman, Moshe's daughter, Malcah (Lamdan) Mandelkern.
From the collection of Ted Fishman.

ROSKES. — On January 9, 1962,
MOLLIE, formerly of Baltimore,
died in Israel, beloved wife of the
late Samuel Roskes and mother of
David and Herman Roskes and
sister of Aaron Demb and Yetta
Schwartz; also survived by four
grandchildren and three great-
grandchildren.   12e
   Funeral services were held in
Israel. In mourning at 4114 Fern-
hill avenue, beginning Thursday
afternoon January 11.
ROSKES.—The Ajax Club regrets
the passing of MOLLIE ROSKES,
mother of our member, David
Roskes.
      MEYER LEVINSOHN,

The Evening Sun Jan 11, 1962 p. 34

Mollie is buried in the Old Cemetery in Rishon Tsiyon (which is just south of Tel Aviv).[117] She was the first of the Demb siblings to come to America. Mollie was survived by her older sister Yenta, who outlived her by ten months, and her younger brother Aaron, who lived until 1972.

פ"נ
עמליה ראסקעס
בת ישראל יעקב
ממלינוב פוליה
ד' בשבט תשעם [?]
תנצב"ה

Here lies
Amalya Roskes
From Mlynov, Poland
4th of Shevat 5722, [age 90?]
(Jan 9, 1962)

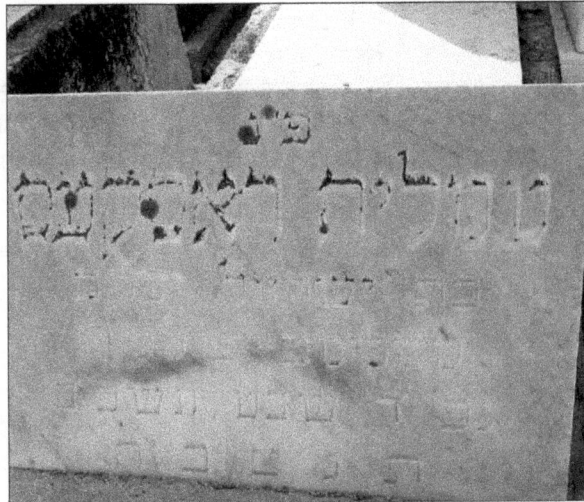

US Records Summary for Family of Mollie (Demb) and Samuel Roskes

1901 Passenger manifest	"Schame Roskis" sailing from Bremen on Jan 19th 1901 on SS Dresden and arriving in New York Feb. 3, 1901, age 27 (implied year of birth 1874), last residence Luck, heading to brother in law Getzel Fox or Fax, 818 E. Pratt St.
1906 (June 25) Declaration of Intention	Sam Roskis declares intention to be citizen. Record found does not include additional information.
1908 Passenger Manifest	Mollie and son David's manifest not located. Clara Fram in her memoir remembers that her Aunt Mollie arrived the year before she did in early 1909.
1910 (April 28) US Federal Census	"Mollie" and Samuel Roskes living at 104 Albemarle Street. Samuel is age 38 (implied year of birth 1872) and Mollie is age 34 (implied year of birth 1876). They have been married 13 years (implied year of marriage 1897). Mollie has given birth to 4 children and only 1 is still alive. Immigration year is listed [incorrectly] as 1900 for both of them. Samuel is listed as a pants maker in a clothing factory. David is listed as age 12 (implied year of birth 1898).

---

[117] Address Al Kanfei Nesharim St 8, Rishon Letsiyon old, Rishon Letsiyon, Israel.

1914 (Jan. 9) Petition for Naturalization	For Samuel Roskis. Living at 104 Albemarle Street, Baltimore Maryland. Listed as "dairyman." Birthday listed as May 15, 1873 in "Loutzk [Lutsk], Russia". Arrived in 1901 in New York on Feb. 20th on the SS Dresden. Wife's name is "Molly Roskes" who was born in "Milanow" Russia. Two children listed: David, born April 5th, 1898 in "Loutzk" and Hyman born Aug. 16th, 1913 in Baltimore. Witnesses: Jacob Sobeloff, upholsterer, residing at 10 Irvine Place, Baltimore, and Harry Katzen, cabinet-maker, residing at 832 [?]anby Street, Baltimore
1918 (Sept. 12), WWI Draft Registration	For "Samuel Roskes" living at 104 Albemarle St. Age 44, Date of birth listed as April 15, 1874. Self-employed in Grocery Store. Nearest relative Mollie Roskes.
1918 Military Record	For David Stanley Roskes, birth date Apr 15, 1898, residence: 102 Albemarle St, Ind[ucted] 10/1/1918, Hon disch[arge] 12/10/18
1920 US Federal Census (Jan 15).	Samuel and Mollie "Oskis" living at 102 Albemarle Street. They are listed as owner of their unit. Samuel is age 49 (implied year of birth 1871) and Mollie is age 48 (implied birth year 1872). Samuel's immigration year is 1901 and Mollie's is 1908. Year of naturalization is 1907 for both (Mollie was naturalized by Samuel getting naturalized before she arrived). Samuel and Mollie are both listed as "keeper" of a grocery store. David "Oskis" is 22 year of immigration 1908 and is naturalized in 1907 (via his father Samuel's naturalization before he arrived). Son Hyman is age 6 (implied birth year 1914) and he was born in Maryland.
1930 (April 7) US Federal Census.	Residing at 2127 Pratt Street. Samuel and Mollie both listed as age 59 and married for 24 years (implied birth year of 1871). Their birthplace now listed as Poland (since Mlynov and Lutsk are part of Poland). Samuel's year of immigration is 1900 and Mollie's is 1907. They are both naturalized. Samuel is listed as proprietor of a grocery. They are listed as owner of their unit. Their son David is no longer living with them. "David S. Roskes" has gotten married and is living in Philadelphia (see next) Their son Hyman who was born in Maryland is now 16.
1930 (April 5) US Federal Census	David S. Roskes, age 32, head, residing at 5827 Beaumont Ave, Philadelphia, Rented, Home Value 45, has Radio, ate age marriage 21, immigration year 1908, Na[turaliaged] occupation Engineer for Electric Co, wife Dorothy B, age 26, age at marriage 17, born in Maryland; Estelle, daughter, age 8 born in Maryland, and lodger Harry Miller.
1940	David Roskes, head, residing at 100 Hurst Street, age 42, same house in 1935, Na[turalized], grocer in grocery store, Dorothy, wife, age 36 born in Maryland, clerk in grocery store, Estelle, daughter 18, born in Maryland, and Marilyn, daughter, age 6.
1940	In Charles Maryland, Herman Roskes, head, 26 born in Maryland, occupation: S[illegible] Government, Mildred wife, age 26 born in Maryland and Saul D son, age 1.
1942 (Feb. 2) WWII Draft Registration	[Samuel and Mollie's son] David Stanley Roskes' WWII draft registration indicates he was born in Lutsk.

***

CHAPTER 9

AARON DEMB, BABY OF THE FAMILY

Aaron Meir Demb (~1876–May 3, 1970) was the youngest son of Rivka and Israel Jacob Demb. Most of Aaron's US records indicate he was born in 1876 (though his 1930 census implies 1880). Aaron died in Baltimore on May 3, 1970, approximately 94 years old. He is buried in the Ohr Knesseth Israel Anshe Sfard Cemetery.

Figure 90 Aaron Demb

Until recently nothing was remembered about the background of Aaron's wife except that her name was Baila on her manifest and that she had a brother called "Mr. Woladad" or "Mr. Waladaid" back in Rowno when she left for America.

Thanks to the excellent sleuthing efforts of her great-grandson, Michael Demb, we now know she was born Baila Woladski from Mervits. Michael discovered her surname listening to an audio recording of Mlynov-born Benjamin Fishman sharing his memories of Mlynov with the children of Lou Demb, one of Aaron and Baila's sons.[118] Benjamin knew a great deal about their grandmother, Baila, because he travelled on the same ship to Baltimore in 1920 along with her and her children.

In US records, Baila's birth year is suggested as 1882 (on her 1920 manifest) and 1888 (on the 1930 census). She died on October 12, 1956, well before Aaron who was later buried next to her.

---

[118] The recording, https://kehilalinks.jewishgen.org/Mlyniv/audio/Ben-Fishman-Memories-of-Mlynov.mp4, was preserved by Aaron and Baila's granddaughter, Debbie Mondell. In Baltimore, Ben Fishman married a niece of Aaron Demb (i.e., Clara Shulman).

Aaron and Baila were married by at least 1908, 1909 or 1911, given the variation in birth years indicated for their eldest son Louis in US records. Their 1930 census indicates Aaron was 50 years old and was married at age 25 and Bessie was 42 and was married at age 17. Doing the math suggests they may have been married as early as 1905. Aaron and Bessie had two sons, Louis and Hyman Demb. Louis later told his daughter, Debbie Mondell, that there were two other siblings, a sister, who died young, and a brother named Moishe who died about 11 years old. Both died before the family came to America.

We can surmise that the two sons, Louis and Hyman, were born in Mlynov since Aaron's last residence on his passenger manifest in 1914 is Mlynov and his closest relative listed there is his wife Beila Demb. On their 1920 manifest, their birthplace appears as something like "Mermoz," probably an attempt by a ship official to render Mervits or Muravica into English, which is where we now know Baila was born. It is true that their son Louis's WWII draft card says he was born in "Rowne" (Rovno / Rivne), but this record was much later and it was probably an effort to name a town that would be recognized.

In his oral account, Benjamin Fishman recalls that Aaron was conscripted into the Tsar's army in 1905 for the Russo-Japanese War. Although he never made it to the front, things were difficult when he returned home because he had no trade. Perhaps this is why Aaron left for Baltimore in 1914 when he did. He also had three elder siblings (Pesse, Yenta, Mollie) as well as several nieces and nephews in Baltimore by this time.

***

Aaron's Migration in 1914

Aaron left Mlynov for Baltimore in 1914 with the intention of sending for his family from America. He left Bremen, Germany on the SS Rhein on February 26, 1914 and arrived in Baltimore on March 13, 1914. There was no hint of the coming War in the front page of *The Baltimore Sun* the day he landed but the War would start that summer and separate him from his family for 6 years, just as his nephew Nathan Gruber had been separated from his.

Aaron is listed as age 38 and his last residence, as noted previously, was Mlynov where his closest relative was his wife "Bsila." We know his parents Israel Jacob and Rivka were still alive when he left, since they appear in a photo of the Shulman family taken during this time. With Aaron as the baby of the family, it must have been a tearful and difficult goodbye with his parents.

Like so many of the other Baltimore arrivals in the prior few years, Aaron was headed to the flat of his "br. i. l. [brother-in-law] Mollie Roskes at 104 Albemarle St." Of course, Mollie was Aaron's sister, but the norm was to refer to the male head of the household, hence the reference to "brother-in-law."

Aron Demb–Passenger Manifest on SS Rhein (Line 3)

Page 2 of Aaron Demb Passenger manifest heading to br. i. l. Roskes Malis 104 Albemarle (Line 3)

WWI broke out that summer and Aaron was among a group of Mlynov husbands, including his nephew Nathan Gruber, who was separated from a wife and children during this time. It must have been extremely difficult for him and the other Mlynov husbands to try to follow the War and see the Eastern Front move back and forth past Mlynov and Mervits.[119]

During the War, Aaron remained with or just across the hall from the family of his sister Mollie Roskes. He was at 104 Albemarle when he signed his 1915 Declaration of Intention and he lists 102 Albemarle when he fills out his WWI draft Registration in 1918. His nephew Nathan Gruber was living there at the time as well.

According to Ben Fishman's oral recording, Baila struggled financially to take care of the kids while Aaron was in Baltimore so she went back to Mervits to live where she had a brother. Yad Vashem records discovered by great-grandson, Michael Demb, show that the name of Baila's brother was Samuel (Shmeel) Woladski (spelled variously in English in the records as Wolocki, Wokocki Wlotocki, Volotzki). According to those records, he was born in 1885 in "Morawica" (Muravica/Mervits). He married a woman named Golda and they had three daughters, Rakhel, Bela, and Kamela. All of them later perished in Rowno during the Shoah.

Like other residents of Mlynov and Mervits during WWI, Baila and her sons were evacuated by the Russian authorities further east and Benjamin Fishman reports losing track of them until April 1920 when he joined up with them again in Rowne in preparation for their migration. In the course of talking about life in Mlynov during the War, Benjamin recalls seeing the Bolshevik's drag the wife of the Count through the streets by a horse until she died.

**

Itzik Lerner Returns to Mlynov

Sometime in 1919 as the War was winding down, Aaron and two other Mlynov husbands in Baltimore (Joseph Lerner and Isaac Marder) began planning to bring their stranded Mlynov families to Baltimore.[120] Aaron's nephew, Nathan Gruber, was also involved in the plan. Joseph Lerner's son Itzik (Isadore) Lerner planned to go back to Mlynov and help his family and the others with their migration.

As you may remember (pp. 74ff), Itzik Lerner was the one who helped Nathan Gruber's wife and two daughters migrate to the US from their shtetl near Novohrad Volinski. Itzik was born in Mlynov in 1896 and arrived in Baltimore in December 1913. He lived with his father, Joseph, for a time at 106 Albemarle Street (with many of the other Mlynov and Demb immigrants).

---

[119] See my discussion of the Eastern Front in "Mlynov in WWI" on the Mlynov web site.

[120] There seem to have been distant filial relationships through marriage between all these men. On his passenger manifest, Joseph Lerner is called the uncle of Israel Herman, the husband of Mollie (Gruber). Isaac Marder's wife was related to Yenta (Demb) Schwartz, as discussed previously.

Itzik entered the US army on August 14, 1918 and his army uniform played an important role in the story of these Mlynov families' migration. A transport record shows he shipped out from Hoboken, N. J. to Europe on Oct. 25, 1918. His emergency contact was his father Joseph Lerner at 104 Albemarle Street. He was overseas from Oct. 27, 1918 until Feb. 23, 1919. He was given an honorable discharge a month later on March 18, 1919. The Treaty of Versailles ending the War was signed soon thereafter on June 28, 1919 and it took effect Jan. 10, 1920.

Itzik didn't waste any time going back to Mlynov once the treaty was signed. On Dec. 16, 1919, "Isidore Israel Lerner" applied for a passport to go back to "Poland, France and other necessary countries" to "bring my mother, sister and brother to America." In the margin someone wrote in different handwriting: "Letters from mother in distress." Itzik planned to leave about Jan. 6, 1920. On the second page of the manifest, he asked that the passport be sent to 104 Albemarle Street, where he was apparently living again.

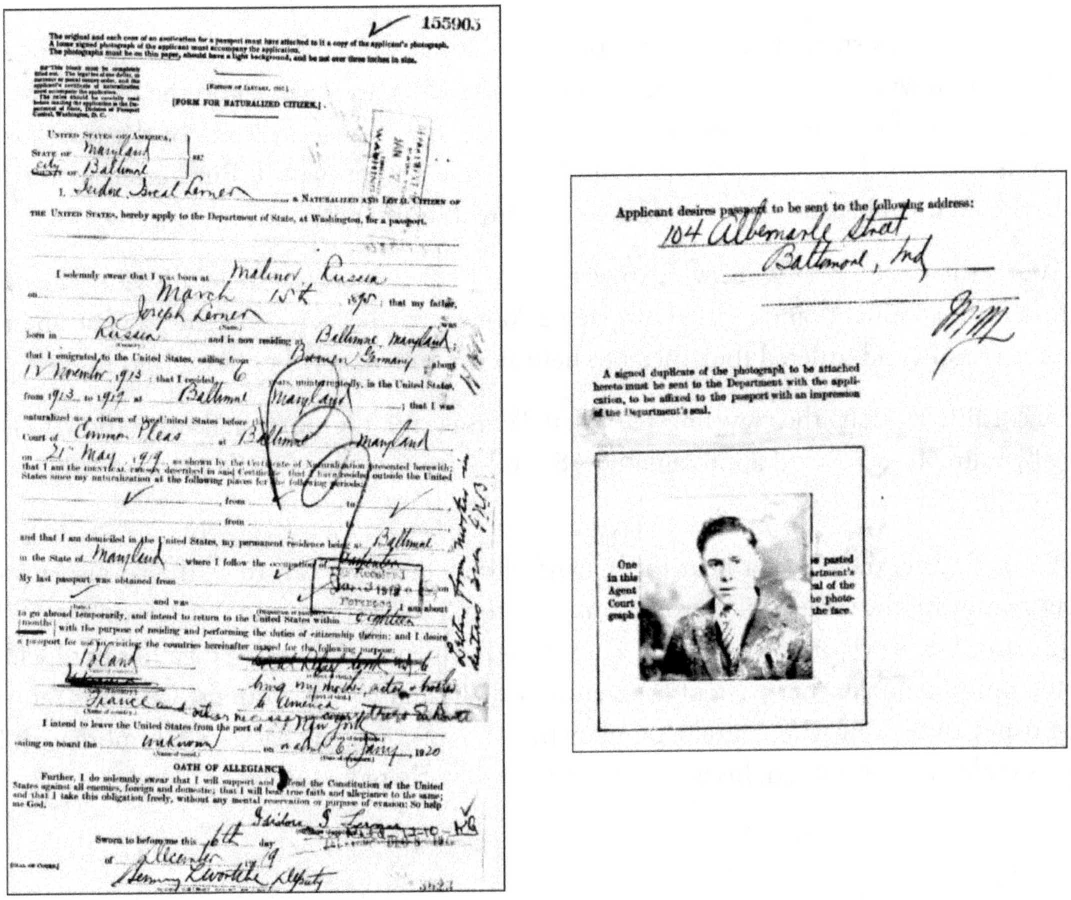
155905
[FORM FOR NATURALIZED CITIZEN.]
UNITED STATES OF AMERICA,
STATE OF Maryland
City OF Baltimore
I, Isidore Israel Lerner, a NATURALIZED AND LOYAL CITIZEN OF THE UNITED STATES, hereby apply to the Department of State, at Washington, for a passport.
I solemnly swear that I was born at Malinov, Russia on March 15th 189?; that my father, Joseph Lerner, was born in Russia and is now residing at Baltimore, Maryland; that I emigrated to the United States, sailing from Bremen, Germany, about 17 November 1913; that I resided 6 years, uninterruptedly, in the United States, from 1913 to 1919 at Baltimore, Maryland; that I was naturalized as a citizen of the United States before the Court of Common Pleas at Baltimore, Maryland on 21 May 1919, as shown by the Certificate of Naturalization presented herewith;
OATH OF ALLEGIANCE.
Applicant desires passport to be sent to the following address:
104 Albemarle Street, Baltimore, Md

Figure 91 Itzik Lerner's Passport application

***

The Migration of Aaron's Wife, Baila Demb

In early 1920, Aaron Demb's wife, Baila, and the wives of Isaac Marder and Joseph Lerner, began planning their trip to America with their children. They were the first of a new wave of Mlynov residents heading to Baltimore now that the War was over. One day while they were planning, Ben Fishman and his friend Hertz Shulman were sitting around listening to the preparations. For some reason, there was an extra spot or ticket available, according to the story Ben Fishman told his son, Ted.

Hertz Shulman nudged Ben and said as a kind of lark, "Why don't you go?"

Ben thought about it for a minute and then said, "Sure, why not?"

As a result, Ben "Boks Fishman" ended up traveling with the three wives and their children to America. The travelers included Aaron Demb's wife, Baila, and her two sons, Itzik Lerner's mother, Radie (Rose) and his three siblings, and Isaac Marder's wife, Karla (Clara) and their three children.

It is from Ben's storytelling that we know a bit about what their journey was like. Ben met up with Baila in Rowne in April 1920. From there, Itzik Lerner got them all on the train to Warsaw and placed them in first class, according to a story his son Ted recalls. None of the travelers had ridden trains first class before and they felt uncomfortable and protested. But Lerner insisted and no one bothered them because Lerner had his US army uniform with him.

When they made it to Warsaw, Ben went into the Polish official to get his visa. The official made antisemitic comments and refused his papers. When Itzik Lerner heard this, he put on his US army uniform again and ordered the official to help Ben. Immediately Ben was given his visa.

According to Ben, the traveling party left Warsaw for the port of Danzig (now Gdansk) probably by train. They covered approximately 588 miles from Mlynov to the port, probably mostly by train.

From Danzig, they took a boat to England. From there we can trace their journey with a passenger manifest. The group sailed from Southampton, England on June 9, 1920 on the SS New York and arrived in New York on June 19th. There were 13 members traveling together not including Itzhik who appears on another page of the manifest dedicated to US Citizens. Itzik was returning from the trip with his new wife, Gittel Czainik, whom he was bringing back to Baltimore with him. Since he was already naturalized, his wife Gittel was grandfathered in as well.

Figure 92 Journey of Baila and fellow travelers

In the traveling party, Bejla Demb is listed as 38, with an implied birth year of 1892. Her son Zipe (=Louis) is age 11, and her son, Chaim, is age 9. Their last residence is "Rowno, Poland" and her closest relative there was her "brother Mr. Woladski."

As noted earlier, their birthplace is listed as something like "Mermrz" [i.e., Muravitz/Mervits /Muravica]. She is headed to her husband Mr. Demb at 104 Ave Canale St. in Baltimore. I'm guessing this address was probably a mangled version of "104 Albemarle near the Canal" (perhaps referring to the harbor or Jones Falls River) which is where her husband Aaron was staying. Traveling with Baila was Isaac Marder's wife, Clara (Tessler), and her two daughters and son,[121] as well as Itzik Lerner's mother, Radie (Rose) Lerner, and her other four children.[122] At the bottom of the list is "Boks" (Benjamin) Fishman.

---

[121] Sore Girla (Sura Gitla?) (married name Sarah Mutter) age 17, Pesra (married name Pauline Samuels Bargteil), age 15, and Hutin (Nutin?) (=Nathan Marder) age 9. The children's mother, Clara Marder, was born Clara Tessler and was an aunt of Holocaust survivor, Liba Tessler, who appeared in the 1929 photo with Yenta (Demb) Schwartz when she went back to Mlynov in 1929, as discussed above (pp. 138ff). The Marder child "Sore Girla" became the mother of my informant Sheila Mandelberg whom I met in Baltimore and told me that her family were relatives of the Schwartz family.
[122] Hene (married name Anna Miller) age 18, Sosra (married name Sophie Glick), age 13, Mojsche (Morris Lerner) age 10, Spre (Sarah) age 11.

According to Ben, when they arrived in New York, Itzik Lerner abandoned him and he was left alone by himself until a landsman, Zhavel Schwartz,[123] who happened to be in the balcony, spied him wandering around and helped get him on a train to Baltimore.

When I later asked Ted why his father Ben thought Itzik had abandoned him at Ellis Island, Ted told me the story he heard from his father. According to Ben, the women asked him to keep track of the money Itzik was carrying for them during the trip and he concluded that Itzik was angry he was being monitored by the young Ben.

I asked Ted whether his father ever asked Itzik whether this was true. But he never had. An alternative and more plausible explanation arises from another set of records. Itzik was on a separate list of the ship's manifest with other US citizens. As a US citizen already, he probably passed through customs through a separate process than the other travelers who were aliens. In addition, Itzik's mother and siblings appear on a list of aliens held for special inquiry as did Aaron Demb's wife, Baila and her two sons. It seems likely Itzik was trying to figure out how to get them out of detention. For all of those reasons, Ben naturally felt abandoned at Ellis Island.

Figure 93 Isadore "Itzik" Lerner
and wife Gertrude in 1920s
Courtesy of Cheryl Lerner

---

[123] Zhavel Schwartz turned out to be Sam Schwartz, a son of Michael Schwartz, a brother of Chaim Schwartz. Sam arrived in Baltimore in 1912 and I doubt he was in the balcony by accident. I suspect he was probably there to meet Ben who was a nephew of Sam's Aunt Sarah (Fishman) who married his uncle Israel Schwartz. Ben was in fact headed to his Aunt Sarah's address. It is of note that one of Sam's daughters, Mildred, married into the well-known Luskin family in Baltimore. A book, *Flowers for Mrs. Luskin*, was written about a grandson of his, Paul Luskin, who hired a flower delivery man to kill his wife in 1988 after a bitter divorce battle.

LIST OR MANIFEST OF ALIEN PASSENGERS FOR THE UNITED

ALL ALIENS arriving at a port of continental United States from a foreign port or a port of the insular possessions of the United States, and all aliens arriving at a port of said insular possessions from a foreign port, a port of continental United This (white) sheet is for the listing of

List _____

S. S. "THE YORK" _____ Passengers sailing from SOUTHAMPTON _____, JUNE 8th _____, 1910.

The manifest of Bejla Demb and her sons Zipe (Louis) and Hyman traveling with the Marders, Lerners and Benjamin Fishman

Page 2 of manifest Bejla Demb is heading to her husband Mr. Demb at 104 Canale St [probably 104 Albemarle St?] Baltimore

***

Settling into Baltimore

After Aaron was reunited with his wife, Baila, and his sons in June 1920, he disappears from US records until 1923. He and Bessie reappear at a new address: 2036 e Balto and Aaron is now a plasterer. The family is still there in the 1930 census and Aaron is listed as a bricklayer in the construction industry. The family remained at the East Baltimore address until after 1940. By the 1950 census, Aaron and Bessie are living at 3622 Spaulding, with their son Hyman and his family. Hyman married Ida M. Arenberg and their daughter Harriet Gloria Demb (married name Rosenbaum) was born in 1945.[124]

Aaron and Baila's son Louis married Priscilla Caplan who was at least 11 years younger. Their son Marvin was born in 1947. In the 1950 census they are living at 3506 Spaulding, a few houses away from Aaron, Bessie and Hyman. Louis is listed as having a retail hardware store and their son Marvin is 2 years old. They had two daughters, Debbie (married name Mondell) in 1950, and Rona in 1953.

Figure 94 Aaron Demb and Baila (Woladski)

---

[124] Ida Arenberg's niece, Helene Arenberg, also married into a Mlynov line. She married Alan Meren, who was the son of Boruch Meren and Amelia (Shargel) both born in Mlynov.

*Figure 95 Aaron and Bessie's sons and families
Courtesy of Marvin and Sharon Demb*

*(back row l to r) Baila, Louis Demb, Priscilla
(Caplan), Hyman Demb his wife Ida (Arenberg),
Aaron Demb; (front row l to r): Harriette (married
named Rosenbaum), Deborah (married name
Mondell) and Marvin Demb.*

*Figure 96 Aaron Demb (right) wedding of granddaughter,
Harriet
Courtesy Jami Rosenbaum*

Figure 97 1967 Wedding of Harriet (Demb) Rosenbaum

1. Aaron Demb
2. Hyman Demb
3. Ida (Arenberg) Demb
4. Harriet (Demb) Rosenbaum
5. Jerome Rosenbaum
6. Louis Demb
7. Pricilla (Caplan) Demb
8. Sol Gorman
9. Molly (Brownstein) Gorman[125]

[125] Michael Demb also uncovered a forgotten/lost family connection to a Gorman Family from Detroit through Hyman Demb's Obituary. Bailah Woladski's niece was Molly Brownstein Gorman. The Gormans used to visit the Dembs on Spaulding Ave on a regular basis.

Figure 98 Hyman Demb and Ida (Arenberg).
Courtesy of Jami Rosenbaum

Summary of US Records for Aaron Demb and his family

1914 (March 13) Passenger Manifest	Aron Demb, leaving Bremen on Feb. 26, 1914 on the SS Rhein arriving in Baltimore, March 13, 1914, age 38 with implied birth year of 1876, farmlab[orer] (faint handwriting: "miller") last residence: Mlynov. Closest relative there: wife: Demb, Bsila. Destination br. i. l. [brother-in-law] Roskes Mollie? 104 Albemarle St.
1915 (Nov. 11) Declaration of Intention	Aaron Demb, 38, Plasterer, white, complexion dark, 5' 4" 140 lbs, hair black, eyes gray, born Mlnenov, Russia on August 15, 1897, resides at 104 Albermarle [sic] Street, Baltimore, emigrated from Bremen, Germany on the vessel Rhein, last foreign residence ws Mlenov, Russia, arrived at the port of Baltimore March 23rd, 1914. *his Declaration is next to the Declaration of Hyman Nathan Fishman from Mlynov.
1918 (Sept. 12) WWI Draft Registration Card	Sept. 12 1918, Aaron Demb 102 Albemarle age 42, DOB Aug. 8, 1876. Declarant (for naturalization), Bricklayer, own employer, place of employment everywhere, nearest relative Samuel Roskes 102 Albemarle St.
1920 Census	Not located. See discussion.

1920 (June 9) Passenger Manifest	For Aaron's wife and children: Leaving Southampton June 9, 1920 on SS New York arriving in New York on June 19th. Destination Husband Mr. Demb 104 Ave, Canale St. Baltimore [probably a mistake for 104 Albemarle St near the Canal], "Bejla Demb," 38 with implied birth year of 1882 in "Mermrz"[Muravitz or Mervits], last residence Rowno, Poland, [Children]: Zipe [Louis] age 11 with implied birth year of 1909, and Chaim age 9 with implied birth year of 1911.
Petition for Naturalization	Not located
1930 US Federal Census	2046 Baltimore Street Aaron N. Denb, head, O[wns] home, home value $4580, age 50 with implied birth year of 1880, age at marriage 25 with implied year of 1905, immigration year 1916 [incorrect] Na[turalized], Bricklayer in Construction Co; Bessie wife, age 42 with implied birth year of 1888, age at marriage 17 with implied marriage year of 1905, son Louis, age 19 with implied birth year of 1911, born in Russia, Clerk in Hardware store, son Hyman born in Russia age 17 with implied birth year of 1913.
1940 (Oct. 16) WWII Draft Card	Serial Number 1163. Louis Demb. 2036 E. Baltimore St. Baltimore. Telephone Broadway 8547. Age 31 years, Place of birth "Rowneo", date of birth Aug. 31, 1909. Closest relative, Bessie Demb (same address). Employer's name: Louis Demb, Hardware. Place of employment: 1033 W. Baltimore St.
1940 (Oct. 16) WWII Draft Card	Serial Number 1519. Hyman Elie Demb. Address: 2036 E. Baltimore St., Baltimore. Telephone: BR-8547, Age 29, date of birth Jan. 1, 1911. Russia, Closest relative: Mrs. Ida Frances Demb, wife, same address, Employer's name: Louis Demb, Place of employment 1033 W. Baltimore St.
1950 (April 18) US Federal Census	Aaron M. Demb, head, 71, citizen, Bessie E., wife, age 60, citizen, Residing at 3622 Spaulding Ave. living in same address with [son] Hyman E. Demb, head 36, citizen, manager retail hardware store, Ida, wife, 32, born in Maryland [incorrect], and Harriette G. , daughter age 4, born in Maryland.
1950 (April 19) US Federal Census	Louis G. Demb, head, age 38, manager in retail hardware store, residing at 3506 Spaulding, naturalized, Priscilla, wife, age 27, born in Maryland, Marvin H. son, age 2, born in Maryland

***

APPENDIX

THREE GENERATIONS OF THE DEMB FAMILY

The following linear Demb Family Tree records three generations of descendants of Rivka Gruber and Israel Jacob Demb, the matriarch and patriarch of the family. The dates are based on records where available and on communications with descendants where they could be tracked down. Because birthdates of those born in Russia were fluid in US records, I have tried to signal that some of them are guestimates with the symbol ~ which indicates the date is approximate.

> Key: **m.**–marriage; **m1**–first marriage; **m2**–second marriage; **d**–died; **dv.**–divorced, **c1**–child of first marriage; **c2**–child of second marriage; **sc**–stepchild; ~–estimate

***

Moshko-Leib (Moshe-Leib) Gruber (1824-?) m. Sura (?) (1826-?). Rivka Gruber was one of their daughters.

Rivka Gruber (1842 – d. after 1913) m. Israel Jacob Demb (1838? – d. after 1929), wed ~ 1863. They had nine children. Six of those children came to Baltimore and the children of a seventh.

❖ **[1] Pesse Demb (married name Bessie Hurwitz) (~ 1864– Jan. 20, 1932, Baltimore[126]) m. David (Rivetz) Hurwitz (~1867– June 1, 1933, Baltimore), wed ~1882**

  ➤ *[2] Gulza (or Gulzia) Rivetz (~1884– Oct. 28, 1978) m. Leizor Mazuryk (Louis Mazer) (Apr. 15, 1883– Oct. 25, 1946), wed 1904*
    ▪ [3] Martin Samuel Mazer (Nov. 8 1913, Beresteczko, Russia–Apr. 11, 1976, Baltimore) m. Mollie Shindel (Oct. 6, 1912 – Mar. 22, 1991)

  ➤ *[2] Menucha (Minnie) (~1886/1887–Feb. 8, 1977) m. Samuel Fox (Aug. 27, 1882–June 28, 1966), mar. license May 29, 1909*
    ▪ Martin Fox (Minnie's stepson) (Oct 28, 1904–March 21, 1987 Pompano Beach) m. Lillian Scherr (Feb. 14, 1902–Jan. 12, 1992 Fort Lauderdale), wed Mar. 4, 1925
    ▪ Earnest "Ernie" Fox (Minnie's stepson) (July 10, 1907 Baltimore–March 15, 1998 Baltimore) m. Marie Mathilda Kaiss (June 5, 1907– Sept. 16, 1996)

---

[126] The dates of Bessie and David Hurwitz's deaths and burial locations were located by Carol Engelman in the Jack Lewis Funeral Home Records Collection hosted by the Jewish Museum of Maryland. http://jewishmuseummd.org/wp-content/uploads/2013/06/Jack-Lewis-records-index.pdf, retrieved May 18, 2023

- [3] Sarah Anna Kappelman (daughter of Minnie and Sam) (July 3, 1910, District of Columbia-Aug. 5, 2013 Baltimore) m1 LeRoy F. Kappelman (July 2, 1909-Dec. 14, 1974 Baltimore), wed Apr. 13, 1938; m2 S. Herbert "Bucky" Harris (Apr. 21, 1907-May 23, 2008) wed in 1980
- [3] Jack (Jacob) M Fox (son of Minnie and Sam) (May 14, 1914 Baltimore-Mar. 9, 1982 Baltimore) m. Ruth Finkel (Jan. 6, 1915 Maryland-May 31, 1998), wed July 2, 1939
- [3] Michael (also "Michel") (son of Minnie and Sam) (Oct. 8, 1911-Aug. 27, 1973 Baltimore) m. Anne Cohen (Feb. 28, 1911-Mar. 23, 1978, Baltimore)

➤ [2] *Yitzhak Rivetz (Isaac Hurwitz) (~June 16, 1886-Dec. 23, 1918) m. Celia Kramer (Dec. 4 1887 Lithuania-May 8, 1966 Baltimore) [Celia m2 Louis Shapiro (Mar. 12, 1876-Feb. 5, 1955) and became Sheila Shapiro and had three additional children)*
- [3] Howard Hurwitz (son of Isaac Hurwitz and Cecilia) (Aug. 5, 1913 Baltimore-Nov. 25, 1995, Pittsburgh) m. Bertha Minna Shymlock Posner (Nov. 14, 1918-Aug. 24, 1996) wed 8 June 1941, District of Columbia
- Eva Shapiro Spiwak (Mar. 15, 1909-Dec. 1 1989) [*daughter of Louis Shapiro and his first wife Sophia] m. Harry J. Spiwak (Nov. 27, 1907-Jan. 20, 1998)
- [3] Dorothy "Dora" Schapiro [daughter of Celia and Louis] (June 14, 1916-Feb. 28, 1985) m. Sigmund Katz (Dec. 16, 1912-Feb. 28,1985)
- [3] Leslie (Shapiro) Smith (daughter of Celia and Louis) (Apr. 13, 1921-Dec. 31, 2005 Randallstown) m. Louis Smith (Louis Zditowsky) (Dec. 25, 1907-Apr. 30, 1985)
- Jack Shapiro (Apr. 22, 1922-July 11, 1944, Normandy) (son of Celia and Louis)

➤ [2] *Ruchel (Rose) Hurwitz (~1899-Sept. 2, 1995) m1 Harry B. Finkelstein (Apr. 15, 1891-Apr. 10, 1939) m2 Haim Margalith (-Oct. 23, 1974, Jerusalem*
- [3] Sylvia (Finkelstein) Scherr (Aug. 10, 1920-Feb. 13, 1990) m. Stanley Scherr (July 17, 1912-Feb. 7, 1996), wed Sept. 4, 1940
- [3] Alma G. (Finkelstein) Lewis (Jun. 24, 1923-Feb. 8, 2007) m. Dr. Paul Lewis (Dec. 30, 1919-Dec 3, 2006), wed Sept. 10, 1944
- Gilbert Finkelstein (March 27, 1929 -Feb. 28, 1997) m. Joann Kolodny (Dec. 7, 1933-Oct. 25, 2010) wed Feb. 21, 1954;   d. circa 1955 (she remarried William Furman May 29, 1955)
- [3] Joel "Buddy" Finkelstein (Feb. 28, 1933 - Apr. 24, 2014) m1 Ellen Stempler (22 March 1933-3 Apr. 1998), wed 7 Jun 1953, m2 Gloria "Goody" LaBorwit (nee Setren)

➤ [2] *Keila (Clara) (May 31, 1901, Mlynov-Sept. 30, 1994) m. Philip Fram (Mar. 21, 1900 Lithuania-Feb. 13, 1964, Baltimore), wed Oct. 11, 1931*
- Betty Iris Fram (b. Aug. 29, 1932) m. Jerome Korpeck (May 26, 1924, Rochester-Jan. 25, 2001, Potomac MD), wed 1953

- David H. Fram (Apr. 13, 1937 Ft. Worth, Texas-Aug. 8, 2019, Reston, VA) m. Marcia R. Levy (b. Sep. 29, 1938 NY), wed June 21, 1959, dv. July 12, 1974; m2 Carol Diane Weissenberg (b. Apr. 1949), wed Nov. 21, 1976

❖ **[1] Pearl Malka Demb (May 12, 1865–Mar. 4, 1933) married Tsodik Shulman (Apr. 12, 1863– Mar. 13, 1947), wed ˜1885**

➢ *[2] Nehuma (Mar. 14, 1887-˜1942) m. Saul/Shaul Miller/Meiler/Malar (?-˜1942), wed ˜1910*
  - [3] Tamara (˜1913-˜1942)
  - [3] Nina (˜1917-˜1942)

➢ *[2] Liza Shulman (Aug. 20th 1889- ? Russia) m. Shia/Shaya Koszhushner (Oct 13 1885-? Russia), wed ˜1912*
  - [3] Etta (Ethel) (˜1914-d. after 1992)
  - [3] Mikhail / Misha (˜1915-d. after 1992) m. Clara
  - [3] Nina (˜1919- d. after 1992) m. Shaul / Shia Orlosorova
  - [3] Yefim (˜1923- d. after 1992) m. Ada

➢ *[2] Shimon (Simon) Shulman (Nov. 6, 1890- Mar. 14, 1970) m. Edith (Alta Ides) Fixman (May 15, 1895-Oct. 8, 1986) wed ˜1919 in Russia*
  - [3] Tessie Shulman (Aug. 2, 1922 Baltimore-Sept. 10, 1966) m. Theodore M. Kremer (May 8, 1913-Nov. 8, 1973)
  - [3] Dr. Melvin ("Big Melvin) Shulman (Nov. 1, 1923 Baltimore-Aug.9, 2015) m. Claire Kantoff (Feb 23, 1926-Aug 16, 2020) wed Apr. 13, 1948
  - [3] Herman Shulman (Jan. 17, 1929 Baltimore-Mar. 9, 2022 Baltimore)

➢ *[2] Harry (Ertz/Hertz) Shulman (Dec. 25, 1894- Apr. 15, 1964 Baltimore) m. Yetta (Eta) Perelson (March 6, 1900 Rovno-Oct. 6, 1967), wed May 5, 1921 in Kovel*
  - [3] Bernard "Bernie" Shulman (Sept. 14, 1922 Baltimore-Nov. 27, 2018, Highland Park, IL) m. Phyllis Mann (Nov. 25, 1926 Chicago-Mar. 23, 2019 Highland Park, IL), wed Dec. 7, 1950
  - [3] Melvin Shulman (Mar. 20, 1928, Baltimore- Sept. 11, 1952, Baltimore) m. Loraine Silver (wed ˜1950

➢ *[2] Sarah "Sura" Shulman (Sept. 5, 1898- Nov. 23, 1988, Baltimore) m. Paul Shulman (Pesach Zutelman) (Dec. 20, 1895, Mervits–July 10, 1988), wed Jan. 17, 1922*
  - [3] Betty Shulman (Feb. 25, 1924, Baltimore-Mar. 21, 1997, Baltimore) m. Samuel Edlavitch (Jul 25, 1914, Baltimore- Dec. 2, 2005, Baltimore) wed June 14, 1946

- [3] Shirley Shulman (Nov. 4 2016 Baltimore–Nov. 4, 2016, Baltimore) m. Alexander J. "Zandy" Leaderman (Mar. 11, 1919, Martinsville, Virginia-Nov. 5, 1999, Baltimore), wed May 16, 1949
- [3] Jonas "Jack" Shulman (Sept 1936, Baltimore-   ) m. Wendy Eppinger (Sept. 9, 1936, San Francisco-), wed Aug. 31, 1958

➤ [2] *Clara "Chaika" Shulman (b. ~1902/1903–July 19, 1990) m. Benjamin "Bennie" Fishman (son of Moishe Fishman) (Apr. 19, 1902- Aug 15, 1993), wed Apr. 13, 1924*
- [3] Theodore "Ted" Fishman (Apr. 11, 1927, Baltimore-Aug. 12, 2020, Baltimore) m. Anabel Siegel (Aug. 9, 1929, New York-), wed Dec. 21, 1952
- [3] Paula Fishman (Mar. 7, 1932, Baltimore - Oct. 4, 2006) m. Allen Brodsky (Nov. 5, 1928, Baltimore-), wed July 1, 1951

➤ [2] *Pepe (Pauline) (~1904/1906, – Feb. 20, 1985, Baltimore) m. first-cousin Paul H. Schwartz (Mar. 6, 1903–Sept. 14, 1992), wed Jan. 3, 1926.*
- [3] Neena Schwartz (Dec. 10, 1926, Baltimore –Apr. 15, 2018, Evanston, Illinois), partner Harriet Claire Wadeson (Jan. 9, 1931-Jan. 26, 2016). No children.
- [3] Leon Schwartz (Apr. 26, 1928-Apr. 1, 2003, Newport Beach, CA) m. Joan Schinker (March 3, 1932-Sept. 23, 2013, Newport Beach)
- [3] Pearl (Schwartz) Imber (Feb. 24, 1935 Baltimore-) m. Bernard M. Imber (Apr 14., 1934 Baltimore-May 11, 2004 Baltimore)

❖ **[1] Simha Gruber (~1863 to 1865-d. after 1912) m1 Chava (?-~1895), m2 Chaindel (? - ?)**

➤ [2] *Mollie "Malia" Gruber (~1882– Feb 14, 1959) m. Israel Erbman/Herman (Apr. 6, 1881-Dec. 20, 1942), wed ~1889*
- [3] Jennie Herman (Oct. 30, 1900, Mlynov-Oct. 28, 1947, Baltimore) m. Michael Bernstein (Jan. 12, 1892-July 19, 1954, Baltimore), wed by 1920
- [3] Herschel Herman (1905-1907 Austria)
- [3] Sarah Herman (Mar 26, 1907 Toprev, Austria-Sept. 28, 1992, District of Columbia) m. Simon "Si" M. Newman (Feb. 3, 1906, New York-June 6, 1985)
- [3] Al (Albert/ Hyman) (Aug. 6, 1908,[127] London- Apr. 9, 1979, Baltimore) m. Carlyn Weinberg (Apr. 16, 1913, Maryland-Sept. 24, 2007), wed August 6, 1936
- [3] Rebecca ("Betty") (May 20, 1910 in London-Oct. 20, 1973, Baltimore) m. Dr. Nachman Davidson (July 12, 1910, Baltimore-Dec. 17, 1992, Baltimore), wed Apr. 4th, 1936

---

[127] According to his daughter Lynne, Albert celebrated his birthday on August 6 but found out years later that was not his real birthday. His mother, Mollie, always said he was born a certain number of days after Tisha B'Av - that's how she knew his birthday. When they looked it up, it was a different date but they decided to keep it August 6.

- [3] Joseph H. Herman (June 14, 1913, Baltimore-Apr. 4, 1981, Baltimore) m. Dorothy "Dora" Altshul (Dec. 24, 1910 Cuyahoga, Ohio- July 21, 1994, England), wed Nov. 25, 1937)
- [3] Sadie "Sally" Herman (Jan. 23, 1915, Baltimore-Dec. 19, 1993 San Diego) m1 Aaron Sokolove (Dec. 10, 1907 Baltimore- Nov. 29, 1982), wed before 1940, dv. ~1940 | m2 Martin Chancey[128] (~1900 New York City- May 26, 1971, San Diego), wed May 16, 1942, Fredericksburg, Virginia

> [2] *Nathan Gruber (~July 18, 1885–Jan. 28, 1971, Baltimore) M. Gertrude (Gitel) Garfinkel (1882 Novohrad Volinsky (Zviahel)- Jan. 27, 1944, Baltimore)*
- [3] Jeannie Harriet Gruber (~Sept. 10, 1908, Novohrad Volinsky (Zviahel)-Sept. 16, 1992 Easton, MD) m. Harry Feinberg (Sept. 29, 1910, Baltimore-Feb. 27, 1996, Baltimore), wed May 3, 1934, District of Columbia
- [3] Doris V. (~Feb. 5, 1910, Novohrad Volinsky (Zviahel)-Jan. 20, 1995, Baltimore) m. Benjamin J. Fishman [son of Joseph and Ida Fishman] (Jan. 3, 1911, Mlynov-Oct. 13, 1995, Baltimore),
- [3] Sylvia Gruber (May 1, 1921, Baltimore-2016) married Joseph Kadish (1915-2004)

> [2] *Samuel Gruber (b. between 1889/1893 – June 2, 1973, Silver Spring) m. Bessie (Gospin 1891-Dec. 5, 1966, Silver Spring) wed ~ 1910 ~Berdychiv*
- [3] unnamed child who died before Bessie's migration
- [3] Jean Gruber (July 17, 1914-Dec 10, 1984) m1. Julius Kirson (Feb. 7, 1911, District of Columbia- Apr. 19, 1969), wed Aug. 22, 1937, m2 Harry S. Schwartz (Jan. 5, 1910 Chicago-Nov. 23, 1976, Miami), wed Nov 1, 1973, Miami
- [3] Ida Beatrice Gruber (Feb. 29, 1916, Baltimore-Mar. 11, 1999, Silver Spring, Md) m. Louis (Goldstein) Gaylor (Nov. 9, 1916, Baltimore-Sept 7, 1991) wed Feb. 28, 1937.
- [3] Nathan Gruber (Oct. 9, 1917 Baltimore-Apr. 22, 1989 Silver Spring, Md) m. Miriam Holzman (Jan 27, 1919, Hoboken, NJ-Oct. 2, 2001, Brookeville, Md), wed January 27th, 1946.
- [3] Morris Aaron Gruber (Apr. 15 1920, Baltimore-Nov. 8, 1980, Silver Spring, MD) m. Fay C. Brown (Jan. 3 1925- Feb. 26, 2009), wed Nov 3, 1946.
- [3] Vera Bernice Gruber (May 13, 1925, Baltimore-May 14, 2003, Rockville, MD) m. Jerome Mendelson (September 1, 1926-June 13, 2012), wed Nov. 3, 1946

---

[128] Martin Chancey was arrested as a Communist organizer in the 1950s. His release from prison was associated with a Supreme court decision that no one could be punished for their beliefs. He is identified in Sadie's marriage record as a labor organizer.

❖ **[1] Yenta (also Yetta) Demb (1870–Oct. 21, 1962, Baltimore) – m. Chaim (Hyman) Schwartz (~1863–Apr. 18, 1946)**

➢ *[2] Benjamin Schwartz (Sept. 22, 1891, Mlynov–OCT 8, 1937, Baltimore) m. Anna Fishman [later Anna Kushner and Anna Gilden) (Feb. 1894, Mlynov–Sept. 30, 1966, Baltimore), marriage license Sept 1, 1914.*
  ▪ [3] Lillian ("Lilly") (Oct. 9, 1917, Baltimore–Apr 2, 2002) m. Sidney Lutins (Jan. 20, 1918, Baltimore - May 3, 1988), wed **Oct.18, 1936, District of Columbia**
  ▪ [3] Selma Schwartz (Sept. 5, 1922, Baltimore–Dec. 2, 1988, Tamarac, Fl) m. Henry H. Hyman (Apr. 9, 1917, Baltimore–May 9, 2007), engagement announced Sept. 12, 1943

➢ *[2] Norton Schwartz (Dec. 8, 1893, Mlynov– Nov. 24, 1978, Baltimore) m. Kate Spector (~Aug. 10, 1899–Feb 03, 1999, Baltimore), wed July 7, 1925*
  ▪ Marvin N. Schwartz (Sept. 28, 1926, Baltimore-) m. Thelma Rose "Temmy" Greber (September 17, 1926, Baltimore–Apr. 12, 2022), wed Nov. 2, 1947
  ▪ Nesanel "Sonnel" / "Sonny" Alvin Schwartz (May 8, 1928, Baltimore–Aug. 5th 2011, Jerusalem) m. Ivy Ebenstein (1932- living in Jerusalem), m2 Mimi (Fuerstein) Teplow (b. May 7, 1935- living in Jerusalem)
  ▪ Milton Schwartz (June 11, 1930, Baltimore–Feb. 15, 2018, Baltimore) m. Millie Weinblatt (Aug. 9, 1932–Apr. 8, 1985), wed August 3, 1952, m2 Phyllis Clair (Ginsburg) Zippin (Dec. 29, 1933 New York City–Dec 11, 2017 Clearwater, Florida)
  ▪ Dr. Mayer Schwartz (Apr. 4, 1937, Baltimore- living in Naples, FL) m. Alice Phillips (1942 Baltimore–living in Naples, FL), wed ~ 1962

➢ *[2] Paul H. Schwartz (Mar. 6, 1903–Sept. 14, 1992) m. first-cousin Pepe (Pauline/Ethel) Shulman (~1904/1906, – Feb. 20, 1985, Baltimore), wed Jan. 3, 1926.*
  ▪ [3] Neena Schwartz (Dec. 10, 1926, Baltimore –Apr. 15, 2018, Evanston, Illinois), partner Harriet Claire Wadeson (Jan. 9, 1931–Jan. 26, 2016). No children.
  ▪ [3] Leon Schwartz (Apr. 26, 1928–Apr. 1, 2003, Newport Beach, CA) m. Joan Schinker (March 3, 1932–Sept. 23, 2013, Newport Beach)
  ▪ [3] Pearl (Schwartz) Imber (Feb. 24, 1935 Baltimore-) m. Bernard M. Imber (Apr 14., 1934 Baltimore–May 11, 2004 Baltimore)

❖ **[1] Motel Demb (aka Max Demming) (˜1870/71 Mlynov–Jan. 17, 1928,[129] Baltimore) m1 unnamed sister of Freida (?–) m2. Freida Herman? Kozusnia? (˜1881–Nov. 15, 1966, Baltimore)**

➢ *[2] Sylvia Demb/Demming (˜1900 Novohrad Volinski–March 16, 1980, Baltimore) m. Abraham B. Penn (Sept. 2, 1897–Oct. 19, 1994), wed 1922 in Springfield*
  ▪ [3] Mitchell Eli Penn (Dec. 10, 1924, Massachusetts–July 9, 1991 Baltimore) m1 Etta Pfeffer (1925–Mar. 12, 1969), wed Mar 28, 1954, m2 Janice Silverman (
  ▪ [3] Marlene Penn (July 6, 1931, Springfield, MA–Dec. 31, 1998, Maryland) m. Ralph Mollerick (May 27, 1930 Kassel, Germany–?) dv. date?

➢ *[2] Julius Deming (Mar. 2, 1908, probably Novohrad Volinski–Nov. 11, 1990, Baltimore) m. Ida Wiener (July 23, 1904, Novohrad Volinski–Aug. 27, 1978), wed Oct. 18, 1930 Brooklyn*
  ▪ [3] Martin Deming (June 4, 1932, Baltimore–May 8, 1998, Baltimore) m. Esther Levin (Dec. 30, 1934, Maryland–Sept. 24, 2014, Baltimore), wed **Aug. 8 1954**

➢ *[2] Marion Demb / Demming (Aug. 26, 1914 Novohrad Volinski–Apr. 3, 1981, Baltimore) m. Joshua Laken (Mar. 16, 1916 Baltimore–June 5, 1985, Baltimore)*
  ▪ [3] Mark Laken (b. July 27, 1940) m. Sandy Wiener (b. Sept. 7, 1941), wed ˜1964
  ▪ [3] Barry Laken (b. 1944, Baltimore) m. Sharon Ann Toney (b. Dec. 26, 1944–), wed Aug 21, 1966.

❖ **[1] Mollya (Mollie) Demb (˜1872, Mlynov–Jan. 9, 1962, Rishon LeZion, Israel) m. Samuel Roskes (May 15, 1873, Lutzk–Mar. 13, 1938, Baltimore, buried Chernigover Congregation New Cemetery, Rosedale), wed ˜1897**

➢ *[2] 3 unnamed children who died according to 1910 Census*

➢ *[2] David Shimon Roskes (Apr. 5, 1898, Lutsk–Dec. 28, 1964, Baltimore) m. Dorothy B ("Dora") Cluster (July 13, 1903, Maryland–July 28, 1963, Baltimore), wed ˜1921*
  ▪ [3] Estelle Roskes (Aug 9, 1922, Baltimore–Jan 21, 2021, Baltimore) m. Abe Z. Greenberg (Dec. 26, 1914, Wilkes Barre, PA– Feb 20, 2003, Baltimore), marriage license May 1, 1953
  ▪ [3] Marilyn Phyllis Roskes (Oct. 24, 1933, Baltimore–June 9, 2006, Baltimore) Charles Kerpelman (?–?) engagement announcement Feb. 22, 1953

❖ **[1] Edle Demb [drown young]**

---

[129]Listed under Max Denning in Jack Lewis Funeral Home Records: http://jewishmuseummd.org/wp-content/uploads/2013/06/Jack-Lewis-records-index.pdf

❖ **[1] Hanna Demb (?-?)**

➢ *[2] Edith (?-?)*

❖ **[1] Aaron Demb (˜Aug. 8, 1876 Mlynov–May 3, 1970, Baltimore) m. Baila Woldaski (˜1882 Mervits–Oct. 12, 1956 Baltimore), wed between 1905 and 1908**

➢ *[2] Moishe Demb-died young about age 11*

➢ *[2] Unnamed sister who died*

➢ *[2] Louis Demb (Aug. 31, 1908, Mlynov– Apr. 1, 1999, Baltimore) m. Priscilla A. Caplan (Nov. 3, 1921 Maryland–Feb 17, 2009, Baltimore)*
  ▪ [3] Marvin Demb (b. Aug. 1, 1947) m. Sharon Kruger (b. Feb. 15, 1952), wed Dec. 1972
  ▪ [3] Deborah "Debbie" Mondell (b. Aug. 23, 1950) m. Ben Mondell (b. Aug. 1953) wed. Aug. 1974
  ▪ [3] Rona Demb (b. Dec. 19, 1953) m. Marvin Barrash (b. Sept. 1953) dv.

➢ *[2] Hyman Demb (Jan 1, 1911, Mlynov–Mar. 27, 1988, Baltimore) m. Ida Arenberg (May 25, 1917 Baltimore-Apr. 1995 Baltimore)*
  ▪ [3] Harriette Rosenbaum (Sept. 29, 1945, Baltimore-Jan. 11, 1989, Baltimore) m. Jerome Rosenbaum (b. 1944), wed ˜1967

NAME INDEX